Awakening the Woman Within
1988-1994

Veronica's Adventures – Book III

VERONICA ESAGUI

Copyright © 2024 Veronica Esagui, DC

All rights reserved. No part of this book may be reproduced or transmitted in any form or by any means, electronic or mechanical, including photocopying, recording, or by any information storage and retrieval system, without permission in writing from the copyright owner. No patent liability is assumed with respect to the use of the information contained herein. Although every precaution has been taken in the preparation of this book, the publisher and author assume no responsibility for errors or omissions. Neither is any liability assumed for damages resulting from the use of the information contained herein.

Library of Congress Control Number: 2024900047

ISBN: 979-8-9896910-1-2
Second Edition

Editors: Chory Ferguson, Maria E. Chitsaz
Book Cover & Graphic Design by James M. McCracken

PAPYRUS PRESS, LLC

West Linn, OR 97068

To order additional copies of this book www.veronicaesagui.com
Printed in the United States of America.

*To my friends, Dr. Peruzzi, Dr. Holdman,
Dr. Clari Fearman, Fay Zealand, Terri Flannigan,
and Mr. and Mrs. Ounuma.*

Author's notes

The people and the stories portrayed in this book are all true as to my recollection when I began writing my diary in Portuguese, Saturday, April 26, 1986 in Howell, New Jersey. Upon translating my diary to English I have kept it as it was written, but I have changed some individuals' names to protect their privacy.

Mix your hopes and dreams with hard work, blend them well with lots of passion and persistence, and your wishes will come true.

~Veronica Esagui

CONTENTS

Chapter One	It's Show Time!	1
Chapter Two	Returning to Egypt	38
Chapter Three	Castaways in the Old World	102
Chapter Four	The Chiropractic Miracle	169
Chapter Five	Freedom has been Granted	229
Chapter Six	College, Dating, and Sex	303

~ *Chapter One* ~

IT'S SHOW TIME!

1988

Lakewood, New Jersey USA

Spring of 1988

While translating this diary from Portuguese to English, throughout the course of nine months, it gradually dawned on me that much of my past experiences were the source of my present situation. Moved by such discovery I inquisitively re-read my first two diaries, *The Journey of Innocence* and *Braving a New World,* and came to the conclusion that I was not only the product of my DNA like everybody else, but also of my ethnic upbringing compounded by an endless enthusiasm toward any of life's hindrances which I considered nothing but stimulating challenges to keep me from getting bored. This new enlightenment or what some people might call, a personal discovery made me recall the spring of 1960, when Nelly my mother's sister, after living in the US for forty years, came to Lisbon, Portugal and lived with us during her three weeks' visit. Meeting her was an exciting event in my young life of sixteen and unknown to me at the time, the start of many more. Her unwrinkled two beige tailored outfit, perfectly coiffured light brown hair and flawless make-up, were to me an example of what American women looked like, even after a long, transatlantic flight. Besides a purse, she had brought two-large leather suitcases and a matching carry-on just for toiletries. One contained her wardrobe and the other presents for every member of the family. We saw her as the epitome of a rich American even though she had been born in Portugal.

Nelly gave me a dress, a very simple front button light green cotton dress with short sleeves, but I found it deliciously American. It was my first dress, where I did not have to be fitted. In those days, ready-made clothing was too expensive for the lower and middle-class and it made more sense for women to hire a seamstress and men to go to a tailor shop. Lisbon boasted of fabric shops at every street corner and learning to sew was an important part of a girl's education which started as soon as she could hold a needle with her fingers. Mama used Maria Antonia an old dressmaker, who lived a block from us and charged half the price of the other seamstresses. My problem was that when Maria Antonia spoke her foul-smelling breath, combined with a strong fish like body odor forced me to hold my breathing for as long as she pinned or stitched around my sleeves or neckline. The experience was as dreadful as going to the beauty shop to have a hair perm and in the process; they burned my hair, scalp and the tips of my ears. The answer to my problems was to wear my hair naturally straight and the same old clothes. In high school, my schoolmates called me *existentialist* but I didn't mind, if anything it was like calling me an American. I had seen at least ten movies depicting life in North America to know that existentialists liked dark clothes like me but lived a simple life in New York City, making a living from dancing to the sound of jazz in badly lit nightclubs. The rest of the population was very, very rich and I took it for granted when Nelly bestowed me with multiple gifts such as a large box of dark chocolate covered thin mints, a whole seven-stick pack of Wrigley's fruity chewing gum, a shampoo bottle with the delicious scent of flowers, a pair of long silver earrings and a dainty perfume flask, with Chanel No. 5 her favorite fragrance. One morning I witnessed her shaving under the arms with a dainty razor blade and without the need for shaving cream. I was flabbergasted. She was only two years younger than my mother, but she had a lively spirit and did not hold back her loving feelings toward me. Nelly's daily kisses and hugs of affection was something I had never experienced from my parents not even Aunt Heydee. Nelly gave me self-confidence when she said I was smart and pretty too and if her son Al met me, she knew he would fall in love with me right away. Except for some of the men that walked by me in the streets and pinched my bottom if they had an opportunity or whistled and called me sexy no one had ever paid attention to me. Until I met Aunt Nelly, I considered myself invisible.

The day before Nelly left, we were walking arm-in-arm in downtown Lisbon, and she said, "I'm going to miss you. I wish I could take you with me to America." I put my head on her shoulder. "Thank you, Aunt Nelly, I wish I could go with you too."

When Nelly's son Al and I were married two years later, in the spring of 1962, I had just turned eighteen. True that it was a pre-arranged marriage but I couldn't wait to leave Portugal and go live with Al and Nelly, in the land of cowboys, movie stars, rock and roll music and Elvis Presley, even though I preferred Paul Anka. I was in love with the English language and the American culture. Some people might say I had seen too many American movies but, in those days, I felt that if anything I had not seen enough.

There was no real culture shock when I came to the US, I was happy to let go of Verónica my given name and welcomed the nickname Ronnie, with open arms. I threw away the three home-made dresses brought from Portugal, including the expensive layered tulle petticoat my uncle Augusto had bought me as a wedding gift. I began to wear jeans, lipstick and teasing my hair in the beehive style and learned how to use an electric can opener and how to remove clothes from a dryer fast enough that I didn't have to iron them. We lived the first year in Jamaica, Long Island, where I gave birth to Ralph in 1963, and our family was still picture perfect—there is, until we moved to Freehold, New Jersey and Steve was born a year later. Nelly and Al expected my second child to be a girl and the mere idea that I had not produced one made me a failure in their eyes. Such occurrence aggravated by Nelly's change of heart toward me while living with us, caused what I'd later classify our household, as a dysfunctional family.

Now 26 six years later I no longer identified myself with the naïve, innocent Verónica growing up in Portugal, who had been taught that complete submission to her husband and elders was the only acceptable way to a congenial life. Time had passed us by in giant leaps, with Nelly graduating in 1986 from a heart attack complicated by sudden internal abdominal bleeding. There was no return from the dead but it was nice to hint some form of continuity.

At seventeen, both Ralph and Steve joined the armed forces. Ralph was the first to enlist in the Air Force and Steve went into the Navy the following year. When Ralph returned to civilian life, he worked as an engineer at Bell Labs close to Freehold, where we lived, and Steve joined Al and I as a partner in our new business, the Howell Music Center.

Al was still managing Ronnie's Music Den at the Collingswood market on weekends but counting the days when he could retire. My time was divided between the Howell Music Center, and the Simy Dinner Theatre I had founded in 1985 at the Kobe Japanese Restaurant, in Howell, right on the border of Lakewood Twp.

But the past was still alive, nothing had been forgotten, just temporarily buried in case its contents needed to be exhumed and when Mama's letter arrived from Portugal today on my forty-fourth birthday it did exactly that. "Verónica," she had written. "I'm so proud of you! You went from your white school uniform to the white wedding gown, never touched by a man."

I did not know whether to cry or laugh when I read her avowal. While growing up, Mama had kept me away from any type of social activity which could put me at risk of meeting someone from the opposite sex that was not Jewish. Big deal not being touched by a man before getting married! How about allowing me to know the future father of my children, more than three days, before getting married for life?

But in all fairness, in 1962 I was a teenager with the mind of a child mesmerized by the idea of going to live in the land of my favorite movie stars. As I look back, I doubt if given a chance I would have known what to do or say to establish a relationship with any man. Al's undivided attention when he came to Portugal to marry me was like a dream come true, and it was easy to fall in love with him. He was my American prince in a white horse, what more could I wish for? That was until I began to grow up with my two sons. When they were young children they were my playmates, and when they grew into teenagers I was one of them. Winter of 1977, just eleven years ago, I was faced with putting my sons in a private school far from home, to save them from Nelly's abuse, and I ran away. Nelly who had been living with us for fifteen years, was forced to move in with her son Joe and his sister Ruth, in Long Island. My sons were back, but my marriage still did not improve. I was not tied down like a prisoner, I had all the freedom anyone could wish for, but what good was freedom when Al and I had nothing in common. I came home from work, and he was already sitting in front of the television, eating peanuts, his favorite snack. And there he remained for the rest of the evening, after I served him dinner on a TV tray because he did not want to miss one of his cops and robbers' shows. There was a lack of oxygen inside our apartment, he liked to keep the windows closed even in the summertime, and I was not allowed to open them. He loved cooking spaghetti with meatballs, stews, and chicken soup. It did not matter what he prepared, the kitchen was left in a chaotic mess. We had a dishwasher but the sink was piled high, the counters needed cleaning and the kitchen cabinet were splattered with food or oil that spread to the walls and floors. He had his own way of cooking and oil was his main ingredient for everything. As I came to be a more hardened housewife I went from cleaning daily, to once a week, usually on Sunday mornings. Talking to each other had become nonexistent, the only subject he spoke with some passion was re-telling me the news he had heard on television or read in the newspaper's front page. He had always done that as far back as I could remember, but now it had become an excruciating broadcast even when I blocked most of his tedious rambling on, "Did you hear about the senator…his secretary and took …the money… the Blacks… a rampage at…It's about time…the Puerto Ricans… send them back to… no good for nothing…the lousy Jews…The prices keep going… a question of…the lousy Cubans… You hear about the fires?

At the end of a day's work, I had no motivation to go home.

But I was a good wife. I kept all negative thoughts where they belonged, in my diary, and I had a certain pride for always sending the best of my world to Mama, through the letters we exchanged every two weeks. I found no reason to bother her with my personal life; she had enough issues to contend with, Papa's health, her health, and my younger brother José's mental health.

More than twenty-nine years ago Mama had been involved in a serious motorcycle accident with Papa, which put her in the hospital in a state of coma for several weeks. She did recover, but never to the full extent of what she had been prior to the accident. Her younger days of being active and having a normal life were gone; she had become dependent on a caregiver. She no longer painted. Her creativity was limited to one form of expression: writing poetry. She and Papa still lived in Lisbon, Portugal and I knew the last trip to the US had most likely been her last. In my mind's eye Mama was living like a little bird inside a gilded cage for the rest of her life, never to return, never to be present in my life. I could blame it in the distance keeping us so far from each other but when I was living in my parents' house as a young girl, there was no mother and daughter bond either. Yet, I still dreamed of sharing my life with her. I wanted Mama to see The Simy Dinner Theatre, which I was the founder and producer. I wanted her to be proud of me. I wanted to put my arms around her, give her a hug and then have her walk beside me. My only chance of being successful at such impossibility was to create her visit through the letter I wrote one late evening.

Dear Mama,
I have sent you several pictures of the Kobe Japanese Restaurant building where I have been producing plays and musicals for the last three years. But pictures, playbills and newspaper reviews can never do justice. Please have someone read this special letter to you. Close your eyes. I'm right next to you. Hold my arm and walk with me to the theatre I named after you, but you haven't seen until now.
You and I stand at the entrance of the Kobe Japanese Restaurant, a large white building that stands tall and proud facing route 9 in Howell. The wide glass double doors open for us with just a little push of my left hand. We enter its lobby of white glass-like marble floor. To your

right is the red-lacquered checkroom where you leave your coat in the care of Susan, a young American girl dressed in a green and white Japanese kimono. She welcomes you with a smile, and hands you a small, numbered ticket which you must return to get your coat back before you leave at the end of the evening. As you turn to your left, you admire the large moon-shaped glass window taking the full length of the wall and facing the outside lush green garden. Inside, to the corner of the window you can't help noticing an upright fish—an unusual, four-foot-tall, dark brown ceramic fish, except for the scales, which have a hint of dark green. You wonder if it is a replica of some rare type of sturgeon. He proudly displays his prominent male genitals, which is acceptable since he is wearing a silly hat and has a jolly fish face. He stands among various types of live plants and bamboo shoots, which are cleverly growing by a narrow river-rock path set along the lobby wall. An older couple entering the restaurant, obviously for the first time, remark they have never seen such a big fish and exchange a smile.

From the lobby where we are still standing, do you see the steps going up? I just want to let you know that the stylish Brazilian-wooden steps covered with a red carpet runner and with red-lacquered handrails on both sides, leads to your theatre, The Simy Dinner Theatre, on the first floor. Now, look up and straight-ahead. Amazing huh? Yes, hanging from the ceiling and draping over the balcony upstairs, is a luxurious, bigger-than-life, red and white imperial looking Japanese silk kimono, with fancy peacocks embroidered in gold. I agree with you, it's monumental.

Let's not go upstairs yet. On your immediate right there's a tiny red-lacquered wall mantelpiece where Mrs. Ounuma displays her pride and joy, an arrangement of huge maroon silk flowers, she created. Later you'll get to see more of her original arrangements. Let's take the steps to the restaurant below. They match the ones going up to *the theatre. I understand you must be anxious to go upstairs to see your theatre, but Mr. and Mrs. Ounuma, the restaurant's owners, are at the bottom of the steps and they can't wait to meet you. Mrs. Ounuma is your height and a little hefty in stature, the opposite of her husband who is also her height but very slim. Don't worry; I'll hold your arm as we walk down the six steps. Oh, before I forget I must tell you Mr. and Mrs. Ounuma's culture dictates that they bow instead of shaking hands. If you bow back they will appreciate it. They tell you in Japanese that they are honored to meet you. Mrs. Ounuma smiles and then she apologizes as she has errands to attend in the kitchen, and Mr. Ounuma turns to welcome four customers that just arrived. It's dinner time, that's why they are so busy. I'll be glad to show you around. Jerry, the bartender behind the small bar on your right, was born in Japan but he is Americanized; he kind of reminds me of a young and trim Groucho Marx. Do you agree? Okay now, try not to laugh. He shakes your hand and tells you how delighted he is to meet you. He asks you to sit at one of the comfortable bar stools and hands you a tall delicious strawberry smoothie decorated with a little colorful paper umbrella inserted into a chunk of freshly cut sweet pineapple and a strawberry. Go ahead take a sip from the straw. I know, absolutely delicious, those are your two favorite fruits. Mine too. There's no rush, take your time savoring their sweetness. You can keep the little umbrella as a souvenir. I then ask Jerry to show you a sample of his artwork. At first, he acts shy, but then he quickly grabs his portfolio from behind the bar with lots of exquisite black and white detailed pencil drawings. I particularly love the one showing a street of Chicago. Jerry is a very accomplished artist, and I just know someday he will be very famous. C'mon, let's say goodbye to Jerry and sit at the sushi bar. You can take your drink with you. Yes, the sushi bar is big; it takes the full length of the wall to your right. The sushi chef wearing a* white top hat is very proud of his creations, which are considered sushi masterpieces by his clientele. You will notice people eating sushi leave $20 and an occasional $50 bill makes its way into the glass tip jar. That is a true sign of how much they appreciate the chef's undivided attention to every detail he puts into their meal.

I know you have never had sushi, but you love fish, and you are always ready to try something new. What better opportunity then to try a Ronnie Roll? A year ago, my favorite sushi chef at Kobe created it, especially for me. He makes them with extra avocado pieces, and one whole sliced shrimp, little crunchy fish eggs on the inside as well as on the outside of the rice and also around the seaweed strip. He tops it off with crispy fresh greens for color. With a Ronnie Roll, I am guaranteed to find fish eggs between my teeth even an hour later after I ate. You are smiling. I love it when you smile. Oh no, Mama. Wait! Hold on! The round green paste on your plate is not pistachio candy. It's wasabi, Japanese horseradish! Trust me, it's not made for human consumption by itself, it must be diluted with soy sauce, before dipping the sushi into it. I must tell you, the first time I had sushi; I couldn't help noticing the small green glob on my plate. Well, you know how much I love sweets and since it looked like a mini side of pistachio dessert, for after the meal I decided to start with it. That's how I learned all about wasabi. Luckily, my eyeballs did not fly out of their sockets as it took my breath away. There were lots and lots of tears. But it feels good to laugh about it now. I should have a t-shirt saying, "I survived swallowing a chunk of wasabi."

Now, let me guide you through the two large dining areas and into the Hibachi rooms. Yes, I love the view from the dining room's five large windows too, and no you're not imagining that the river is a bit too close for comfort. Mr. Ounuma personally planted the beautiful bamboo trees along the river and the side of the building, in an attempt to retain the land, the river has not already washed off. Twice last year it rained a lot and the river inundated the restaurant as far as the kitchen, way in the back. A lot of water damage happened to the building as you can imagine. The carpets had to be replaces because of that. But Mr. and Mrs. Oununa are hard-working people and they're not going to allow something like a river overflowing to destroy everything they have worked so hard for. They've been saving money to purchase an outdoor water pump to prevent it from happening again. No, their landlord is not offering any help; he just wants the rent money.

As we enter the hibachi area, you'll notice there are four hibachi tables in each room. They work like grills and up to ten people can sit comfortably around one of them, while the hibachi chef performs the cooking in front of the hungry patrons. You've never had hibachi? Mama mia, you have got to experience this. Have a seat. What would you like; chicken, lobster, steak, or shrimp? Okay, if that's your choice, shrimp it is. Jack is our hibachi chef tonight. Wow, you are right; the way he throws those knives in the air and moves the fresh veggies and shrimp around is like being at the circus. What a show, hum? Oops, one of the shrimp just flew onto your plate. Jack is giving you an extra shrimp because you are my mom. Isn't it fun to see your food being prepared? Can you taste the delicious flavor of the fresh shrimp? And what do you think of the fluffy rice with those sweet peas and small bite-size carrots? Isn't it delicious? Here, have some of my fresh bean sprouts. I love their crispness. I'm glad you like them too. They're supposed to be very healthy for you.

The show upstairs starts in a half-hour. But don't worry; I already have a table reserved just for you and me. Did you notice that when we crossed the restaurant the dining room tables were covered with colorful silk tablecloths depicting fine Japanese artwork? Well, I hate to tell you this, but some customers love the tablecloths so much that sometimes they steal them. Mr. and Mrs. Ounuma were forced to cover the tables with a heavy glass top. Still, once in a while, a tablecloth will disappear right from under their noses, which means the crooked customer had the nerve to pull the large tablecloth from under the glass, and most likely hid it under their coat on the way out of the restaurant.

 Mama, look at the green bamboo growing in large containers as partitions between the two large regular dining rooms and the mini arrangements of dried flowers mixed with wheat, nuts and dried corn inside the low ceramic containers on the corner shelves of the dining room on your left were also Mrs. Ounuma's creation. Now that you have seen the restaurant downstairs, you understand why I loved it here, but wait until we go upstairs. C'mon, let's take the steps up to your theatre, The Simy Dinner Theatre.

 At the atrium upstairs there's a long table covered with a white linen tablecloth and a low but wide glass bowl with water and fresh rose petals, once again one of Mrs. Ounuma's artistic touches. Along the wall behind the table are several 12"x14" black and white pictures of the actors and actresses that have performed in your theatre. That's Tracey, my theatre associate and best friend, you have seen her picture as well as Michael's my other partner in theatre. She is busy seated behind the table collecting the tickets from our theatre patrons. She comes over and gives you a hug and tells you she's glad to meet you in person. In theatre we always hug each other; it's part of being in touch with our own emotions, and it shows we care for that person. Just then, Michael comes out of the theatre and shakes your hand. Then he says, "Ronnie's mom, hum?" He gives you a long hug.

 Did I just catch a wink telling me you approve of my theatre partners? I'm glad. Yes, I'm very lucky; I couldn't *do it without them.*

If you are wondering about the closed red-lacquered double doors, from where Michael came out, they open into your theatre. Let me do that for you. Sure, you can stand in the doorway and take an overall look of the room; the audience dressed in their finest have already finished dinner and are enjoying their drinks. The ceiling and the back of the stage are painted black to give the illusion of infinity. Michael taught me that.

Come, the small table close to the stage has been reserved just for you and me. This month's show is a musical comedy.

Shhhhhh, the house lights are dimming. Have a seat and I'll be right back. I have to make an announcement on stage.

"Ladies and gentleman, welcome to The Simy Dinner Theatre, and the company's original production of, 'That's Entertainment.' It's show time!"

When Mama wrote it could be as much as twelve handwritten pages. After years of my one or two-pages she was impressed with my seven pages.

"Thank you, Verónica, for taking me to the Simy Theatre, it felt as if I was there walking beside you. You're the best daughter a mother can wish for. I'm very proud of you."

I had accomplished my mission and could only hope that once in a while Mama would read my letter and let her imagination carry her to a world where pain did not exist, only unlimited possibilities.

I perceived a subtle sadness in Michael's face. We'd known each other for four years, as friends and theatre partners and all those years had taught me to read his eyes and since he was shy and too busy to have a girlfriend, I took it upon myself to play the part of matchmaker. I told Denise, the stage manager—who was single and nineteen years old—that he liked her, and then I told Michael that Denise liked him.

"You want me to go out with her?" His brows curled up slightly as if surprised with my idea.

"Yes, I do. Everybody needs someone special in their lives. She is about your age, and she likes you, and so why not?"

I knew I really cared for Michael since I had gone out of my way to bring some happiness into his personal life.

They went out Friday night after the show, and I crossed my fingers it would go well. They were young and it was spring. Love was in the air.

On Saturday night I did not ask Michael how the date went. I had already done my job as cupid. After the play, he looked for Denise since they had set a second date that evening; she had left with my son Steve, who had attended the show. Michael told me not in so many words what he thought of Denise as a person.

"I'm sorry it didn't work out." I felt like a fool.

"You're never again to play matchmaker. I'm very capable of getting my own girlfriend."

When would I learn not to interfere in other people's lives, I asked myself. I wanted to cry.

"Ronnie, I apologize for being angry at you." He put an arm over my shoulder. I know you meant well, okay?" We hugged briefly, for moral support more than anything else and after setting the props and cleaning the theatre for the next day, we waved goodbye to each other.

Steve couldn't help if the girls were drawn to him like bees to flowers. He had told me several times, "Mom, if a girl is not attracted to me it's because she's a lesbian."

Designing the set for the production of "Don't Drink the Water," a comedy taking place inside an American Embassy behind the Iron Curtain, took me on a trip down memory lane. A year prior to coming to the US, I started going to the American Embassy in Lisbon, two to three times a week for the sole purpose of being familiar with the culture I would soon embrace. At the embassy I diligently read magazines, newspapers and books by American authors. I listened to a variety of music records, from country to classical and serious plays, like "Death of a Salesman," and "Cat on a Hot Tin Roof" which left me bored to death. The American ambassador heard from the staff about my pre-arranged marriage and the weekly visits to the embassy and invited me to his drawing room. A picture of President Dwight D. Eisenhower, hung behind his dark wooden chair with the American flag on one side and the Portuguese flag on the other. There were no other decorations on the worn-out bluish walls. On top of the massive mahogany desk was a black phone, a small framed picture facing him, a rotary desk calendar with two fancy gold color pens, inserted on each side of the calendar and several piles of what looked like documents waiting to be signed. I figured the reason for the lack of décor had to do with neither the ambassador nor the staff living there; most likely their homes were decorated just the opposite. He was a pleasant middle-aged man but, in those days, I lacked social skills of any kind and with only three years of English in high school I felt tongue tied. I answered his questions but maintained my gaze down as if studying the patterns on the carpet. Feeling anxious and embarrassed, I could tell I was blushing. Most likely he thought I was retarded, because he didn't keep me long in his office.

The set designs always received great reviews, for which I took great pride in being the stage designer but I also knew that without the actors bringing to life the characters, the set would be a corpse without a heartbeat. A few years back I had tried working with a professional set designer, a very sensitive guy who could not stand the thought of the actors using *his* set. Since I did not like dealing with difficult people I took over the position of set designer for all my theatre productions.

One day, Ralph invited Al and me for a tour at Bell Labs. I got to wear some of the gear he used to work in the whiteroom and I had a picture taken next to him. We looked like two nerds in white.

Al and I were very impressed; our son had survived the crazy days of youth and had become a working, mature, and talented young man. After the tour he invited us to his apartment for dinner.

He cooked a delicious meal of fresh veggies and chicken in a large wok. I had never seen a wok being used for cooking at home, only at the Kobe Japanese Restaurant where Katie, the restaurant manager and hostess, sometimes prepared lunch for us, when we were alone at the restaurant. After heating the oil in the wok, she added thinly sliced onions and shredded cabbage. When tender she threw in previously boiled ramen noodles, a little soy sauce and fresh ginger, simple, quick and delicious. What Ralph made for us was more like a feast of colors and flavors. On the way home Al and I counted our blessings as parents.

Jerry, at the Kobe, told me there were two juried art shows going on the following Saturday, and he wish he had a clone so he could enter both. I offered to help him by representing him at one of them.

Jerry won first prize at both competitions. To express his gratitude, he offered to take me out for dinner. I told him I'd rather have a copy of one of his art works; my very favorite, a black and white, in-depth drawing of a street in Chicago.

I made out like a bandit. I had the Chicago print framed and hung it over our couch in the living room.

What an unexpected surprise when Jason, a student who in his teens I used to teach guitar ten years ago and later participated in the musicals I produced at several high schools, came into our music center wearing a highway patrolman uniform. He had aged a little and looked very handsome in his uniform but had not lost his innocence; he still possessed the childlike quality of an honest to goodness person.

Since then, Jason stopped by once in a while, just to talk about the good old days. One morning he waked in with a big smile, "Ronnie, you're not going to believe this but yesterday I helped a very attractive young lady when her car broke down on Route 9. She asked me if I liked chocolate cookies, and of course I said yes. And then, this morning I received at the police precinct, a box of chocolate cookies and a little note with her phone number. I called to thank her for the cookies and she asked me out for dinner tomorrow night. I need your advice. She's a medical doctor and I'm a bit nervous."

Jason was the kind of a guy I could see getting married to a country girl, the type that would be happy staying home and having his children. He was not the academic type or a suave, sophisticated Don Juan. I loved Jason very dearly, but I had a gut-feeling she had fallen for his uniform. "Just be yourself and enjoy the company and the dinner. If it's meant to be, it will be." And then I sang, "Que sera, sera, whatever will be will be..." Jason joined me singing but we stopped when a customer walked in.

"I can't tell the difference between one white customer or another, they all look the same to me," Jerry wore a straight face as he handed me a club soda without ice and with a slice of lemon. After a performance or rehearsals, I liked sitting at the bar, talking to him. He made me laugh.

Before I left the Kobe that evening he called me over. "I'm not happy just giving you a poster-copy of my artwork for helping me out with the art fair. I'd like to invite you to have lunch with me, here at Kobe. Does tomorrow sound okay?"

I accepted his invitation.

I ordered a Ronnie Roll sushi and seaweed salad and Jerry got his favorite, Udon Noodle soup. He ate the noodles while making loud slurping sounds. "Since we are friends," he said. "I'm comfortable eating this way. If I were on a date, it would not be romantic for me to eat in this manner. But, I don't have to worry about that, because I don't have the time for a girlfriend." He kept slurping the noodles.

"You live a very lonely boring life." I bumped my shoulder into his as Yoko the waitress walked by us carrying a serving tray of Miso soups. "Why don't you ask her out? She's single, beautiful, and definitely very nice."

"They're all very nice until you have to live with them, and then the truth comes out."

I had never heard him talk like that. It sounded like he had a bad experience in the romance department and didn't trust anyone. I felt sorry for him.

Michael and I were alone putting a new set on stage when we heard a loud banging on the large glass doors of the restaurant downstairs. The Kobe restaurant was closed and we ran to see what was going on. There were four enraged old men screaming their heads off outside. "It's bad enough we have a Japanese restaurant in our town, but if that is not enough of an insult, these Japs have the audacity to put our American Flag upside down!"

Thank God Mr. Ounuma was not at the restaurant, he would have been lynched. Michael and I did our best to calm them down by telling them over and over again that it was an innocent mistake since the Japanese flag just had a red ball and whoever had put up the two flags, took it for granted and didn't bother to look up.

"We're World War II veterans and we're going to let the township know about your disrespect toward our country. Nobody, neither family nor friends, will ever set foot in your crappy Japanese restaurant. We're going to have this place shut down."

We lost the argument; they were still in the war zone and the restaurant was at fault for the war itself. Michael brought the flag down and up the correct way. But the damage had been done as I was soon to find out.

Jason's romance with the doctor did not last long. After the first date she called, "it's not going to work out between us." He was heartbroken. I told him, "For everyone there's someone out there; it's the law of Nature."

"You believe in that?"

"I make you a bet, before the end of the year; you'll meet the right woman. Trust me." I did not have to cross my fingers.

I could tell that Al was upset when he walked into our music center after taking Steve out for lunch. "Ronnie, I swear I'm never going to take *your* son out again. First, he ordered a huge breakfast and when he was done eating, he ordered an even larger lunch. It was disgusting seeing him eat like a pig."

"Did he eat everything?" I always got irked when he referred to Steve as my son and Ralph as *our* son.

"Yes, and like I said, it was disgusting."

"Maybe he was very hungry," I said.

When Steve was a child he was a bit picky about his food. He always served himself a small portion from the large tray I served in the center of the table, and then if he liked it he would try to get a second serving, I say try, because Al would yell at Steve, if he went for more. Ralph never had to contend with that, he always filled his plate to the brim. While growing up Steve went through a lot of emotional and physical abuse from his father and Nelly his grandmother. But I was also guilty too. In those days I was nothing but a subservient weakling and lacked the courage to put a stop to the way they treated him.

I was no psychiatrist but to me it was a clear case of Steve trying to say, I'm not a kid anymore and now you can't stop me from eating as much as I want.

Al and I got a real surprise gift for our wedding anniversary. Ralph called us at four in the morning and told us not to ask any questions. "Just get your coats on and bring your video camera, I'm outside waiting for you."

Ralph waived at us from the window in the back seat of a long, shiny, black limousine. He wore a mischievous smile and refused to tell us where we were going. The chauffeur drove us to an open field. A large white van pulled in front of us, and from the back of the van a flat balloon got pulled out, which to my amazement turned into a hot air balloon.

I hadn't shared this with anyone, but since reading, "Around the World in 80 Days" when I was a kid, I had always dreamed of traveling in a hot-air balloon expedition of some kind. I eagerly jumped inside the basket, holding on tight to my video camera, and proceeded to motivate Al to get into the basket with me. He was not as enthusiastic. But it did not take long for Ralph to convince him. When Ralph said something to Al, it automatically became God's spoken word.

With the video turned on, I only had one mission in mind: capture the take-off and what would follow next. An open-air elevator feeling came over me as we went up and up. There were no clouds, just clear skies and farm land below. *I'm in heaven.* I told myself. Except for the loud burner on and off there were no other sounds, it felt as if we were floating in outer space. Then, sanity started to settle and I became aware of the hard earth staring from below us. Al didn't show any signs of fear if anything he seemed relaxed and gazed straight into the horizon. I took a swift look inside the balloon and did not see anything even close to a parachute. My next thought was more like an inner prayer; *I'm in God hands and Bob our professional pilot, who I hope has done this more than a few times will keep us safe.*

Over the fields we hovered moving super gently along with the air and everything was going well when suddenly we started losing altitude. Two golfers playing in the field below called out, "Are you having problems staying up? Are you attempting to land?"

"Oh no," answered our calm pilot. "It's nothing to worry about, we're just losing a little altitude, but we'll soon be up on our course." Bob was working hard at maintaining the air balloon up by opening the propane valve. "It's a lot like a gas grill," he announced to Al. "The bigger the flame to heat the air the faster the balloon rises."

La di da, who cares, this is fun, la di da, I sang inside my head keeping the video camera going. Up and up we went again and then just as we were gliding smoothly over a farm the balloon began losing altitude quite rapidly and I heard our pilot say the s word and Al doing the same, followed by a fairly rough landing on what looked like a potato farm. As we hit the field below, I did not let go of my camera and kept it going, capturing every detail of our exciting crash.

The "potato" farmer came out of his house in pajamas with a shotgun pointed at us and screamed at the top of his lungs, "You bastards! I'm going to kill you all for waking up my baby with that entire racket. You f…… idiots and your hot air balloons! Get the hell off my property!"

Up we went again, high enough to get over his fence and off his property but not too much farther. We landed gently in the middle of a side road in front of us. Luckily it was very early in the morning, most likely why no traffic coming our way. The van and the limousine with Ralph had been following our trip along the road and were waiting for us. A champagne bottle was opened and everyone had a glass in celebration of our safe landing.

Summer of 1988

An official from the Howell Township called me this morning at the music center. He had called the Kobe Japanese restaurant and gotten my phone number from Mr. Ounuma. "We are planning to close your theatre because the curtains, set, and stage are not fireproof," said the township official.
"You can't just close us down." And then I bluffed, "I can have that fixed in two weeks. I'll call you when it's done."
I looked into the cost of fireproofing everything and we lacked the funds. We had three exits; what more did they want? Considering the size of the theatre, we had more than enough exits to make us the safest dinner theatre in the world. That kind of request from the township was totally unreasonable. I bet the old-war veterans were behind the whole scheme.
Neither Michael nor Tracey had an easy solution for the dilemma, and I did not know what to do either. We were in serious danger of losing the theatre and everything we worked so hard for.
Staying awake night after night, thinking how I could keep the theatre from closing down was getting me sick. My father's voice rang in my head, "Verónica my daughter, how many times do I have to tell you that staying awake trying to find an answer to a problem is a complete waste of time? In the morning you'll be refreshed and clear minded after a goodnight sleep and the solution will come to you as clear as a bell."
He was right. When I awoke the next morning a most

daring idea flushed into my mind. I called the township and told them the stage, curtains, walls, and everything else had been fireproofed just as they had requested. They were going to send over an inspector, the following Monday.

"Everything has been fireproofed?" asked the so-called inspector as he walked up to the stage and stared at it. "You used flame retardant material for the curtains?"

Oh, how I wanted to shout, *it's a dinner theatre, for goodness sake! Can't you see we have no curtains? Inspector, my foot!* What was he going to do, start a fire on the stage floor to see if it burned? My heart pounded so hard, it surprised me he couldn't hear it.

"Yes, of course the curtains and everything else have been treated," and I added quickly, "By the way, would you like two complimentary tickets to our next production?"

"That's very kind of you. Would you mind giving me another extra ticket so I can also bring my mother?"

We had some very good productions through the years, but some were more unforgettable than others, like "Same Time Next Year." Barbara Schiavone got the heel of her right shoe caught in one of the cracks on the stage floor and landed flat on her face. The audience believed she was supposed to fall in that manner and at that specific moment. Not a sign of pain was seen on her face. She smiled and stood gracefully with the help of her co-star. The bruises on her arms and legs lasted weeks before they were gone.

Because of what happened to Barbara, Michael took on the job of repairing the stage immediately, but we made plans for the following month to raise it two feet higher for better audience view.

"Fools," was close to a fairy tale, even the cast had a certain innocent look. The audience loved it and we were sold out every night. One of the performances brought a standing ovation as the old wooden bench where seven actors were seated—broke. Everyone slid down to one side and managed to remain with a dumbfound look on their faces. The response of the audience was pure amusement since it was a comedy.

"1959 Pink Thunderbird," and "Play it Again Sam," went on without any glitches. When it came to running extra smooth, these shows deserved an award of faultlessness to the full extent of the word, the same director for both plays took it upon himself to build the set and bring in the props. I enjoyed just being the producer.

"Love, Sex, and the IRS," brought in full houses every weekend. People wanted to see what sex had to do with love and the IRS. But talk about glitches, Debbie the stage manager, found a syringe and a couple of needles backstage—which cleared the mystery of why Tom, the main character in the play, would hide backstage most of the time besides arriving late for every show. Debbie told me heroin was being used. One night it did not look like Tom would be making it. The audience had finished their dinner and we were missing the main character. There was only one solution to saving our necks. Took a bit of convincing but I finally got Tracey to drive over to the Strand Theatre, in Lakewood where I had heard Mr. Van Zandt, the playwright of our play, just happened to be directing one of his plays. I figured he might be gracious enough to come over and cover for the missing actor. Meanwhile, thanks to Mr. Ounuma, we kept the audience busy with complimentary plum wine. Tracey returned twenty minutes later. She never even got to see Mr. Van Zandt. She was told by their stage manager that he had left strict orders not to be disturbed while directing his play. To our relief, Tom showed up just then. Our show went on after I announced to the audience, "My apologies for the delay, but due to a serious traffic jam it made one of our actors arrive late…" A spokesman for the audience cut me off, "We don't care honey, just bring us another glass of plum wine." After the run of the show was over, Tom knew better than to audition again.

I hope he is still alive and doing well. He was actually a very nice person.

"Alone Together," was one of those solid comedies theatre patrons loved watching and returned several times, much like a really good book that you love to read over and over again.

"Barefoot in the Park," ran by popular demand for two straight months. But it caused the theatre staff and me to use profanities when we tried to sweep the stage floor, between performances. The shredded white Styrofoam Tracey brought in to be used as snow falling, did look real but those tiny foam particles possessed a mind of their own, and any movement nearby made them fly away and play a game of catch me if you can.

"Shredded white tissue paper is the answer," Michael told me when he found out how frustrated we were. He also showed me how to make thunder sounds by shaking a metal sheet backstage. He was a wealth of theatre knowledge.

I sat for lunch at the sushi bar next to a short, heavy set guy who looked up at me and said enthusiastically, "Ronnie, remember me?"

I stared at him trying to pull a clue from his features.

"I used to live in the corner house from where you lived, in Freehold. Remember Martha? I'm Robert, her son."

I had to take his word it was Robert. He looked like an out-of-shape middle-aged man. But then again, Robert hadn't been in good shape even as a teenager.

"How is your mom?" I remembered her well. She was very friendly, actually one of the few neighbors who would speak to me when I used to walk by her house, but I always cut it short because of her bad breath.

"She died five years ago, from cancer," he said.

I tapped my hand on his shoulder. "I'm very sorry. She

was a very nice lady, your mom."

He put his hand over mine but I instinctively pulled it away. His next words confirmed what I read in his eyes. "I had such a crush on you when I was a kid," Robert said. "I still fantasize about you, in that small silver bikini you used to wear while sun-tanning in your backyard by your pool." He smiled the same gross smile he used to have when he spotted me alone at a store. He would come from behind pinch my bottom and run away. He was only fifteen then, but already sexually overbearing. He went on, "I used to climb your fence and just sit there between the bushes watching you sleep on the hammock. You were a sight to behold."

"You were a freaking peeping Tom and you're proud of that?" I stood and walked away. I sat upstairs in the darkness of the theatre, feeling flustered and angry at myself for not having the guts to punch him until he was unconscious.

Autumn of 1988

After "Blithe Spirit," I produced "Crimes of the Heart." Anthony, the director did not make it to the opening night. I happened to glance at the newspaper three days before opening. There in black and white right in front of my face was a picture of Anthony, and the full story. He had just died from AIDS. The article went on and on. It came to me as complete shock, his picture, his name and it mentioned he had achieved his dream of directing "Crimes of the Heart" before he died. No wonder he looked so sickly and frail in the last two months he attended rehearsals at the theatre. His dark skin blotches had worried me and I had even asked Arlene his co-director and close friend if Anthony had skin cancer. "Yes, he does." And she had walked away.

Now it was clear to me that neither Arlene nor her

husband, who were helping to build the set, wanted the other actors or crew to know Anthony's condition. They were afraid we would not want to work with him. The cast and crew, including myself, were upset that we were not told about his illness; after all, the AIDS virus was something very new to us and we did not know much about it except that it was a death sentence. We were scared we might have caught it just from being in the same room with him.

I called my friend Francis who was an expert on HIV/AIDS. "You don't catch it from shaking hands or hugging," she assured me. "It can only be transmitted through body fluids, like intercourse." I trusted Francis but did not share Anthony's fate with Al; he would have hit the roof even without cause for alarm.

Ahead of their times and against the public outrage who believed HIV/AIDS' victims suffered from a form of leprosy or plague, Francis and Jonathan her husband were looking to buy a building in Newark where they could provide care for parents and their children afflicted by the deadly disease. Of all my girlfriends I considered Francis a saint.

On Monday night Michael came to Kobe to set up the stage lights for the next production. I sat on the stage reading a script and every so often I glanced at him as he stood on a latter aligning the stage lights. I would have died if he had caught me staring. I had always enjoyed his company but lately his presence made me feel more than just partners working together. I missed him when I didn't see him for more than a day. Jane, our stage manager who also worked downstairs in the cloakroom, came upstairs. She wanted to tell me everything about her new boyfriend. I followed her to the lobby where we sat. When Jane talked, all I had to do was nod every so often. Her voice faded in the distance as my spirit carried me away. I imagined a misty warm rain falling softly over Michael and I, like a magnetic field lifting us higher and higher into the sky. Holding hands, we soared over the mountains ahead. The rain stopped and a soft breeze carried us over a blue ocean where a mini island with a single palm tree waved at us. We nodded and smiled at each other getting ready to accept the invitation, but Jane's voice brought me back, and I said the first thing that entered my mind, "Jane, sometimes I need to dance and jump and sing for no reason other than being happy. Do you ever feel the same, from time to time?"

"You're the most understanding person I ever met, that's why I love talking to you." And she gave me a long hug before returning to the cloakroom.

If I could pick a place to escape to, I'd choose the fishing village of Eiriceira, in Portugal, and live in the same tiny stone house, perched on the tip of the cliff overseeing the ocean where my family and I used to stay during the summer months. Just like in the old days, the warm soft sand would be more than enough to lavish my naked feet while walking to my old favorite spot by the sea and sit watching the ocean waves hitting the rocks around me, all day until the sun went down. Then return to my little house, cover myself with a lot of blankets, and sleep. In the morning, I'd get up early enough to catch the sunrise and sit again on the spot where I sat the day before, watching the ocean, the waves crashing like busting champagne bottles of white foam against the rocks below me and wait peacefully for the sunset. This scenario provided me great spiritual comfort.

Al was free of thoughts like that. He lived in a simple world. When he lied down at night, he was fast asleep. I stayed awake, dreaming impossible dreams for as long as I could until I no longer knew if I was awake or sleeping. Francis, and her husband had not given up trying to find someone willing to donate an old building, in the city of

Newark to use as a hospice for HIV/AIDS victims and their families. A week did not go by without seeing each other or talk on the phone. "There are lots and lots of abandoned buildings in Newark," she told me. "It breaks my heart to see those buildings not being put to good use."

She stopped by the Howell Music Center often. We exchanged stories about family and life in general and one morning I confided my fear about Steve's future. "He goes out with so many girls. "I'm afraid he might catch a deadly venereal disease," I said. "I don't know what the heck Steve has that drives women wild."

"You don't see it because you're his mother. He projects a natural sexual energy in the way he walks and talks. A lot of women are attracted to those types of signals. Look at the woman he's talking to. I bet she'll buy anything he wants to sell her."

Francis was right on. Mrs. Sanders came to the Howell Music Center to buy drum accessories at least once or twice a week, and if Steve was not in she walked out. Lately, she had been calling the store to have Steve deliver her order to her house. "I'll be back in two hours or so." He winked at me before leaving the store with a drumhead or a pair of drum sticks under his arm.

Mrs. Sanders lived up the street from our music center, only a five-minute walk. Her three little boys—four, five, and six years old—walked to our mall, on their own. That's how close they lived.

I was scared that one day her husband would come home early and find his wife and Steve in an incriminating position, and kill them both. Then I would have to adopt her adorable three children and the baby she was expecting.

For years I had wondered what was about our theatre productions that made our patrons roll with laughter in response to one funny line after another and other nights the same performance only drew a few raw smiles. I began paying close attention "I know what it is," I told Michael. "When someone in the audience laughs, it's contagious. It's like yawning."

"You're right," he smiled. "And knowing you, what are you planning to do?" He cocked his head sideways just a little as if waiting to hear my answer.

"I'm going to provide the sound of laughter and as such give the shy audience permission to laugh."

I spent the next few days practicing the art of laughing loudly. It was far from easy. Laughing heartily did not come naturally to me. I blamed my vocal inability to produce a loud tone, on the medical batch-up job of cutting out my tonsils when I was five years old, while pinned to a chair like a frog in a dissection lab. That had been the last time I screamed loud enough to hurt someone's ears. Al asked me what in the world was I doing going around the house making guttural creepy sounds.

At the end of the week, he asked me, "What's so funny? What are you laughing about?"

He had recognized it as laughter! My mission had been accomplished.

Friday night I let out a heartfelt giggle, right after the first punch line. Miracle of miracles, the audience relaxed and responded with a boisterous laugh at the next line. Michael gave me a hug after the show and whispered, "You're a miracle worker, congratulations."

Our music center was doing a lot better in the new location. Being in the corner of the mall facing route 9 had its advantages. Visibility, visibility! Also letting people know our whereabouts was the key to our success. Once a week, Steve spent the morning at the mall down the road passing out fliers with our store specials. I named such type of advertisement, *hand-to-hand combat* because the results were immediate with calls for music lessons, and parents coming in to buy reeds, music books, and other items on sale.

Also, with Christmas at our doorsteps, sales were already climbing steadily. Thank God for Christmas and Hanukah, two excellent holidays for retail people like us.

One night, an out-of-the-ordinary couple came to see our show at the Kobe. Barney and his wife Patricia were a middle age retired couple and wanted to volunteer their services as crew members. They were already involved with the Spring Lake Theatre and as such they had a lot of theatre experience. There was one stipulation to their volunteer work, in the near future Patricia wanted to direct a play for us.

Barney was an ex-veterinarian. He had to quit his practice after developing an allergy to animals. My goodness, what a career tragedy! But I couldn't complain, if anything I welcomed him and Patricia with open arms.

We were having Christmas dinner when someone knocked at the front door. A woman in her mid-thirties introduced herself as Sylvia and asked to see Ralph. The disheveled look on her face made me ask her to wait outside, and I closed the door.

"Mom, tell her that I'm not here."

I stepped into the hallway and closed the door behind me. "I'm very sorry but

Ralph is not here. You have to go."

"I know he's there." She pointed to our apartment door. "I need to speak to him."

"Sorry, I'm very sorry but you have to go," I said once again.

"Here," she tried to hand me a brown grocery paper bag. "You're his mom, and this is for you, a Christmas present." I backed away but she stepped forward and shoved the bag into my hands. "Please take it. It will make me happy." I took it and she left crying.

Ralph had met Sylvia at a bar. They had seen each other twice and then he broke up with her when he realized she had emotional issues. Since then she had been following him everywhere with her car.

Inside the paper bag was an old, bluish chipped ceramic bowl. Ralph didn't want it. I couldn't help feeling sorry for Sylvia. Love could be so devastating. I kept the bowl because I loved ceramics.

For the New Year's show, we did an original musical comedy, "The Best of Burlesque." Sam, our featured star performer, not only played a glittering, incredibly beautiful Joan Rivers, but he was even funnier. Two weeks before the show opened he invited the rest of the cast and staff to his favorite gay club in Asbury Park to help promote the show. Tracey already had plans made to spend the weekend with her family and Michael who worked as a night guard couldn't make it either.

Sam put on an outstanding mini performance, at the gay club and then the other members of the cast and I passed the advertising fliers around the tables. It was dark and musty inside the club. The air hung thick, as if brought in as foreign matter. The people inside were mostly men, talking, drinking, and being social. Within an hour I began sneezing nonstop and then a queasy feeling in my stomach took over. Feeling as if I was going to puke I had to leave earlier. Halfway home my head felt like a ton of bricks—sneezing, nausea, stomach ache and unable to lift my head, I recognized the symptoms, they were the same I always experienced when going into the chicken coop I rented in Howell to store the stage props.

According to Barney, I was allergic to mildew, and most likely the club had plenty of it since it was an old decaying building. I began to look for a clean newer place to store the stage props.

Winter of 1989

Al, Ralph, and Steve were having Hibachi at the Kobe with me when Sylvia, came over to our table, opened a small jewelry box, and put it next to him. It was a man's gold diamond ring. She then walked to the corner of the room and stared at us. Ralph went to her, put the box with the ring in her hand and returned to our table. She came over and laid the box open once again next to him and returned to the same corner staring in our direction. It was getting creepier by the minute. Ralph went to talk to Mr. Ounuma who asked Sylvia to leave the restaurant or the police would be called to take her away. She left and we thought everything was back to normal that was until we walked out of the restaurant.

Sylvia stood in the middle of the parking lot under one of the light poles. When our gazes met she dropped to the ground as if she had passed out. "Oh my God," I stepped forward, but Ralph grabbed my arm and held me back. "No Mom, this is what I've been telling you. She's emotionally unstable. Dad, don't pay any attention and don't even look in her direction. Trust me, when she sees us leaving she'll get up."

I did a quick glance over my shoulder as we drove off the parking lot; she got up and stood against the light pole. Ralph was right; she was out of her mind.

Tracey and I liked to sit in the Simy Dinner Theatre lobby waiting for the patrons to arrive, and as always, we found ourselves gossiping about some of the actors and previous funny experiences we had encountered along the way as theatre producers. Tracey possessed a devil-may-care attitude toward life and was a master at telling dirty jokes. She was quite entertaining except for when she made prejudice remarks about religion and or race. I had always remained quiet, unable to confront her. But last night she got to me when she said, "Did you know that the Jews own all the banks?"

"Wow, all the banks. Are you sure? That's a lot of banks." Last week was about owning all the farms in New Jersey. What next, I wondered.

"Mostly foreign banks, Ronnie it's a fact that the Jews like to hide their gold in foreign banks, instead of our good American banks. No wonder Hitler tried to get rid of them."

"I'm a Jew," I announced feeling my throat tightening and my voice barely able to project the words. Her bottom jaw dropped open and her eyes widened with surprise. "Now you know," I added vehemently, "And I don't own a farm or a bank and the only gold I have is my wedding ring. Tracey, my two cousins twelve and thirteen years old were in Holland when the Germans broke into their school and took my cousins, their schoolmates and the teachers and put them in a train to a concentration camp. As they arrived they were sent directly into the gas chamber."

She backed into her seat. "I'm sorry, about your cousins."

"Tracey, your daughter is married to a Jew. You must hate your son-in-law."

"Oh, no I love him, he's wonderful! The best husband and father anyone can wish for."

"It doesn't matter how nice he is, your grandchildren are half-Jewish. If you were all living in Germany during Hitler's time, your grandchildren and your son-in-law would be murdered just like most of my father's family. You better watch your words of hate, they are like seeds, and will spread like stinkweed."

She nodded in silent agreement and after a few moments she said, "You're right. I wasn't thinking." She looked at me as if for the first time. "You don't look Jewish," she said.

At least she didn't call me a beatnik like Al had done

whenever I defended a minority group. Tracey was a good person, but like Al she had grown up in a time when discrimination must have been part of their upbringing, and since neither one of them had any personal experience with losing someone close to them because of religion or skin color, I could understand how they might be detached, but I wasn't going to stand for ignorant opinions.

A small UPS package addressed to Ralph was delivered to our music center, this morning. When Ralph came by, I gave him the package. It was a colorful book of very graphic pictures showing the creation of a baby from inception through its growth in the mother's womb. With it was a letter from Sylvia accusing Ralph of having abandoned her after he had gotten her pregnant, and a prescription note with a doctor's name, stating that she was pregnant.
　Ralph called the doctor's office immediately. According to the doctor she was a patient, but she was not pregnant. Sylvia had stolen one of their prescription pads.
　The whole thing reminded me of the movie "Fatal Attraction." Thank God, the law was on Ralph's side; he put an ordinance against Sylvia to stop stalking him or she would go to jail.

On Barbara Shiavonne's recommendation I began running our stage productions for a month and a half instead of just a month. The work involved in changing the sets was physically demanding on me. The longer I could draw out between shows, the less I had to exert myself. Lately, Michael only came in when I called him to help with something that I couldn't do on my own. Besides working nights, he had started taking day classes at the community college. I missed him terribly but I also understood he had his own life. Barney had become my right-hand with stage work. I purposely had the productions closing on Saturday night so I could dedicate all day Sunday to putting up the next set. The director and the actors for the following show were very appreciative of this because it gave everyone a chance to rehearse and to get used to the new set from Monday through Thursday, before opening night.

    Taking the set down on closing night, took a major toll of pain on every part of my body, from my scalp down to my toe nails. I never got home before two in the morning since on closing night Mr. Ounuma liked to treat the cast and crew to a Hibachi dinner and I did not leave the theatre until I dismantled the set so that the next day the new set could go up. If I called Michael, he would help me but I only called him when I was in a real bind, like I needed a specific size window, or a new door frame built. Tracey came to the theatre to drop off the props, and in rare occasions she would offer to help paint the set. She didn't have the same freedom I had, to spend so many hours at the theatre. She had a very large family and she liked to spend time with her grandchildren.

    I rarely asked Al to help me with stage building of any kind. He complained about everything and being a very impatient person, he made a mess painting and did what I called a half-assed job. He came to the opening night to see the show, and then he didn't return until the next production's opening night. Barney helped me put most of the sets up, but sometimes he was involved with the other theatre and not available. I began hiring high school kids.

I found a clean professional storage unit on Route 9 only three blocks from the Kobe and during the week I moved the theatre props into it. The rent was five times more than the chicken coop, and it was a quarter of the space I used to have, but I was able to fit everything by throwing away items I had not used for the last five years, and those too large to storage, I took them home.

    While taking the stage props from the chicken coop to

put in my van I came upon an old typewriter still inside its original case. When I opened the lid, two baby mice with the eyes still closed laid between the keys in a comfortable layer of soft pink insulation, probably removed from inside the walls of the chicken coop, by their proud parents.

    I rested the lid carefully back without putting any pressure to close it. I removed all the props from the chicken coop, except the typewriter.

Taking advantage of being alone at the music center I played on my acoustic guitar, one of Mama's songs she had written as a young woman. I sang the melody with the Portuguese lyrics, "Like Jesus, his eyes are kind and affectionate. Like Jesus, he speaks softly and caring."

    I was thinking about Michael while I sang Mama's love song.

~ *Chapter Two* ~

RETURNING TO EGYPT

1989

Spring of 1989

The Howell Music Center had reached the highest selling record of Omnichords ever sold throughout the US. The owner of the company called. He wanted to know what we did to sell so many, and what kind of advertising technique we were using. He was very impressed with our selling skills.

I told him we rarely sold any Omnichords at our music center. They were selling like hotcakes at the Collingswood Flea Market, where we had Ronnie's Music Den since 1979. We did very well there because of the large foot traffic of teenagers that couldn't wait to play *Freebird* by Lynyrd Skynyrd on the Omnichord. I played loud enough to attract a crowd and then I stopped to ask how many would like to play *Freebird* that easily. All hands went up. It was a tune everyone wished they could play.

The Omnichords were easy to play and we sold them at a reasonable price. They were the perfect instrument to sell at a flea market.

I finally went to see a Rheumatologist in Red Bank, a town where a lot of doctors had their offices, most likely because of the hospital nearby. I wanted to know why the bones in my legs hurt so much. The pain was not constant but when it did show up, for no reason I could think of, it felt deep and sharp like knives stabbing my legs and it could last for days. Dr. Swanson, the rheumatologist asked me if I drank coffee, alcohol or smoked. I said no to all the above.

I found it interesting that he diagnosed me with Rheumatoid Arthritis, and not Juvenile Rheumatoid Arthritis like my Uncle Augusto, who as a medical doctor in Lisbon, and had prescribed me some sour medicine. Dr. Swanson offered to give me injections that might help with the pain.

I didn't make another appointment, instead I began taking into account what he asked; obviously, he thought I was ingesting something that affected my health. I wondered what kind of food in my diet could be acting like poison in my system.

"Have you seen the way Patricia, treats her husband?" Tracey whispered to me during one of our tête-à-tête moments while waiting for our theatre patrons to arrive.

"I've noticed that. Well, we can consider ourselves lucky that we're not married to her." I laughed.

"She's so rude to him," she said. "Last week, Barney had been working on the stage all morning without a break and when he saw her gorging herself with sushi from the restaurant downstairs he asked her for a piece. She told him point-blank, 'no I'm not sharing my food with you. If you want sushi, you go downstairs and get your own.' Ronnie, she treats the poor man like shit!"

When Tracey left her home in the evening to come to the theatre, she always prepared a healthy hearty dinner for Sam, her husband. He only ate one meal a day and she left it in the refrigerator and all he had to do was warm it up in the microwave. I did the same for Al.

I charted everything I ate and drank. Two weeks later, I found the culprit to my Rheumatoid Arthritis pain. It turned out that two days after I ate a couple of chocolate bars, my legs began to hurt. It was the worst thing I could have discovered. I loved chocolate!

I stopped eating chocolate for two weeks and the pain disappeared. Then, just to make sure it wasn't pure coincidence, I drove to the German deli on Route 9 and bought every single chocolate I could get my hands on.

Only God knows how much pain I endured two days later, after my chocolate orgy. Being an adult did not stop me from crying as loud as I could. Tears rolled down my face. *Oh, my legs. Oh, my hips. I couldn't go to work.*

I rented six romantic movies and spent the day on the couch, eating oranges, pressing my knuckles into my legs to alleviate the pain, and watching one romantic movie after another. I promised myself to never eat chocolate again.

Patricia and Barney wanted me to ask Michael to play Clifford Anderson in "Death Trap."

"I can't do that," I said to them. "He's busy working at night and going to school in the daytime, there's no way he can take the role."

"Honey, Michael would jump off a building if you were to ask him to do it." Barney elbowed me gently.

I glanced away feeling annoyed at being teased.

"Don't tell us that you're not aware of it." Patricia put her arm over my shoulders. "Sweetie, he's in love with you."

I remarked as quickly as possible, "You're confusing his kindness with love."

Barney winked at me. "Yeah, right, trust me when I tell you he only has eyes for you. Besides, we need him to play the part, and if you ask him he'll do it."

Barney and Patricia left the theatre and I sat in the

darkness of the room holding my hands to my head, thinking, this is impossible, this is impossible, it can't be true. I'm in love with him, not him with me.

I called him before leaving the Kobe and did my best to keep my tone of voice casual, "Patricia, the director asked me to call you to see if you're available to play Clifford Anderson in "Death Trap." I told them most likely you couldn't do it."

"I see." I heard his familiar breathing on the other side. I muffled the mouthpiece on the receiver with my hand, afraid he might hear my heart pounding in my chest. "Well, Ronnie, tell Patricia she can count on me."

Wow, maybe he did love me. I had to make sure. "What about school and work?"

"I'm not doing well; I signed up for too many classes and lately I've been thinking about dropping out. I've also been feeling guilty not being around to help you with the theatre," his voice took on a jubilant tone as he added, "but now I'll be able to do it."

"Are you sure about this?" Oh, my goodness, he did love me.

"Believe me Ronnie, I want to."

"Okay then, thanks. I don't know what to say. I guess, I'll see you soon. Tomorrow. Rehearsals for the show, tomorrow night. Thanks, see you then, at the theatre." I knew I had mumbled on too long and a wave of embarrassment took over me as I hung up.

Michael attended rehearsals before going to work at night, and during the day he slept. Since I lived very close to him, from time to time I offered to pick him up for rehearsals. Sometimes he fell asleep while I drove. When that happened, I slowed down and instead of going directly to the theatre I drove around Lakewood and Howell, and what would take fifteen minutes to get to the restaurant could take half-hour or more. When we finally arrived to Kobe, I parked the van but left the engine running so he would feel like we were still on the road. I did my best to keep my breathing as shallow as possible and used that time to study his flawless profile framed by the disheveled dark brown curly hair. The stagnant smell of tobacco emanating from his clothes and overall lack of hygiene fitted his slightly rebellious character and outspoken views. I accepted all his faults, in the name of love.

Michael's mom called last night. "Hi Ronnie, Michael is very sick with fever and with what looks like chickenpox. He asked me to call you and tell you not to worry. He's staying with a friend." I gave her my chicken soup recipe to pass it on to Michael's friend and that evening I went to the movies by myself. The movie *Cocoon* was about some older seniors regaining their health and youth by swimming in a pool. The water in the pool had special powers drawn from the cocoons that just happened to be from out of space and were being kept at the bottom of the pool by aliens. Besides loving fantasy and sci-fi movies, I enjoyed the story line and the happy ending.

There was nothing wrong with getting old, as long as we did it with dignity. But I was also aware that growing old could be one miserable health disaster after another. My parents were a good example of what happened with aging. If it wasn't the heart, it was the circulation, and if it wasn't the hearing, it was the eyesight. Everything broke down or went haywire. And what was the end? Death! I was not afraid of dying; I just prayed I dropped dead when the time came.

Michael returned after ten long days and even though he was very slim to begin with, I could tell he had lost weight. He had one tiny pockmark scar on his forehead. "I was very lucky to have a friend who's also a nurse, taking care of me," he told me.

I was thinking, big deal having an itchy skin rash. Kids have chickenpox and they survive. A tad of jealously toward his nurse friend had creeped up on me.

Al got annoyed every time I looked at our tab before paying at a restaurant. But he had the bad habit of giving the waiter the charge card without even looking at the bill. We got someone else's tab for lunch yesterday. It was from the table with the four drinking businessmen.

I also learned that when eating out it was wise to look at the food before putting it into my mouth. We were at the German restaurant in Lakewood, which was Al's favorite restaurant to have lunch, even though he barely ate anything but bread and butter and then ice cream for dessert; when I happened to look at my spoonful of asparagus's soup. I had to take a second look to make sure, a blonde cockroach laid between the small bite size white asparagus pieces. As I looked at it more closely I could see her tiny little legs sticking straight up, most likely as a result of being boiled.

The waitress wanted to bring me another cup, but I figured it would be from the same cooking pot and most likely other members of her *family* had fallen into the soup.

Sunday evening, Michael and I finished putting up the set for "Death Trap," and then we sat at one of the small tables close to the stage to admire our final work. "It really looks great, thanks for your help," I said.

"It's team work, give me a high-five," he raised his right hand.

"A high-five?"

"You don't know?" He asked I shook my head,

"It's a celebration gesture, raise your five fingers." He slapped his hand on mine. It hit me as the funniest gesture I had ever seen. Americans had some peculiar gestures for expressing their emotions. He walked to the back of room to turn off the stage lights. "I'm thirsty," he said. "Would you like some water too?"

"Yes, that would be nice."

He brought two glasses of water from behind the bar and we sat quietly sipping from the straws. We looked at each other momentarily and then simultaneously looked away toward the stage. We were synchronized when we turned our attention to the glasses of water and then our eyes met again. Time became non-existent and I knew exactly what drew us to reach for each other's hands at the same time. For my seventh birthday my grandmother Rica had given me two tiny Scottie toy dogs, smaller than my pinky finger, one was black and the other white and when close enough they attracted each other. Mesmerized by the way they snapped together, like glue, I said, "Grandma, how did that happen?"

"They are magnetic," she held one Scottie dog in each hand. "Imagine, one is the North Pole, while the other is the South Pole, the two opposites create a magnetic field, and that invisible force of attraction pulls them together." She brought them a little closer and then they held together. And that was exactly what happened to us when we reached for each other's hands. We didn't let go, we couldn't let go even if we tried, our fingers had intertwined as if we depended on them for life support. We couldn't stop talking about the way we felt toward each other and finally how that would affect our future and those around. The consequences brought us back to reality and we agreed that no matter how we felt, we could only be friends. Neither of us wanted to hurt Al in any way, and we agreed to keep our feelings a secret. Still, overjoyed by the mutual discovery that we loved each other, and since we were the only ones in the building, we held hands until we reached the downstairs foyer. Then we hugged each other just like we always did but did hold a little longer as neither wanted to let go. As we were leaving the restaurant and I locked the main glass door downstairs, Michael waved before driving off, just as Al pulled into the parking lot. He was driving home and had seen my van.

I could not sleep that night. Even though we had done nothing wrong except for holding hands, if Al had arrived earlier and seen Michael and I sitting in the semidarkness of the theatre, he could have easily jumped to the wrong conclusion and killed us both for nothing.

I called Michael in the morning and asked him to meet me at the Kobe. He was waiting for me in the parking lot. He put his arms around my waist and brought me closer, as he said, "I love the way my arms go around you. We fit each other like two puzzle pieces."

"I know," I gave him a gentle push and stood against my car door facing him. "We can't hug anymore. Al arrived right after we parted last night, imagine what could have happened if he found us hugging, like we did just now?" I could hardly hold my tears. "I think it's best that when you're finished playing Clifford we go in different directions," and I added with great effort, "It will also be a lot healthier for you to start seeing someone single and closer to your age."

"Our age difference means nothing to me." He opened the door to his car and maintained the distance between us. "Our only downfall is that you're married, a very difficult situation for both of us. Like you I don't want to hurt Al, he's a good guy." As he was getting in his car he turned, "I'll do my best to stay away from you until the play is over. But, if you need me for anything whatsoever, call me." I wanted to run into his arms but instead I said, "Thank you Michael." I didn't think he heard me.

I drove up and down Route 9 listening to the music tape he had given me on my birthday, but I did not cry.

The following week was the longest of my life. He played his part on stage and sat on the opposite side of the table when we had dinner with the cast and crew downstairs. Our relationship was one of politeness as we did our best to ignore each other. I felt brain-dead from lack of sleep. Finally, I came up with a solution for our dilemma. I called and asked him to meet me at the Kobe. We arrived at the same time. The restaurant was still closed. I opened the front door and locked it and then we ran upstairs and sat by our favorite table.

"Ronnie, I missed you so much, what are we going to do?"

"It makes no sense for us to stop seeing each other. We love each other but we are also friends. Friends are supposed to talk to each other and love each other, and hugging is also perfectly normal between friends. I hug the cast and staff. Does it mean I'm in love with them?" And then I added convincingly. "No, so why should we not hug the person we love the most?"

"It makes sense to me," he said. "What a relief to know I'm not losing you. I couldn't bear the thought of never seeing you again once the play was over."

We left the Kobe feeling perfectly happy, knowing our relationship was back to normal.

Michael called the next morning. "I have to go grocery shopping for my mother. If you want to meet me at my house we could go together."

I had been to his house several times to help him with building the sets in his cellar and his mom and I got along great. She always welcomed me with open arms; and served me a cup of tea, while she drank from a large mug of coffee and smoked her cigarette. She had a great sense of humor and always had a funny story to tell about Michael or his older sister Rose a newlywed of two years and living in South Carolina. I asked his mom where her husband was. "I don't know. One day he just left us, just like that." She snapped her fingers cheerfully.

Later on, Michael confirmed her story, "My father left

ten years ago, after he ran out of carpentry chores around the house."

His mom gave us a long grocery list. "You two take your time shopping and have fun," she said in her usual jolly manner of speaking. I had the feeling she was providing us with an all-day alibi. Michael and I held hands while he drove and we stopped at a diner in Belmar. While we were having french-fries covered in ketchup and vinegar he wanted to know more about my life before I met Al and how I had first come to the US. I gave him a condensed version of growing up in Portugal and how my mother had kept me away from having any type of contact with the opposite sex, and when I met Al, I was already married to him, by proxy. My mother and her sister Nelly had pre-arranged my marriage to him.

"I would have run away," he said.

"I tried. Believe me," I giggled. "I was so naïve in those days, I remember going to a travel agency to get a train ticket to Spain, but my allowance was something like a dollar a month. Besides, what could I do in Spain? I didn't speak Spanish."

"Why didn't you get help from a friend?"

"Except for my Aunt Heydee, my mother made sure I had no friends while growing up. I had no one to turn to. And then the thought of breaking away from my mother's reign became very appealing. I began to look forward to leaving."

"Did you love Al?"

"Love, yeah it felt like love." I had never expressed my thoughts out loud. "But I guess, it was an illusion I created. I say that because if true then I'd still be in love with him, right?" Michael nodded slowly. "Even the letters we exchanged for years while we supposedly wrote to each other, were an illusion, my letters to him were dictated by my mother."

"By your mother?"

"I didn't speak or write Spanish and my mother didn't know English, so she wrote all the letters in Spanish and I was told to copy them exactly the way she had written and then Nelly her sister translated to Al, who also responded to me in Spanish. Oh, my goodness, Michael I just realized something," I backed into my chair and said, "Al can't write or speak Spanish that means his mother wrote the letters for him." My mouth had dropped open. "My mother and her sister wrote the love letters to each other while playing the whole thing out!"

"Ronnie, that's beyond weird."

"Wow," I took in a deep gulp of air into my lungs, shocked by my sudden discovery. "Wow," I said again while letting my breath out super slow. "In a scheming way, Al's mother and my mother were playing Greek gods with our lives," I laughed at the thought.

He tilted his head slightly, his sweet face marked by sorrow. He reached over the table and held my hands. "You were so young; I can only imagine how difficult it was for you."

"No, not really, the whole thing was more like a dream come true. I was very happy. Even though he was twelve years older than me, he was very handsome, kind and affectionate; I made him my hero, my savior."

He shook his head slowly. "I'm so sorry, Ronnie, I didn't know this about your life. Basically, you were an order mail bride. It's so sad." He remained gloomy.

"No, please, don't be sad. If I had not come to the US we would have never met."

"That's true," he sat back holding one hand under his chin nodding at me as if he was seeing me for the first time. "You have gone through so much in your life and yet you don't look more than twenty-nine or thirty, it's amazing."

"I know, sometimes when I'm with my sons, people think they're my brothers. I wonder," I paused, and then went on, "Michael, this is going to sound insane but when I turned fifteen years old I worked very hard at building a mental brick wall around me to keep me safe. I know I'm getting older. I no longer look fifteen, but as strange as it may sound I feel like my aging is in slow motion because on the inside I'm still locked at fifteen."

He did not laugh or show concern for my crazy thoughts. He understood me. I knew we would never be a couple in a physical manner, we were like two ships in the night, but our souls had no mortal preconceived ideas and lived side by side. If holding hands and hugging was bad, I accepted my punishment whatever it was. I no longer wanted to look half my age. I wanted to grow old with Michael and even looked forward to it. I chose that very specific hour at the diner with Michael as the moment I had become a woman. Before falling asleep that night I tore down the brick walls covering me all those years, I no longer was afraid to face life, I had awakened the woman within.

Friday evening, when Michael came to the theatre, we hugged each other without any worries of what anyone might think. And we hugged when we said good-bye and made plans to drive into the countryside on Sunday after the show.

Then Al showed up at the theatre on Sunday and stayed to watch the play. Michael and I had to cancel our drive afterward. When Al got home he went straight to the couch to watch television and munch on salted cashews and peanuts. I went to our bedroom and sulked.

The next morning, I drove to New York City. I found a quiet spot on the steps of one of their public libraries where a stone lion summoned me to use his protective shadow. Using a pencil to write on my empty paper pretzel bag, I scribbled,

> When you hug me I can hear your
> heartbeat, and time stands still for me.

Tick tock, tick tock.
In your arms I am a snowball melting in
the heat of the desert.
In your arms I flow like a water spring
From within the Earth
gently sliding into the dry valley below.
But no matter how much I drink from it I
never have enough to quench my thirst
You are the air I breathe.
You are the space that surrounds me.
Without you I don't exist.

Before I left to drive back to New Jersey I dropped the paper bag into a trashcan.

Saturday night I got to the theatre two hours early. Michael had called me earlier in the day saying he wanted to tell me something very important that was going to make our lives less troublesome. We sat on the stools by the bar. "Ronnie, I need you to remain calm and hear me out," he said. "I'm dating a girl who I met a few months ago. She's a nurse, and when I had the chickenpox I stayed with her, and she took care of me." His words pierced my brain like poison darts and I felt a numbness taking over my whole being. "She's a very nice girl, a bit on the heavy side, and doesn't even come close to being as pretty as you." He lit a cigarette.

I put on my public-relations-smiling-face while my thoughts ran rampant. *She is nice, fat and not as pretty as me, is that supposed to make everything alright?* I maintained my smile.

"Ronnie, I'm seeing her on purpose so we don't stir up any suspicions. If I have a girlfriend, people won't suspect anything between us."

"Oh, I see. What a great idea." It wasn't that I admired his Solomon's wisdom. I was confused, sad and angry. But

I was no different from Ralph or Steve's ex-girlfriends, I was a fool in love and I knew it.

Then he invited me to spend the following Thursday at the Renaissance Fair in North Jersey. I didn't give it a second thought and said yes.

I had been in theatre long enough that I could express and act in the happiest, most pleasant manner and yet be dying inside. Every time I fell on my face I learned from it. It was called the school of life, and like Aunt Heydee used to say to me, "You can either take it or leave it."

I'll take it now, I told myself. *But if I have to, I'll leave it.* That night I began building a new protective wall around my spirit. I did not use bricks like the first time; I used feathers, swan white feathers and green duck feathers sown with clear silk thread. Since feathers could repel water I assumed they could also repel tears and as such help to keep away the pain of sadness, sorrow and disappointment.

Then I fell asleep.

The trip to the Renaissance Fair turned out into a fun-filled experience, as I had convinced myself that it was fine for us to be alone together. He had a girlfriend and I had a husband. *Michael and I are friends.* I told myself throughout the day. *We are only friends.*

At the fair there was a small lake with a path of rocks leading into the water. Michael walked on the rocks and stopped on one, then called out for me to join him.

I stayed on the shoreline thinking, if he comes over and takes me by the hand to walk on the rocks with him, we would live happily ever after. He didn't, and I took that as a bad omen. Before we left the fair, he bought me a round silver medallion necklace with a printed fairy and an inscription on the back, "Long life, and may all your dreams come true."

I had done my best as a wife and my two sons had grown fine into adulthood. Al would survive fine without me once he found a normal wife that would be happy just staying home with him. I only had one wish for myself, I wished I was dead.

That night I covered myself with another layer of feathers and double stitched the thread.

I asked Michael if he knew a graphic artist who could paint a large musical theme mural, on the side of the Howell Music Center, the side facing route 9. I wanted something big, something bigger than life size, to draw the attention of the drivers on highway. He recommended his friend Morph who had gotten his nickname from drinking to the point of oblivion. I had a gut feeling that Michael was his drinking partner, because when he worked at the theatre he always had a bottle of beer close by.

I was impressed with Morph's large dossier of very original cartoons. "I'd like the wall to be painted with the caricatures of a full rock band playing their instruments," I told him. "If you can add a sexy singer to it that would be great too."

"Right up my alley," he said. "I'll draw a few ideas on paper and see what you think of it." I couldn't wait.

Al saw me as I was about to leave the house last night and said, "I don't know where you get your energy. I'm going to watch TV and then go to bed. You gonna be home late?"

"I'm going with Michael to see the play, "Little Shop of Horrors," at Monmouth College. I should be back by eleven. Who knows, if it's good maybe I'll produce it at the theatre."

"From the title it sounds like a piece of crap." He sat in the couch put his feet on the coffee table and began clicking his remote control to change the channels.

"Bye, bye," I said before closing the front door.

Michael pulled over to the curb in his old pickup. He

reached over to open the door for me and when I got in he raised his eyebrows slightly and smiled keeping his lips closed the way he always did when he was trying to figure out what I was up to. "I have never seen you wear a sweater..." he seemed unsure of what to say next and then added, "You look so proper... nice."

Just in case he meant it as a compliment I said, thanks. Then noticing he wasn't wearing his usual t-shirt I said, "I've never seen you wear a shirt. New?"

"Brand new," he said.

"Blue is definitely your color, it matches your eyes." I noticed his hair had been washed and combed and his clothes had a starchy appearance, even his dark pants were creased as if just ironed. Maybe his girlfriend the nurse had washed and ironed them. I had gone through several changes of clothes myself, before making up my mind on what to wear that evening. I wanted to look dignified like a librarian but at the same time I wanted to project the look of a college student, since the play was being performed at a college. I settled for a short pleated black skirt, a cotton white blouse and a pink sweater. I thought the white sneakers and pink socks added the perfect touch to the ensemble.

We sat next to each other at the theatre, but we did not show any affection for each other, except for our knees touching. We smiled, we were connected. I found the play a typical juvenile story, and he agreed it would not do well in our theatre, our patrons were too sophisticated.

He drove along the shore and then stopped at Asbury Park where we checked out some of the boardwalk stands. "Would you like to see where I work?" he asked.

"I told Al I'd be home around eleven."

He looked at his wristwatch. "It's still early and the factory where I work is only two miles from here."

The building was closed and the parking lot was barely lit. He parked by one of the tall light posts and then pulled back the one-piece front seat to give us room to stretch out. He liked the play, which made sense to me since he was so young. He shared a couple of funny stories associated with having performed it in high school among many other plays. He had played King Arthur twice, his favorite character. "If you could choose," I had a hunch I knew his response. "Who from the past would you like to be?"

"King Arthur. Legend or not, King Arthur and the Knights of the Round Table are to me the epiphany of chivalry," he said. "I'm drawn to that time period. Men and women knew their roles."

"That's why you wanted to go to the Renaissance Fair." I smiled. He was a bit of a sexist.

He gazed at me inquisitively. "And you, who would you like to have been from the past?"

"Honestly, I don't care to be anyone from the past, too much drama. I may sound a bit philosophical but I prefer the present and who I am."

He stretched his legs out, put his arms up and crossed his hands behind his neck. "Philosophy is just a bunch of words with no conclusive meaning," he said. "That's why philosophers are constantly debating."

"You have such a good sense of humor." I laughed with gusto. But he was serious and the submissive part of me warned me to drop the subject unless I wanted to have an argument with the man I loved. Silence creeped up awkwardly and without mercy but the foggy windshield and windows drew a favorable curtain of privacy around us.

His eyes met mine. I had heard the eyes were the windows to the soul and I looked away. When I looked up again he was still looking at me, and I read in his eyes the desire I also felt for him. "Will you sit on my lap?" he said.

I didn't give it a second thought. His hands slipped around my waist and brought me closer to him. He rested his head softly against mine. We remained that way for a while like two doves crooning. The slight whiskers above his upper lip tickled my cheek as he used his lips to caress my cheeks. Our lips met gently for the first time and then the hunger for each other's touch grew into an uncontrollable lingering passion where our lips remained locked as I always had imagined between lovers.

Am I out of my mind? I asked myself as I moved away from him and sat back in my seat, knowing that I had gone as far as I wanted. I could tell he felt the same way because he had let go.

He wore a solemn look when he turned to me and said, "Ronnie, swear that if you die before I do, you'll wait for me in the next life."

Such statement took me by surprise, since death was the furthest thought in my head, but I answered, "Okay, I promise." And I instinctively reached for the knob on the radio.

But he turned it off. "Ronnie, if you don't mind, rock-and-roll music is not quite proper at this moment. We have just kissed, and…this is very serious, what we have done."

I was an oddball when it came to being happy at the wrong time. A heavy feeling covered me like deadly fumes from toxic waste. He was right; we had just committed the sin of kissing, French kissing no less, but in all fairness, he had been the one that asked me to sit on his lap and brought his lips close to mine.

"I better take you home, it's getting late," he lit a cigarette followed by deep inhalation. Pulled the front seat forward and drove speedily off the parking lot. I remained quiet, unable to express what was on my mind, but he said it for me, "Call me selfish if you want, but I still don't want to stop seeing you. Ronnie, I love you." His voice quivered and I wondered if he was going through an emotional breakdown from being in love with a pretty married woman, and a single not so pretty out of shape girlfriend.

I put my head on his shoulder and closed my eyes. "I

love you too, Michael." We didn't speak during the fifteen minutes' drive back to my apartment. When we arrived, I opened the door to step out of the car when he reached for my arm and said, "I'll be at Kobe's tomorrow night for the show, an hour earlier."

"I'll be there," I replied.

On weekends Michael and I met at Kobe, before Tracey, the cast, and the stage crew arrived. We spent the hour talking, hugging and kissing, not necessarily in that order. During the week Michael and I drove into the countryside, to the shore, or did errands for his mom.

Hugging, kissing and holding hands had turned into a delicious habit we were not willing to give up.

As per popular demand "Same Time, Next Year" was produced at the Kobe, once again. Barbara Schiavone not only shined as the main character but also as the director. Many people probably thought of it as a light romantic comedy with nothing to do with real life. But the play couldn't be any closer to the truth.

Cousin Ruth had been flying once a year, to the same hotel in Florida to meet her lover, a married man she had met and fallen in love thirty years ago.

Summer of 1989

I was at the Howell Music Center when Steve called from the hospital in Red Bank. They went to deliver a piano and he was driving the van and Al sat on the floor in the back "watching" the piano in case it moved. If that were to happen, Al would simply hold the piano with one of his hands. I had told them over and over again that in order to transport a piano safely, they needed to tie it with ropes and attach it to the hooks along the van's wall panels. But did they listen to me, never. I spoke out of experience from my first piano delivery. When I drove on a roundabout, the piano went along with the turn and fell backwards. Luckily no one was in the back "watching" it.

This time the piano didn't turn over but weighing close to a ton, it slipped like a dead elephant into one of Al's legs, crushing it into the van's wall. He was still in surgery when I arrived at the hospital. The head nurse told me that Al's left leg had fractured in multiple places and his foot had been dangling when he arrived at the emergency room.

The next day when I visited Al he was still under the effects of morphine. I called his surgeon and he told me he had to insert special screws to hold the bones together.

A week later, Al was discharged from the hospital. He lied on the couch all day watching television which was about all he really could do. When I came home, I served him dinner, and he watched one television show after another. In many ways his lifestyle had not changed since prior to the injury. If anything, he was enjoying the extra free time to watch more TV. Sometimes I sat through one movie with him before I went to bed.

In the morning I helped Al to get washed and dressed. My days were spent at the Howell Music Center with Steve, and in the evening, I headed to the Simy Dinner Theatre for rehearsals. On weekends I worked at Ronnie's Music Den during the day, and at the theatre for the evening shows. Michael and I agreed to stop seeing each other while I was so busy.

Two weeks passed. I did not tell Michael that Al didn't need me as much anymore, he had gotten used to using his crutches and had become quite mobile. At the end of the day, if I was done earlier with the rehearsals I relished spending time on my own. I drove to the shore and parked somewhere until it was late enough, that when I got home Al would be sleeping. Thank God Al never asked me where I had been. He did care, but he had gotten used to not having me around.

With his left leg no longer in a cast, Al began driving again and returned to work on weekends at the Collingswood Flea Market. During his checkup with Dr. Scramp his orthopedic surgeon, the x-rays showed the leg had healed well and if anything, it was even stronger than before it got shattered. Al was delighted with the good news and encouraged me to take a vacation on my own since he couldn't go with me.

Michael called and said he missed me. I told him the same and asked him if he had any suggestions where I should go on vacation. He recommended Cape Cod, and said he wished he could come with me, but he couldn't take any more days off from work.

Over the weekend I made a large dish of lasagna, boiled a couple of calf tongues for sandwiches, made a Moroccan stew of meat and potatoes with oregano, and tomato sauce with meatballs, and put everything into individual containers and into the freezer like Tracey did for her husband. Al wouldn't have to cook while I was gone and the kitchen would survive clean until I returned. I made sure everything was taken care of at the theatre and planned my getaway for Monday morning.

Before driving north in the Howell Music Center's van, toward my final destination, Cape Cod, I made sure I put my Lynyrd Skynyrd, Rolling Stones and Eric Clapton cassette tapes inside a shoebox on the passenger seat for easy access.

I drove without stopping through New York, Connecticut, and finally Massachusetts. Singing along with *Sweet Home Alabama,* I found my gas gauge hinting that I'd better stop very soon. I was in North Falmouth. I sat in my van waiting for the gas station attendant with a white turban and a painted dot on his forehead to fill the tank. He kept smiling at me but he would not come out of his glass booth.

I finally gave up and walked to his window. "Hello, can I have some gas?"

"How much in gas you want?" "I need a full tank."

"Okay, pay me first."

I gave him a twenty-dollar bill and walked back to the van. I waited and waited and he was still smiling but didn't even budge from behind his booth. I returned to his glass window.

"Excuse me, but aren't you going to put gas in my van?"

"In Massachusetts you pump gas yourself." His smile was impassive.

"I don't know how. I never done that, can you help me?" I pleaded.

"Sorry, can't help, must do yourself." He closed his sliding glass window and remained aloof.

There had to be a good reason why in the state of New Jersey only the attendants were allowed to pump gas. I waited patiently for a customer to show up. A car pulled behind me. I told the driver, "I'm from New Jersey and I have no idea on how to pump gas. Can you please show me? I'd really appreciate it."

I did a good job playing the damsel in distress because he stood by my side guiding me with each important step. First, you pull the latch by the trunk release. Then you open the gas tank and put the cap down where you can see it. Next, you remove the nozzle from the pump and put it in the tank. Remember 87 regular is your fuel grade. Keep a tight grip on the gas nozzle. When the nozzle handle returns to the off position it means it's done.

I put the nozzle back in the hoister. I pumped my own gas! Thanks to the kind stranger I felt as if I had achieved a masters' degree in auto mechanics.

It was eight in the evening when I found a hotel in Falmouth. For forty dollars a night I got what the front desk girl called, the captain's quarters, a white cottage set away from the main hotel at the very top of the hill. The view of the surrounding gardens made me ecstatic; it was perfect. I was in "The Ghost and Mrs. Muir" set.

I found a small quaint restaurant just around the corner from where I was staying. Oddly enough it felt wonderful to have dinner alone and to walk through the small town without any responsibilities or thoughts for anyone else. For sure my sea captain would be visiting me that night, and the passion of love would be as natural as the butterflies upon the garden below.

I awoke the next morning fully energized. Now I knew how Aunt Heydee had felt when traveling on her own all over the world. I was inebriated with my freedom. I grabbed a couple of blueberry muffins and a small container of milk from the free buffet breakfast at the hotel and hit the countryside with no particular destination in mind.

A road sign caught my attention and I followed the directions to an open field where a festive gathering of several Indian American tribes was having their annual powwow. The weather was pure sunshine splendid, with a slight breeze moving slowly across the large open field which felt more like a caress from Mother Nature. Except for Hollywood movies I had never seen real Indians before. My wish to someday see Native American Indians had come true and being alone had one great advantage, I didn't have to rush or worry if someone else, wanted to accompany me. I took my time walking from one craft booth to another and bought a small handmade basket, a pair of black beaded earrings and a primitive looking clay piece of a naked couple sitting next to each other with their legs crossed and one arm around each other's waist. Then I sat on a bench eating a plate of rice and corn, close to the tent of a family with two grandparents and four well behaved children. They wore their tribal garb with pride and I could see they had paid serious attention to the smallest detail of their attire. I watched the different tribes taking turns dancing and after a couple of hours, I found the perfect spot of grass to lie down. I used my pocketbook and a light jacket under my neck for a pillow and lay there listening to their steady vocal sounds accented by the beat of their rattles and drums. When it got a little cooler as the sun was going down, I returned to my hotel room where I dressed to go dancing at one of the many nightclubs around. I called Al to see how things were and I told him my plans. He said I'd be a jerk if I didn't have fun.

At nine sharp I entered the nightclub on Main Street which was packed with people a lot younger than me. The music was upbeat and loud, my kind of music. I danced and danced in the middle of a bunch of people whom, for the most part, were dancing by themselves. When the band stopped for a break, I left. There was another club two blocks away. I walked in as if I belonged and nobody bothered with me. I had become invisible. I danced until I was out of breath and when I looked at my wristwatch it read, midnight, the magic hour to go back to my captain's room. I wanted to get up early and take a drive to Provincetown, famous for whale watching.

The whale watching boat possessed a love-boat atmosphere of people holding hands and kissing their same sex partners. I had never seen anything like it so close to me. I had a lot of gay male actors in the theatre, but I couldn't even recall any of them being with their partner at any of our rehearsals or productions. Kissing between two men or two women was happening in a matter of fact way and soon I stopped staring at a couple of young lovebirds; it wasn't any of my business. My main interest was to see the whales, and there they were, those awesome huge creatures playing with us by diving under our boat and coming up on the other side. I could swear the whales were laughing at us as they sprayed us. A relationship, had been established between the sea creatures and the people onboard, a bond of mutual understanding that each belonged in their own environment. A boisterous joyful emotion ran free in the hearts of everyone on board when we witnessed one family of whales showing off their offspring as they jumped up out of the water and then fell back with a huge splash. The echo of ohhhhh's and ahhhhh's were followed by our intense clapping of appreciation.

The so-called Portuguese soup sold onboard had much to be desired. I was forced to spit a mouthful of sour veggies, into a garbage can. After paying the outrageous price of five dollars for a cup of spoiled food I felt entitled to get a refund. I told them when Portuguese soup was sour it meant it was spoiled. The response was *their* Portuguese soup was supposed to taste just like that, sour.

When we docked I walked to the center of the town to find a place to have an early dinner. A long line of people stood waiting to get seated at a seafood restaurant, and I figured it had to be good. The lobster stew was delicious and I used the French bread to soak in the broth.

I found Provincetown to be a very artistic town with lots of unique trinket shops. I didn't buy anything just had fun hopping from one to another and talking to the friendly store owners and salespeople. While walking on the main avenue, I found a theatre. The name of the play didn't ring a bell, but I thought it would be enjoyable to see a theatrical production I had nothing to do with. Bought a ticket and sat at the center of the second row, the only seat available. I was the only woman in the audience. I was surrounded by men; men of all ages. Most of them were young and very handsome. It wasn't until the play started with two men and the subject at hand that I realized I was in a gay theatre. Finally, I was going to learn more about homosexuality which has been taboo all my life.

There was no air conditioning inside the theatre. I felt sorry for the two actors on stage sweating profusely under the heat of the stage lights. Within half-hour into the first act, I started sneezing. I pressed my nose up with one of my fingers to stop the affliction. I even held my breath between sneezes but nothing helped.

I heard the usual God bless you, from the crowd. But after sneezing more than a couple of times the blessings stopped and the silence around told me I better stop or get out. I couldn't help being like my father who used to be booed off the movie theaters in Lisbon, when he suffered a sneezing fit. After ten sneezes I left, most likely to everyone's relief. I only had one scary thing prevailing in my mind as I drove back to my captain's quarter; I had most likely caught the AIDS virus. The sneezing would not stop, and my head felt as if it was going to explode every time I coughed out phlegm. I ran out of tissues in my car and had to stop at a convenience store. What if Francis was misinformed about catching AIDS only from body fluids and my running nose was the beginning of my deadly symptoms?

To my surprise, when I awoke late the next morning I was cured. I spent the rest of the day by the pool relaxing until the heat got to me. I retired to my air condition room and fell asleep until midafternoon.

After dinner I asked the girl at the front desk if there was any kind of entertainment besides dancing clubs. She recommended a theatre only an hour drive from the hotel. When I got there I almost died; it was "The Pirates of Penzance," the most awful musical I had ever seen. Tracey and I had seen it at the Strand Theatre in Lakewood a few years back and had been so bored that we kept counting the painted bricks on the stage wall so we wouldn't fall asleep. I told the ticket lady my disappointment after having driven an hour to get there.

I experienced a déjà vu feeling when she said, "You buy your ticket and see the show. If you don't like it, I'll personally refund your money back in full."

The show was more than fun to watch, I laughed with

tears and my feet kept dancing along with the music. I should have known better, a production relied solely on the quality of the director and actors, and that was one of the best musicals I had ever seen—besides my own productions of course. Before leaving the theatre, I stopped at the ticket booth and thanked the woman for encouraging me to stay. The only problem I encountered was finding my way back to the main highway. Out of desperation I simply followed the car in front of me. I got the idea from reading Douglas Adams, "Dirk Gently's Holistic Detective Agency." Michael had given me a copy as a Christmas present.

The following morning, the front desk girl informed me that my captain's cabin had risen to $80 per night because it was the Fourth of July weekend. I decided to head home, but not before visiting Martha's Vineyard which was very close to Falmouth. Turned out the cost of taking my van on the ferryboat was too costly and I opted to leave it on the mainland and then use the island's public transportation, once I got there.

When we docked at Martha's Vineyard, I was mesmerized by a row of tiny gingerbread-like homes. Like a foolish tourist I headed straight to one particularly pretty pink and purple home and opened the front door, ready to walk in when a big black dog came running down the steps barking excitedly with way too much saliva dripping from his mouth. Thank God, I closed the front door in time not to become dog food as the owner yelled at me for being nosey.

I wished I had learned to ride a bike as a kid, since they had lots of them including motorbikes for rent. Instead, I had to depend on their bus service and felt like I wasted a lot of time which could have been used to see the island. Still, I loved the time I had alone and I didn't think about Michael except for when I bought him a kaleidoscope at one of the shops.

Driving home I couldn't help smile, thinking about the pirates on stage, the way they jumped up and down singing and dancing as if wearing springs in their boots. They had used large trampolines strategically hidden behind the stage set, painted to look like ocean waves.

I opened all the car windows and said to the earth beneath my tires and the sky above my van, *thank you, God; for everything and most of all, thank you for allowing me to enjoy this incredible vacation by myself. I feel brand new.*

When I got home, Al wanted to spend a day in Atlantic City, but he didn't think he could walk the boardwalk for more than ten minutes with the crutches so I told him we would rent a wheelchair from one of the casinos.

Too bad the old pier was gone, because that was the best part of going to Atlantic City. In the old days I used to drive with my two sons and my mother-in-law to Atlantic City three to four times a year, it was only an hour and a half drive from Freehold where we lived. We always went to the pier amusement park and spent the day watching the amateur musical shows and finished the day waiting patiently to see the horse with the pretty girl jumping off the pier and into the water below. One day the whole pier burned down, interestingly enough, just prior to the casinos taking over the boardwalk. Then the casino owners had another pier built but no more fun shows, no more horse jumping off the pier, and only boring stores with junk. One store was no different from the next one, as if owned by the same company. Like the song says, "Nothing lasts forever but the earth and sky."

I pushed Al's wheelchair up the long ramp leading to the new pier, which reminded me of a cheap shopping mall with expensive, junky souvenirs. There wasn't much to see, so I proceeded to bring him down the ramp. But I didn't count on gravity and the weight of the wheelchair with Al seated. I lacked the muscle strength to hold the handles on the wheelchair and I was forced to let go. Al screamed, "Not so fast, Ronnie." I ran after him but couldn't catch up. He was lucky the wheelchair didn't turn over or hit an innocent bystander as it went down the ramp like a roller coaster into the boardwalk's crowd.

He was fine but very upset with me, as if it was my fault I had been born a weakling.

Michael called and asked me to meet him at one of the parks in Toms River. He kissed me as if I had returned from the dead and made me swear never to leave again for so many days. I gave him the kaleidoscope and we sat on the park bench talking and exchanging kisses between sentences. I was glad he had missed me. Then he said, "While you were gone my girlfriend moved in with my mother and me. We couldn't say no, she offered to help us with the mortgage and the sharing of the house bills."

"That sounds like a good financial arrangement. You and your mother must be very happy," I displayed full facial serenity while my innards constricted as if he had punched me in the stomach.

"I'm trapped, Ronnie. I've never felt so unhappy in my life." He hid his face in his hands. "She's a nice person and I feel bad saying this but, I don't love her, I'm not even attracted to her.

Oh, what a pity. He loved me but he was stuck with her. How terrible. But obviously not being attracted to her didn't stop him from sleeping with her. He's gotten what he deserves, misery. Yeah, misery! Okay, so I did feel sorry for him, but only a little.

"I know you and I are an odd couple because of our age difference, too" he said. "But when I'm with you it's the only time I'm truly happy." He held me in a close embrace. "Yes, we're odd," I said. It wasn't my fault that he'd been born later than me.

There was no medicine or cure for what I had. It was

called, being in love, and it sucked.

The next day Steve wanted to talk to me in private and asked me to take a drive with him during lunch break. He drove the backroads to Freehold. We talked about his ex-girlfriends and dating. Then he brought out marriage. I had a gut feeling that he knew more about my situation than I gave him credit for. "Mom," he said. "You and dad are truly a rare case, all these years still married. I don't know of any other couple married for so long and still happy with each other."

"Dad may be happy, but I'm not. The last fifteen years we have steadily grown apart."

"I understand. Dad can be hard to live with, but where are you going to find a better man than him? As a matter of fact, where's he going to find a better wife than you? Mom, if you get into a relationship with another man, at your age, it's only for one thing, sex! How long do you think that will last?"

I did not share my inner thoughts with him. The reason for my marital status being on the rocks was simple: our marriage lacked romance, passion, mutual interest in thoughts and beliefs, and most important the physical and emotional chemistry that came from being true soulmates. At the same time, I had to ask myself if what I felt for Michael was real love since he was my first real boyfriend. Perhaps I would not be in such predicament if I had been allowed to date before getting married. I had missed the link between being a girl and becoming a woman.

Steve said sex was the only reason a man would go out with me. But he was mistaken. Michael and I were in love, and yes, we kissed, and hugged, and held hands, but that was it.

Comedy plays like "Murder at the Howard Johnson's," were well worth doing over and over again. Neither the audiences nor I ever got tired of it. Bill Daniels the director and his wife Janet the co-director, were of the same professional caliber as Barbara Schiavone, except they lacked Barbara's aggressiveness and demanding manners. Bill was also a talented actor. If he were a movie actor he would be a superstar. Katie Grau a young actress I had the privilege of having in our theatre company stood in the same category of superstars. I guess I could just keep adding names to the list since I worked with many gifted people. But I had also learned that no matter how talented a person was it all depended on whether or not they were lucky enough to meet the right person who had the pull to get them to the top.

A good example was, when I met Paul's parents. Paul and Ralph were schoolmates and friends at Valley Forge Academy. His parents invited Al and me to dinner at their home. Paul's mom was a well-known movie star, and his dad a very successful agent in the entertainment world. His father heard I was a guitar teacher and asked me to play on one of his acoustic guitars. I chose a classical piece I had composed and he and his wife reacted as if it was the greatest song they had ever heard. He asked me to send him a tape with my composition, and then he assured me it would be out in the musical market as soon as he received it. The whole idea scared me at the time and I never sent him the tape. Opportunity had knocked at my door to have my music published, but I chose to ignore it due to my lack of confidence in my aptitude as a composer.

I knew I had reached my goal in set designing when Mr. Ounuma asked me where I had purchased the outside porch siding for the production of "The Gin Game." I told him I made it by following Michael's instructions. I cut long strips from the piano cardboard boxes I had collected from my music center, and then overlaid the strips by stapling them one by one like siding. Then I painted them gray and rubbed newspapers over the surface while it was still wet to achieve the outside weathered beat-up effect. Mr. Ounuma couldn't believe it and climbed on the stage to touch the siding.

"Bus Stop," was another unforgettable production with an excellent director and cast that year. I couldn't even think of anything more fulfilling than producing theatre. Our theater patrons left the Kobe with a smile of satisfaction on their faces.

"The Nerd," turned out great but it was partially directed. Kind of an inside joke since the director rarely attended the rehearsals. It came true only because the cast didn't give up and they basically directed the play themselves. The very young Ann Marie Alliano who played the part of a spoiled bratty kid, kept everyone inspired to have fun with the play instead of getting all stressed out. It received critical acclaim in the Asbury Park Press, and the director took full credit for it.

Autumn of 1989

I loved going to New York City every chance I had. I rarely took the bus; it was only an hour drive from where we lived. I always drove my van which passed as a commercial vehicle and I could park for an hour in front of any business as long as there was a sign, "Parking for Deliveries." One day while driving through Greenwich Village, an interesting sign above a black painted door, "Witchcraft and Vessels," caught my attention.

I parked the van right in front of the shop even though there was no authorizing sign. I opened the thick heavy front door, with daylight on my back until I closed the door. It took a few seconds for my pupils to adjust to the darkness. My nostrils began tingling in response to the stagnant odor of old books, candles, dried herbs in metal containers and burlap bags, staggered through the long but crowded narrow shop. I reckoned that soon I would be sneezing uncontrollably. A very skinny, young man with a pale greenish complexion wearing a black hooded cape was on his knees hunched over in one aisle aligning mini glass bottles in the bottom shelve. I walked up to him and said, "Hi, nice place you have here." He looked up but didn't respond. His back was still curved forward as he silently walked away like a slithering shadow. He would have been the perfect wizard character in a medieval movie. Just then, three men entered the store. From the way they were dressed in dark blue suits, white starched shirts, ties, and each carrying an attaché case, there was no doubt in my mind that they were businessmen on lunch break. They were chatting in cahoots with each other and chuckling as they passed by me. I could tell they were looking for the secrecy of something concealed from us mere mortals; the genuine dark world of the occult. I followed them.

"Look," I pointed to the young man I had seen earlier in the aisle. I lowered my voice, "He just came out from behind that tall bookcase cabinet, and maybe it's a door to a dungeon. C'mon!" I gestured with my hand.

Chuckling, they trailed behind me and when we reached the bookcase I fearlessly pushed it toward me. It made a grating creepy screech like that of a rusty metal castle door. On the other side was a badly lit room. "Oh, oh!" said the man on my right, the other two remained speechless.

I needed them for protection in case I was entering a real dungeon or some kind of torture chamber. I tempted them with, "This is definitely a secret passage. We should check it out together, don't you agree?"

"We're with you," said one of them.

They followed right behind me as I crossed the threshold slowly. "Is anybody here?" I called out. I was waiting for bloodthirsty bats to strike at us and kept my hands in front of me in case I had to fight for my life.

It was a storage room. Nothing but a badly lit storage

room! We walked through it, and quite disappointed but in some way relieved—at least that was how I felt—we got out of the store laughing a bit nervous from what we had just done and not being caught. They took turns shaking my hand, and the quiet one said, "You're a remarkable lady."

I drove back to New Jersey with a smile of accomplishment on my face.

I don't know why I shared my New York experience with Al. In his opinion, I could have been killed by the three so-called businessmen.

I should have known better than to tell Al anything, but sometimes I forgot he was a party-pooper. Michael, who was my soulmate, would be amused and most likely say he wished he'd been there with me.

Michael found a beautiful out of the way park by Ocean County College where we met whenever we could get away. We played hide and seek, jumped over water puddles, and I walked on the narrow two-foot high curb around the small pond and he held my hand so I would not tumble over. We had a favorite park bench, situated under a large willow tree and hidden away from the main pathway. I loved to climb on the bench and then drop into his arms. We sang songs and did a bit of harmonizing. I danced for him while he smoked. On our bench, we talked and sometimes just stared into each other's eyes and kissed without the worry of being seen. I did not expect more than what we had.

I had heard that in some religions, like in India, they believed in reincarnation. I needed to find the truth. Maybe my present situation was a repetition of my previous life and I could make a change for the better so I didn't have to return over and over again.

Two sleepless nights passed as I did my best to keep my eyes open while letting my spirit wander through the ages of time, but it wasn't working. Then, last night I saw myself as a child in a place I felt comfortable enough to call home. I stood among papyrus grass towering over me. I could see the same terrain on the other side of the river. I felt the warm muddy waters on my naked feet as I walked toward my two older brothers and sat next to them to play with the mud. We spent most of those sunny warm days playing by the river and running in and out of our hut a few steps away. Our hut was barely big enough for my family and me. There were no windows, our only source of air came from the doorway entrance where an old broken-down wood door half stood as if about to fall off the hinges. My father, brothers and I shared the sparing straw on the ground to sleep next to each other. There were no furnishings not even a tiny stool to sit on, but we did not go hungry, we always had either raw or sundried fish, and my older brother cooked delicious lentil soup with onions and garlic inside a clay pot, outside on an open fire. Then one day for no reason the river began to dry. We were barely surviving. Food was scarce. My father was not in condition to do physical labor. His legs were covered with sores and he used a stick to hold himself up. I couldn't remember my mother's face. Perhaps she had died when I was too young to remember her?

I wondered if I had dreamed the whole thing. I didn't recall falling asleep, only existing in a different dimension, a different time. Maybe it had been a dream after all.

I couldn't wait to go to bed the following night and see if I could go back to my dream, which felt as if I had lived through it.

I found myself sitting by the river as my right hand held the wet clay. My two older brothers were no longer around, they had been sent by our father to help build the pyramids. My father was the only family I had left, and he no longer could take care of me because of his age and health. His only recourse was to sell me to Senetenpu, the temple woman on the hill. She handed him several large coins and a basket of grain. I cried scared of my new surroundings until Senetenpu, said, "Will you be my friend?" And she ran her hand over my head. She was a very beautiful lady, draped in blue and gold cloth. I was entranced by the aroma of her perfume and admired her beautiful dress; I couldn't help but smile back at her. Two young women came into the marbled floor room and took me to a small pool of water and there they scrubbed me down with some kind of spicy soap and rubbed me with scented oils afterward.

I was Senetenpu's companion. I got to do errands for her, and I was present at her bath. They even let me pour rose water over her shoulders. Afterward I watched as the other girls massaged her body with oils and herbs and then style her dark wavy long hair up with silver pins decorated with pearls.

Senetenpu oversaw the temple where men came to be washed and entertained and then taken to private rooms for further body care. I was like a pet to the girls or perhaps more like a daughter to them. Senetenpu herself took me under her wing of protection and taught me to read and write, and after a year I was able to read to her some of her favorite poetry books.

As Senetenpu's favorite I had special sleeping privileges, I was allowed to use the bottom of her bed with Annipe and Mekal, her cats. Her room was my favorite in the whole temple because its large windows opened like doors to a wide veranda, with steps that led to the garden below. I loved standing under the stone arches where soft see-through blue curtains with gold trim (blue was Senetenpu's favorite color) hang from overhead, and when it was a little breezy they would brush gently against my face. Every day I sat on the two top steps between two nymphs' marble statues and watched in awe, birds of all colors and sizes landing on two large white towers in the garden, that Senetenpu had a cousin build for her. The towers provided a home for all kinds of birds, even falcons and it was amazing to see how well they got along as they made their home with their families until they were ready to fly away further into the skies.

Whenever possible I made little sounds from deep within my throat to get the peacocks in the garden to show off their feathers. It always worked because they were very vain. At night they were housed inside a large cage and they made sounds like those of a child yelling, it made me think that they were talking to each other and I couldn't help smiling.

One day Senetenpu walked into her bedroom unexpectedly and caught me using her lipstick and rouge. I told her I wanted to look pretty like her. She gently took the make-up from my hand and said, "You don't need all this junk on your pretty face," she wiped my face with one of her makeup removal creams. "Besides, these things were made to attract men, and at your age you should enjoy my love instead."

She laid me down next to her on the large bed and she kissed and hugged me tenderly and she told me that from that day on, I could sleep next to her as the daughter she never had.

Two years went by quickly. I enjoyed reading and making simple jewelry, I even made an amulet for Senetenpu. She took great pride in letting me ride with her in her private carriage. Those were the simple happy days of my young life.

Each night I found myself going back in time by just closing my eyes, it was that easy but I had no control over the fact that I would find myself in the same spot as the previous night, and the new chapters ran its course.

I was reading to Senetenpu in her seating room, when one of her cousins, a middle-aged man who came to visit us once a month, insisted on seeing her immediately. He warned her that the Romans were taking over the villages as they rode toward our town and he and his family were fleeing north for safety. Senetenpu decided she was not going to run away and told those working with her at the temple that they were free to leave. Except for two girls, everyone else stayed. Senetenpu cut my hair and dressed me as a slave boy.

When I asked her why she did that, she said, "So that you remain a virgin." She cried and then hugged me. Then she kissed the amulet I had given her, took it off and put it around my neck. "This will protect you. I don't know why men have to be so cruel," she said. "They like to burn and kill and make people suffer."

And that's what they did to us the next day. They laughed as they ransacked and torched our temple. When Senetenpu tried to hold on to her favorite vase, a knife was thrown at her back and she fell down. I ran to her crying. She said, "Quick, hide in the kitchen in one of the cupboards." Blood was coming out of her mouth and then she just stared at me and wasn't moving. The girls got their clothes ripped off and the soldiers were on top of them taking their turn at hurting them, some girls got beaten and others taken away as prisoners. I quickly hid inside one of the wooden cabinets in the kitchen. I could hear the girls screaming and the chaos surrounding me when suddenly, to my horror, someone opened the cabinet door and a large hand came in my direction. A Roman soldier grabbed me by the hair and pulled me out of my cubicle. Oddly enough his eyes showed no anger, if anything they appeared to ask me to forgive him. "Boy, you don't have to hide," he said.

I must have fainted since everything went black.

I looked at the clock on my night table, it was six in the morning and Al was sleeping next to me.

By the end of the day, I couldn't wait to return to where I

had been the night before. I didn't share my travels with anyone, I was afraid it would break its continuity and I couldn't go back ever again. I knew that being away was only temporary and felt safe even though while on the other side I had no recollection of my life here. Maybe now I would know what had gone wrong and I could fix my present life from my past experience.

I climbed anxiously into bed and went from darkness to opening my eyes as I found myself lying on a thin rug inside a tent. I stood ready to run away when I noticed the same Roman soldier standing in the corner and beginning to take his breastplate off.

"Boy, I see that you're feeling better. I could use your help here," he gestured with a hand to approach him.

He thinks I'm a boy, this is good, I told myself. *Thank you Senetenpu, you saved my life. I* reached for the amulet around my neck, it was still there.

His name was Damasus. I helped him to undress and I found that men had a different anatomy from women. I gave him a massage like I used to give Senetenpu—when she was tired from running the temple, which was a lot of responsibility and work—I noticed his skin was not as soft and white as hers and his hands were bigger and calloused. Afterward he fell asleep just like Senetenpu used to. I felt content that I had done a good job and laid on the floor next to his cot waiting for his orders.

In the next few months I learned more about Damasus' position in that miserable war. He was not to fight, but to stay safe and busy as a carpenter and toolmaker among many other things, like fixing the chariots' wheels, and maintaining the weapons by fixing broken ones, and making new ones. Because I had nowhere else to go, I found no reason to run away. Even though I was legally his slave, he did not mistreat me like some of the other Roman soldiers who could be quite brutal toward their slaves. I felt very lucky being Damasus companion and assistant carpenter. At the end of the day I sat outside the tent with a hand adze and a spoon with sharp edges and carved birds and cats from small wood pieces. I gave Damasus my best ones.

    When my breasts started to develop, I bound them with a cloth around my chest to keep them from being noticeable. Then the dreadful day came when I found blood coming out from between my legs. I immediately inserted a thick piece of cloth inside my pants and used a roped around the waist to hold it up secure. I had no idea what was wrong with me I only knew that I would soon be as good as dead. It was a very hot muggy night and we were having our meal outside. I drank two cups of wine along with Damasus. The wine loosened my tongue and got me to go into an elaborate explanation of what death meant to me. After trying to finish my third cup of wine which dropped from my hand spilling its content over my robe, I confessed, "I'm sorry to have to tell you this, but I'm bleeding to death. Goodbye Damasus." I fell off my stool. He picked me up and carried me into his tent where he took my clothes off. In the three years I had been his companion it was the first time he saw me naked. He filled a metal tub with cold water and asked me to get in. He handed me several cloth towels before leaving. "Wash yourself properly. I'll be back."

    After getting cleaned up I positioned the thickest fabric between my legs and got dressed. He looked tired when he returned to the tent. He pointed to the only stool available. "Sit," he paced back and forth. I could tell he was thinking. "You're not a boy. You lied to me." Before I could say anything in my own defense he stretched his hand out toward me. "I realize you did what you had to do, it wasn't your fault, the whole thing happened as part of the circumstances involving us." He kept pacing. "I don't like war. If I had my wish, I'd be home instead, working at my craft." He noticed my inquisitive look. "Furniture," he said.

"I enjoy making furniture. This job here is just a way of making a living so I can send my meager pay to my parents." Then he explained that my bleeding meant I was a woman, which was what women did once a month. If they didn't, they were with child.

The next day, after serving Al's dinner, I told him I had a long day and was going to bed earlier. To my relief he stayed up watching television. I couldn't wait to go back to Damasus' side. I closed my eyes.

Against my will Damasus took me to his parent's house where I became their servant, and his mother taught me to cook and sew and take care of her small herbal garden. The months passed without seeing Damasus and one day he stopped by briefly and to my disappointment he was gone for the next four years. I had lost all hopes of ever seeing him again when one morning while carrying a load of clothes I had washed in the river, I saw him on the road to his house. He wore plain clothes and walked slowly next to his horse; they looked like two worn-out friends back from a battlefield. I put my basket of wet clothes on the ground and after calling his name I ran to him. We looked at each other momentarily. "Are you coming home to stay?" I asked. The Roman world had stretched out too far and the conquerors were returning to their homeland. He wanted to know how his parents were doing and I told him his mom was doing well considering that his father had passed away a month prior.

Just two days after being home, Damasus received a special order from a rich merchant for a bedroom set. He had me helping him like in the old days, but our relationship was no longer the same. I could feel his masculine presence taking over my senses and I noticed he was not relaxed either when we worked side by side. I no longer looked like a little boy; I was a nice looking eighteen-year-old girl, in love with her master.

One morning while assisting him with some cabinets I handed him a small wooden drawer and dropped it by accident, on one of his feet. I fell to my knees. "I'm sorry I hurt you," I cried out. He lifted me into his arms, "The only pain I feel is in my heart, from not knowing if you love me."

From that day forward, we were lovers and saw each other every night.

A few months later his mother invited a well-respected family from our town for dinner. With them came their daughter-ready for marriage.

"No wonder she's still single," he told me that night. "She's larger than a sack of flour." He laughed.

But life worked in mysterious ways, and one night he said, "Since my father died, as you know, we're in a lot of debt. I'm afraid we're going to lose our house and property, if I don't marry Demetria. We need the dowry. When my mother first suggested this, I was completely against it, but now I realize that I was being selfish. But don't worry," he caressed my face with his lips. "I'm not leaving you. You're staying with us. You're the only one I love."

His marriage was a farce, a contract of convenience, and in the middle of the night he would leave Demetria and join me in the small room next to his carpentry shop. Sometimes we would talk about our future as a couple, a fantasy, a total impossibility but it was good to dream.

Demetria hated me right from the first day she set eyes on me. She took pleasure in making my life miserable, ordering me to do the most menial tasks that the other servants were not asked to do. When she found me washing the floors one morning, she kicked the bucket of water with her feet. Then she picked the bucket and hit me over the head with it. Everything went dark. When I opened my eyes, I was back in my bed.

I wondered if I should pursue my so-called past life any

further. It had changed a lot in the last few nights, but at the same time my curiosity took the best of me.

Damasus needed to go to Rome to pick up some metal and marble. The latest style in furniture required the combination of wood with those two elements. He told me he would be back in one month, maybe less.

A week had gone by of physical abuse under Demetria's hands and I was sleeping in the barn when two men came in and forcefully slipped a rag into my mouth and proceeded to tie my hands and feet together. They dropped me in the bottom of a carriage and I heard one of them say, "Not bad, we get paid to take her away and then make more profit by selling her." Their laughter mingled harshly with the sound of the horse's leather straps and the wooden wheels that waved sideways as if ready to fall off the axis. After two days on the road, I stopped spitting and trying to bite them when they approached me with water and food. I apologized for my rudeness and even offered to be their cook. Anything was better than being beaten daily by Demetria. By the time Damasus returned from Rome, I would most likely be dead. They laughed. Demetria had told them to do whatever they wanted with me, preferably cut my throat, but they were businessmen not criminals.

The short one with a flabby belly said, "A very wealthy man in Egypt is looking for a bride and we've already sent word ahead that we have the person he's looking for."

"We're getting too old for this kind of life," said the oldest, with only one front tooth. "But with this transaction, we'll be able to finally retire." I acted interested but only had one thing in mind, at the first opportunity that came along I intended to run away. But it wasn't that easy, I had become their precious cargo and through the months we traveled, every night they tied my hands and feet and slept next to me, one on each side.

It was nighttime when they wrapped me in a thick blanket and carried me aboard a boat, where I remained locked in the cabin below, and lost track of time. They explained that in a boat with a crew of undesirable men, I was better off not being seen. When we reached land, they used the same blanket to carry me out. At night they were still keeping me tied when they slept. I had lost all hope of escaping.

I knew I was back in my country when I recognized my old village. Upon reaching their destination they took me to a bathhouse and had me washed and dressed by an older but friendly woman who I took for being part of their clan. She told me that Amir my new husband had been married twice and both wives had died without providing him an heir. "He's desperate for a family. Give him a son and he'll give you anything you want."

"Who is he, my new husband?"

"He's the town mayor and as such he serves as the high priest of the nearby temples but his main duty is to set up the pharaoh's mortuary temple. There is no higher job status in our land." She stepped back and looked me over, and then lowered her head. "Dear lady, you're beautiful and soon to be very rich, please remember me. You have met my two sons, they saved your life and now I hope you'll have a kind word toward them and me so we can be rewarded accordingly."

Two tall young men wearing white loincloths and looking like soldiers were waiting outside. They escorted me in silence through town and then a large courtyard where cornflowers and daisies, fruits and vegetables were growing. A girl not much older than me but dressed as a slave, stood in the doorway of a large white house that glittered under the sun rays. The two men remained outside posted at each side of the door. I followed her to the central room in the house, where green wide leaf plants and a narrow-elongated pond with brightly colored fish, provided a serene, cool environment. She bowed and left. I touched the water and smiled at the fish, then looked up and saw

Amir across the pond. He had been watching me.

He stood from the bench and gestured to come and sit next to him. I expected an old man or someone mean and cruel that would beat me without mercy, but Amir was pleasantly handsome and only twenty years older than me. He confirmed what I had been told. It was important to him that I was young and could give him the children he longed to have, he also liked the idea that I could read and write and be part of their education.

If the man that professed to love me could get married to someone else for money, I could do the same for the adulation I felt in Amir's eyes. At my reach were all the promises of wealth that made life so much better to be enjoyed. Everyone that had meant something in my life had been taken away. Amir did not ask me to love him. I felt safe to devote myself to him.

I was nursing my firstborn a baby boy, when upon closing my eyes briefly, I found myself back in my bed.

I no longer question if it was a dream or traveling back in time.

All day I wondered what happened to Amir and me. Did we live happily ever after? When still living in Portugal, Aunt Heydee had done some research concerning our family tree, and she told me she had found the Esagui's had originated from Egypt and then traveled to Morocco as perfume merchants. That was probably my ancestral connection to Egypt. It made sense.

I couldn't eat dinner, I told Al I had a headache and went to bed. Before I knew it, I was back in Egypt where I now belonged.

Amir was loved and respected by everyone and most of all for his close position with the Pharaoh. The years went by as I kept busy overseeing my two sons' education, the monthly parties, our homes, and the people that worked for us. Once a week I walked through our poorest neighborhoods to drop off clothing and food. One late morning as I left one of the mud huts, I saw a beggar sitting at the street corner. I stopped next to him and noticed he was a foreigner from his clothing. "Are you looking for work?" I asked.

He gazed at me as if he had seen a ghost and as he murmured my name he fell to his knees and cried. Damasus face burned from the desert sun and marked by starvation made me cringe back. I looked around to make sure no one was watching and asked him to follow me. I called my chamber girl and asked her to get him settle in the apartment close to the kitchen and to bring him soup and bread and then to take him to the bathhouse with a set of clean clothes. He was to be made comfortable and allowed to rest.

I awoke with my heart racing as if I had run a marathon. I wanted to go back but no matter how hard I tried nothing happened. Finally, the sun peeked through the shades in our bedroom and I knew I had to be patient and wait until nightfall.

I told Al I had a long day at work and needed sleep. I pulled the shades down tight on our bedroom window.

Damasus had been brought to my receiving room. We stood apart, looking at each other, and then I motioned for him to walk with me.

We took the marble steps leading to the garden behind the house and walked silently for a while. We sat at one of the benches by the outside pond and then he held my hands in his and told me how he felt upon returning from Rome to find me gone. His wife told him I had run away, but he knew I would never have done such a thing. He knew she hated me and there had to be foul play, but he couldn't prove it. A year ago, at her mother's deathbed she confessed to him that Demetria had paid two men to have me killed, but later on when she managed to find out that I had been sold as a bride in Egypt, and felt it was better not to tell him. She reasoned with herself that I could be living anywhere in Egypt or died. After his mother's burial, he began traveling from town to town, hoping to find me. We kissed without regard for anyone seeing us. We would never be apart again. Taking my carriage, we drove down to the river, the same river my two older brothers and I used to make mud pies as children. The old hut barely stood, empty like a ghost from the past. We swore our love for each other and in that hut; we made love, realizing that without each other we would never be happy again.

How Amir learned of my infidelity I had no idea except for our indiscretion in the garden, most likely one of the servants turned us in. The next day I couldn't meet Damasus at the hut, I was to be punished according to the laws of the time. I had no fear of death, what bothered me mostly was that I couldn't die in Damasus arms. With my hands tied behind my back I was taken to the main square outside and there I stood next to the water hole surrounded by an angry crowd.

One of them yelled out, "Whore!" The stones flew from all directions.

My sons were not present. I had done wrong and they were never going to forgive me. Amir stood on the open roof of our house and I could have sworn I saw him cry. As the stones kept hitting me, the world around slowed down and then stopped rotating and all the pain vanished. For a long time, I was part of a peaceful and silent space.

Then, I found myself in my bed alive and that in itself amazed me. I pondered for a while on how real my other life had felt.

I prayed not to be reincarnated again if that's what had happened. I couldn't even imagine having to live, over and over again. I mean, how many times did it took to finally learn a lesson, if that was the purpose of rebirth. It sounded more like what the Catholics referred to as Purgatory.

But I couldn't help wonder if Michael and I had been Damasus and the Egyptian girl, and Al had been Amir because in our case except for being stoned to death, the story did repeat itself in many ways. If true, how pathetic that as human beings we were the re-embodiment of our past lives, no wonder history kept repeating itself. I could only hope my other life had been a figment of my fertile imagination.

For as long as I could remember I had known that I projected a "goody two-shoes" image most likely created by people's perception of what they wanted to believe. They always apologized if, by accident or habit, they used a curse word. And I always tried my very best to make them feel comfortable with their verbal communication. "My ears are not pure." Or "I have heard those words before." Or "I have used those words several times when a bad driver cuts me off the road."

"But you're so sweet, I can't even imagine you doing such a thing." Their usual response made me smile politely but it also annoyed me. I blamed my slight foreign accent and poor grammar for giving me a saintly image.

No one told me dirty jokes except for Tracey, who kept me in stitches laughing when we got together. Sam her husband, had a good sense of humor and didn't mind her jokes, but Al had a fit when I came home one day all keyed up to share one funny story I had heard from Tracey. It was a reminder of what happened when at ten years old my father cut me off from expressing my stand-up comedian streak by lecturing me how a proper young lady didn't tell jokes that might be considered risqué.

Once Al reinforced my father's philosophy, I no longer could repeat a joke without totally screwing up the punch line.

Morph finally got started. It took him over a month to

finish the full-wall painting of a five-piece rock band in caricature format. But artists could not be rushed, and when he signed his name on the right side at the bottom of the mural he was not the only one that was impressed with the final product. No one could drive by Howell Music Center without taking a second glance. It was a very entertaining and colorful form of advertisement and it brought us many customers that otherwise would have driven by without even knowing we existed.

I called my parents every Sunday. But when I talked to Mama it turned into an emotional trauma to my psyche. I wanted to create a bond between us but it didn't work. I came to the conclusion that I would never understand her. We were from two different worlds and would remain that way. Papa rarely came to the phone; he'd rather write a letter.
Papa had been born with a defective voice box and had to have surgery of the larynx when he was six years old. He was self-conscious about the tone of his voice which, had been mistaken several times in the past, for that of a female and no matter how many times I told him that he sounded fine to me he preferred not to speak unless absolutely necessary.
After talking to Mama, I felt depressed and without energy, like a dead battery. I cut down my phone calls to Portugal to once a month.

Barbara Schiavone called at two in the morning last night. It took me a while to realize it was her on the phone yelling at me about Tracey not bringing her the props on time for rehearsals and she'd just had it with her.
Whenever I had to experience confrontation, blood ran cold in my veins and prohibited me from expressing my real feelings. I wanted to say, call me tomorrow and we'll talk. But being a coward, and a non-assertive blob, I said,

"I'm sorry, Barbara. Yes, of course, I'm sorry, so sorry. I'll talk to Tracey tomorrow, I promise. Sorry about all this." She didn't hang up until forty-five minutes later.

I laid back, staring at the shadows on the walls. Rolling from one side to the other feeling emotionally battered. I looked at the alarm clock; it was three-thirty in the morning and I couldn't let go of the gripping stress twisting my innards. One of Aunt Heydee's favorite parables came to mind: Once upon a time there was a married couple that couldn't sleep. The husband kept his wife awake telling her over and over again, "What am I going to do? I owe one hundred escudos to my neighbor across the street, and I won't have the money tomorrow like I promised him. I use it to pay the rent."

"Stop worrying about it," lamented his sleepy wife. "You can't draw water from a stone! Just talk to him tomorrow."

"No, you don't understand. He's going to raise hell if I don't pay him tomorrow. What am I going to do?"

"Look, good man of mine, it's three in the morning! I need to sleep, and so do you. Just open our bedroom window, (the houses in the small village were very close to each other, one good reason why they didn't need a telephone to communicate) and after you call his name out loud, let him know that you can't pay him tomorrow and he has to wait until you can. Then come back to bed and go to sleep."

The husband got up, opened their bedroom window, and at the top of his lungs yelled out, "Hey, João! Hey João, wake up! I got something to tell you!"

João opened the window yawned and squinted his eyes. "What the inferno are you screaming about at this forsaken hour of the night?"

Mario yelled out from the top of his lungs once again, "Hey, João, I don't have the money to pay you tomorrow morning. I'll give it to you next week... if I have it. Good night!"

Mario closed his window and fell asleep like a rock next to his wife who was already snoring.

The moral of the story, as Aunt Heydee would say, is one should never hold anything back that can take away a good night's sleep. Yes, how dare Barbara take away my sleep to complain about stupid props in the middle of the night? Her phone call had been an inconsiderate and selfish act.

I dialed her number. It took a while to answer. "Hello…? Who is this?" her bass-like muffled voice answered as if she was still in a dream stage.

I told her Aunt Heydee's story from start to finish and then added, "Don't you ever call me again in the middle of the night! Good night!"

I lay down with a smile on my face, empty of anger, and fell asleep like a rock next to Al—who slept through anything.

If anyone had told me I could make a living out of selling chopsticks I would have laughed my head off.

It all began when after doing my usual walk around New York City I drove to Chinatown and found a place to park. I loved the Asian culture and enjoyed hopping from one gift shop to another. I happened to enter a larger store and noticed steps up to another floor. It was a dilapidated building, outside and inside but it was jammed packed with clothing, toys, grocery items and all kinds of household wares. It reminded me of a ten-cent store type of Chinese Salvation Army, except that everything was Asian.

I had to control myself from jumping for joy as the feeling of being in China-wonderland took over me, especially when I found the most beautifully handmade lacquered chopsticks, with engraved mother-of-pearl intertwined with other colorful stones. I bought one dozen for a dollar a pair, figuring on saving them for presents during Christmas and birthday gifts. But when I showed them to Mr. Ounuma, he was so taken by their beauty that he offered to buy them from me for ten dollars each. He said he would have no problem selling them for twenty-five dollars each set.

A month later I returned to Chinatown, to buy three dozen chopsticks. The store owner offered me a dozen chopsticks if I bought a total of six dozen pairs. Mr. Ounuma bought all the chopsticks from me. I made out like a bandit but so did he.

Michael's room was located in the cellar of his house and except for his twin bed, the room was more like an overfilled storage. His two cats had the run of the room and they strutted around waving their tail, and meowing as they jumped from one box to another.

I had been there once to help him carry an antique gutless floor radio to be used in one of our productions. He had reached into one of the boxes piled on the corner with all kinds of stage props and thrown me a rubber chicken which I caught in midair like a professional football player. The room was seriously crammed with old broken-down furniture, costumes from different eras hanging on a clothesline, tires, and lots of car parts. His collection included two old engines, three transmissions and several car bumpers he had bought from a junkyard in Toms River he liked to frequent, whenever he had extra money to spend. His bedroom smelled like a greasy garage with a cat scent.

One morning I got to his house too early and while waiting for Michael to get ready, his mom invited me to join her in the kitchen. To my disbelief she confided, "Ronnie, I have to tell you this. When Michael introduced Joanne to me, I just about passed out. Michael has always liked petite women, and if they're wearing a mini skirt he goes nuts over them. I mean, don't take me wrong, she's very nice, but they're not made for each other."

Then she looked around the kitchen to make sure we were still alone and whispered, "I think he started going out with her because she took care of him when he was sick. Now she's living with us and helps us with our bills, which I really appreciate, but I don't think that things are working out between the two of them. I hear them fight all the time."

I couldn't help feeling sorry for Joanne.

Our winter show kicked off our fifth season with a repeat of our first smash hit production "Plaza Suite," by Neil Simon. As always, with Barbara directing and starring in it we were guaranteed a successful run. If I were a lazy producer I would run that show all year long.

On November 9th to be exact, the Berlin Wall came down. One less separation between mankind! Little by little my wish will come true.

I knew it would take time, but with each step forward, we were definitely getting closer to having a perfect world. I couldn't be happier.

Two large straw fans hid Sherri's body in "The Best of Broadway." Her skin-colored body suit gave the impression that she was naked as she danced to a very sultry popular sax tune. One musical scene after another of dancing and singing with professional singers and dancers brought a few emotional moments to my memory bank of the days when I used to produce musicals with young people that had never been on stage and yet they were the best one could ever imagine. But those days were gone, and when people were paying a good price for their ticket, they expected their money's worth. I could honestly say that our patrons did receive the best of entertainment and the food was also top quality. Mr. Ounuma drove all the way to Canada and back within 24 hours without much of a break, just to purchase certain fish eggs and fish that fit his approval when it came to sushi quality. The chef was no different, if anything he was even more demanding.

One afternoon the restaurant ran out of meat for the hibachi, and Katie, the hostess and restaurant manager, drove to the market up the highway to buy a rump of meat. Katie had to run off the kitchen with her hands covering her head so she would not get a concussion when the Kobe chef threw the meat at her as he yelled, "Not acceptable in my kitchen! You can give that meat to your dog!"

Winter of 1990

Al's favorite food to eat out was Chicken Lo Mein. He could eat it every day, and the opportunity came along when a Chinese restaurant opened right next to our music center. Chicken Lo Mein was one of the foods in the buffet-style lunch, and he was there at least three times a week. I didn't want him to know I was not eating, so the few times I joined him, I put one or two pieces of broccoli on my plate but used my chopsticks to play with it. He asked me why I wasn't eating, I told him, I had a stomachache or I was still full from breakfast.

Michael asked me if I was sick because I seemed too thin. I lacked the courage to tell him that I was trying to shrink so when we hugged I could melt into him like magic. Even though he was the only one that understood me, I doubted he would comprehend my logic.

Without the desire for food I went from a size nine to a size three. Sleep became non-existent and if I did sleep I awoke shaking. I started having doubts about my sanity and since Barney used to be a veterinarian, I asked for his medical opinion without going into details. "Not eating and not sleeping, huh," he scratched his head. I wondered why some people had to do that while thinking. "It sounds to me like, depression," he said.

That scared me. I didn't want to be like my Aunt Ligia and be put in a mental hospital where the doctors would give me electric shocks to put my brain back to normal. And then, the next morning, Al walked into the bathroom, while I took a shower and screamed, "Oh my God, you look like a skeleton! Ronnie, you're skin and bones! What's happening to you?"

That afternoon I made spaghetti and meatballs for dinner and had two heaping plates.

We arrived at the Howell Music Center on Monday morning and found the police and three officials from the Howell Health Department taking away in handcuffs the restaurant's owners, next to our music center. Mr. and Mrs. Zhang and two other employees tried desperately to explain to the cops that, in their country, cat meat was a delicacy.

A neighbor had called the police department after hearing loud meows during the night coming from our building. The cops found cats kept in cages in the cellar and vestiges of the dead ones.

Thank God, I never ate the meat they were serving. But sometimes I did swallow the broccoli that had stewed for hours in the cat juice. "I always thought the sauces were too gummy," I told Al.

"I swear I'm going to puke," Al made a sour face. "I'm never going to eat Chinese food again."

I loved when people were honest enough to give me criticism. I throve on honest assessment and analytical opinions. The success I experienced with all my endeavors were due to that. I listened and then did what made sense. On the other hand, I had people telling me that I was too easygoing and Tracey even suggested I take a class on assertiveness. But I didn't want to be assertive. I loved making people happy and I went out of my way to do that. Maybe it was stupid of me, like Tracey had told me several times, but I liked myself better that way. I also believed I had changed a lot in the last few years. I felt more secure, more open to expressing my opinion even if not one hundred percent of the time. I also recognized that I could be very assertive when I had to fight for what I believed. I just needed a good cause to fire me up.

What possessed me to have nose surgery? I wanted a button nose, like Doris Day. The doctor made it sound easy and never explained how he was going to fix my deviated septum, as he called it, or how painful it would be after the surgery. They should have kept me in the hospital overnight so that I could at least sleep it off but the surgery was classified as an outpatient procedure and even though a blasting snow storm had been coming down for the last two hours making the roads a serious hazard, I was discharged from the hospital.

Al couldn't drive straight on a clear summer day much less on slippery ice with chunky snowflakes flying straight into the windshield. After ten minutes of stop and go, and slip sliding from one side of the road to the other, I knew I wasn't going to make the forty-five-minute drive back home. Besides feeling sick of my stomach, the pressure inside my skull, pushing through my jaw, my eyes and facial muscles made me beg Al to stop at a motel for the night. I needed to lie down.

All the motels were full. We found a hotel, for the exorbitant price $295 dollars plus taxes. It was the worst night of my life. I could not sleep because of the pain inside my brain, and it didn't matter if I had my eyes open or closed, dozens of ugly scary monsters and death-type roller coaster visions took over my senses and all I did was cry and sweat into episodes of pure panic. Whatever drugs they had injected me with; it drove me completely out of my mind. Poor Al, he couldn't watch television, any type of light or noise made my head hurt even more. In the morning I proposed that with what we had paid for the night, all their towels and the Bible were ours to keep. He agreed.

Bill Daniels was directing the next play for me, and as always Janet was with him. She worked as a nurse and I told her about my reaction after the operation.

"Oh, that's because he inserted cocaine into your nose, after the surgery." she smiled.

"Cocaine? Are you sure? Cocaine up my nose? No wonder I had horrible visions and thought I was going mad."

"It's a normal standard procedure to help stop nosebleeds during surgical procedure. It sounds like you had what they call, a "bad trip." Maybe he used a little too much, I don't know."

There were more surprises. Michael said if I had told him what I intended to do, he would have discouraged me. He had the same surgery done for a deviated septum eight years ago, and the cartilage inside had grown haywire making it difficult to breathe through his nose. But the worst was still to come. Al said this morning, "Ronnie, I know you're not going to like it, but since the surgery you have been snoring every night."

After one month the bridge of my nose was still sensitive to the touch. I couldn't wear glasses. I tried contact lenses, but I had stigmatism and only hard lenses worked. The lenses felt like glass fragments cutting into my eyeballs. I was forced to drive without glasses. Luckily, I didn't need them to see up close.

What a major task building the set for "Brighton Beach Memoirs!" We had to extend the stage on both sides, but I couldn't complain. Michael built the extra pieces needed to extend the stage floor from wall to wall and Barney helped me with building the set. I also had a great team of directors working together for the first time, Sandi Van Dyke and Barbara Schiavonne.

Michael called Thursday night. It was his girlfriend's birthday and she wanted to come on opening night, would I mind? "Of course, I don't mind," I couldn't wait to meet her.

She was not obese, just chunky and I didn't find her ugly either. Like Aunt Heydee once told me, "When you're young it doesn't matter what you look like. You can wear a toilet bowl for a hat and still be a charming beauty."

His girlfriend didn't smile and my intuition told me that she was aware of the love/friendship between Michael and me. Women have a sense for those things. After he introduced her I stayed away from them.

I had been eating and had gained a few pounds but sadness still filled my heart. I began thinking that it would be nice to go back to Portugal. In Eiriceira, the fishing village where I used to go in the summertime as a kid with my family would be far enough to hide away my lack of happiness. The sun would keep me warm and the sea would provide me company. But without money to pay for housing and food I had to stay amid the turmoil of my hopelessness. The feathers were not helping as much as I had wished for but I did not want to build another brick wall either. *Grow up, and stop whining* I told myself, before I fell asleep.

Francis and her husband finally found a building, in Newark, where children and families with AIDS could have the proper care. Al was upset with me for co-signing for the building. He didn't want me involved with anyone in contact with people with AIDS. He forbade me from going to Francis's house. What he didn't know it didn't hurt him, I still visited her.

We had a devoted group of theatre patrons, but I was also aware that people were not spending like they used to. Every once in a while, we didn't have a full house at the theatre, and we had the horrible experience of putting on a show for two or three people. But as they say in theatre, the show must go on.
   The Howell Music Center was not doing the greatest either. Two stores in our mall closed last week. The media announced that we were going straight into a recession. I felt we were already in it and the idea of opening a music center in Marlboro came to me as a possible salvation. Marlboro's population was in a higher level of finances than in Howell where the average salary was at the bottom of the totem pole. "I wish I had thought of this a few years back," I told Steve. I crossed my fingers we might still be able to get our heads out of the water before the boat sank. I began to look for a place to rent in Marlboro.

I received a letter with an invoice from a company in New York wanting me to pay an exorbitant amount of money in royalties for all the songs we had used in the musical prior to "Baby." I didn't know I had to pay royalties for songs we heard on the radio. I thought we only had to pay for professional musicals. The company kept track of every production around the country by having newspaper clippings mailed to them on a monthly basis. They had found us when the Asbury Park Press mentioned by title what great tunes we had presented on stage. Since it was my first offense, they let me off the hook, but from then on, any song out there in the music world was no longer available, unless our theatre paid royalties.

I asked Al several times to take on a hobby so we could have something to talk about besides listening to him telling me the news, but he had no other interests. I began playing with the idea of asking for a divorce, but I lacked the courage since he didn't even know that I was unhappy. I felt sad all the time, but nobody knew it, I wore a permanent smile—and I must have been doing a pretty good job at it, because my family and friends believed that I was the personification of happiness. Several times it had crossed my mind to leave a simple letter explaining to everyone that I was weird and needed to run away from it all.

Maybe I was like my mother more than I wanted to admit it. She had never achieved perfect happiness and her refuge had been writing passionate novels and poetry, an expression of her soul-seeking fulfillment. I had Al's love and support, but we were the result of twenty-seven years of marriage that had turned into a stagnant pool of emotions. I had two sons that loved me and were my best friends but now that they were adults, they had their own life. I also had Michael's love/friendship, but he was taking advantage of the girl he professed not to care for, so he could get financial help, and that bothered me to no end. It was painful to admit that everybody had a price and Michael the one I looked up to, was no exception. But I had good solid friends, and was doing well with my business endeavors, the Howell Music Center, Ronnie's Music Den and The Simy Dinner Theatre, and we were all healthy! I should've been satisfied but something was missing. I didn't know the answer. But I knew one thing for sure, there had to be more to life than just existing.

Not knowing where to run to, I began thinking about visiting my parents.

Al was not interested in expanding our business but I had Steve's complete support. "Mom, we can sit and wait until we lose everything or we do something about it, either way we have nothing to lose."

I found a building for rent in Marlboro, facing Hwy. 9, it couldn't be better situated. All we had to do was move some of the merchandise from the Howell Music Center into it. Basically, we didn't need to invest much except for the monthly rent. All the small businesses around us were closing. Steve and I crossed our fingers that our new Marlboro Music Center would keep the one in Howell from going under. This would be our last effort to keep us afloat until the economy got better.

I stopped going to New York City by myself after a young woman came into the Howell Music Center and told me she had been mugged and severely beaten while walking in the city by herself. It happened when she was twenty-three years old. She had been in coma for two months from the beating. If they had no pity and attacked a pretty young girl in the street, I would definitely be easy prey. I couldn't fight myself out of a paper bag.

Over the years, Al had been telling me over and over again not to go to New York City alone, crime ran rampant there. I didn't believe him because I had never seen anything bad happen while in New York, but after meeting a victim of a senseless crime, that did it for me. I still drove to New York or took the bus but only with company, like a friend. While one was being beaten the other could run for help.

We opened the music store in Marlboro but business was not good there either. We had a good size sign facing the road but no one was coming in. I was the chosen one to manage it. The sound of the music on the radio made me happy, and since there hadn't been any customers all morning I got busy dancing between the pianos.

The German side of me spoke first, "There's a lot to do here, stop dancing and go dust the guitars."

The Portuguese side laughed about it. "Don't worry. The

dust is temporary, clean it later. Dance and be happy!"

Both sides fought for a while and then my inner wisdom came to my rescue proclaiming; under the economic situation the country is in, you have done your best, now go ahead and take a well-deserved vacation.

When I got home I called Mama and told her about my plans to visit them in the spring. Ralph heard me and said he would like to go with me.

Instead of going alone to Portugal for a week, like I had planned, Ralph and I made plans to spend one week with my parents, and the other week traveling through Europe.

I stopped collecting new clippings from newspapers and magazines about me and the theatre. It was nothing but a bunch of paper clippings getting yellow and I did not see any purpose keeping them. Also, with about ten shows a year at the Kobe I had started running out of space where to store the VCR tapes. They were nothing but dust collectors and I had no intention of sitting down to watch the same show I had already seen performed for over a month.

There was always someone filming opening night and then all the actors and directors wanted to buy a copy. I was too embarrassed to say I didn't want a copy. I was such a nerd. When they offered me one as a present I couldn't say no either. Then with a guilt-ridden-feeling they all went into the bottom of the hallway closet, with all the other production tapes.

"Butterflies Are Free," turned into a brain twister because of the set. The low ceilings made it impossible to fit a bunk bed on stage. Barbara was adamant about having one with a hippie look even if I had to knock out the ceiling and the roof of the building along with it.

I wound up at a fence company buying metal pipes and had them cut to make a downsize bed frame, that could fit the height of the stage without looking too crowded.

Michael built the frame for me and it looked great. I did have fun painting in graffiti format a rainbow across the backstage wall.

Barbara couldn't be happier with the way I created the hippie set. The show was a success and as always, we received great reviews about the play and the set.

Lucky for me, Barbara offered to direct the next play, "Educating Rita." There wasn't much for me to do so I made plans to use that opportunity to get away with Ralph to Europe. The only thing that had not been easy to find was someone to take my place to run the stage lights and sound. Michael and his mother were making plans to sell their house. We still saw each other, but I had no intentions of bothering him to run the lights for us when he needed all his spare time to make much needed repairs on the old house. He had enough on his plate to contend with. Tracey offered to take care of collecting the money for the tickets, while I was away. I called Bill Goods and asked for his help; after all he was the one that worked with Michael designing and setting the stage lights at the township stage, when I was a member of the Cultural Arts Committee in Howell.

To my great distress I found that Bill may have been great at designing and mounting stage lights in the old days, but when it came to actually running the stage lights on cue, during rehearsals for "Educating Rita" he was too slow. Two weeks into rehearsals and he still couldn't coordinate the light panel with simple things like turning the lights on or off when an actor touched a light switch on the set. Bill was either too early or too late to be on cue.

Meanwhile, Ralph and I had already bought the plane tickets. I prayed for a miracle the only thing I could do.

Monday, Bill called in sick with the flu. Jean, the stage manager's assistant, offered to learn how to run the stage lights and sound. Jean learned the whole process that evening. Barbara and the actors were beyond happy and asked me not to have Bill back.

Bill came in Thursday and I was faced with the nasty part of my job as a producer. I told him I was worried about his health and felt better having someone else do the lights. I couldn't have been more delicate.

He turned his back on me and left without saying a word.

~ *Chapter Three* ~

CASTAWAYS IN THE OLD WORLD

1990

Spring of 1990

The whole mess with Bill, made me gloomy, but like Barbara said, business is business. I called Bill, but he wouldn't come to the phone, and his wife told me he wasn't going to talk to me ever again. Sadly, I had to accept the loss of Bill as a friend.

Barney's wife asked me to bring her two hand soaps. She swore that the Portuguese soap was the best she ever used. I planned on bringing lots of soap for presents, it was inexpensive, and they wouldn't take much space in my luggage.

While Ralph and I were in Europe, Al offered to take care of the Marlboro Music Center during the week and Ronnie's Music Den on weekends. Steve would handle the Howell Music Center. And when it came to leaving The Simy Theatre it was in good hands. When I returned, Al would be off from work for two weeks and I would cover for him.

With Al's blessing, Ralph and I got on the plane to Portugal. We had the kind of flight only kings could afford. The plane was half full. I took two Benadryl capsules and stretched myself across three empty seats. Ralph followed my example on the next aisle. We slept through most of the trip. I awoke with a man's foot close to my face. He had been sleeping on the seats next to mine.

Spring in Portugal was unquestionably the best time of the year to visit, the weather was sunshine perfect. I knew we would arrive at seven in the morning, and had written ahead to my parents, telling them not to bother coming to the airport to pick us up that early.

No matter how many years had gone by, I would always remember how to get around the city of Lisbon, where I had been born. From the airport we took the local bus to Praça do Chile, which had lost its frightening roundabout traffic jam, thanks to a new subway entrance. We walked up the Rua Antonio Pereira Carrilho a long steep street, which I used to run up and down in my younger days with the easiness of a mountain goat. Carrying a heavy backpack on our shoulders and pulling our rolling suitcases on the broken cobblestones was not an easy task, but as we stopped to catch our breath it gave us the opportunity to check out the meat and fish stores along the way, which threw Ralph for a loop since they showed their goods hanging behind glass windows with no apparent refrigeration. There were a lot more clothing stores and quaint restaurants along the way, since my last visit. And I was shocked to see an eclectic clothing store had taken the place of the old corner tavern, as we crossed Rua Carlos Jose Barreiros to my street, the street of my childhood, Rua Ponta Delgada. My apartment building #72, no longer resembled what I had described to Ralph. True that it was twenty-eight years later, but it still made me sad. The ten-foot-high pink marble exterior had turned a dirty gray, and the bright green exterior around the windows had faded into a peeling yellowish olive shade as if suffering from serious sunburn.

I rang the doorbell downstairs for the first floor on the right and the familiar buzz I remembered so well came along with the click of the door opening for us. We climbed the shiny waxed wooden floors. Papa stood alone in the doorway of the apartment waiting for us. He stretched out his arms toward me and cried when we hugged. That day he was expressing his happiness and longing for us. It was the third time in my life I had seen my father cry and it broke my heart. The first time, after his partner in business stole from him and ran away to the US, leaving our family destitute. The second time, he had cried after apologizing for having worked day and night to provide food and the basic needs for his family and in that process, he had lost the opportunity to know my brothers and I while we were growing up.

I found Mama seated in her rocking chair next to her bed. She was too weak to get up. Most likely drugged, (one of the benefits of having a family of medical doctors) because she cried calmly, without the usual drama I used to witness in the past.

By staying with my parents, Ralph got to watch them fight over the large fish head during dinner. They were willing to share the brain and the fish eyes, but Ralph refused to try either. They gave me the eyes. Poor Ralph didn't know what he was missing.

I was very disappointed and might even add angry at Maria Fonseca the maid that took care of Mama. I should say employee, their new job title as Papa corrected me. It had always bothered me when people professed how religious they were when in actuality they were the furthest away from God. Mama told me that Maria Fonseca, was helping her with bathing one morning and she said to Mama, "I'm a Catholic, and every time I have to touch you, it turns my stomach to know I'm touching a Jew."

When the employee gave notice that she had to leave for a week to have a tumor removed from her neck I said to Mama, "I guess God gave her what she deserves."

Papa heard me. "God doesn't give pain and misery to

anyone. Each of us gets what we do to ourselves. God is good and forgives everybody for their sins."

He was right. I had spoken out of anger. I asked Mama why she did not fire her employee for speaking to her in those terms, and Mama said, "She's very religious and can't help herself. Overall she's a good person."

Yeah right, a devoted Catholic making another human being, feel like dirt.

At breakfast, Papa told us, "Lisbon reminds me of an old mouth with rotten teeth." Papa had lost his dry German outlook on life and had become dramatically Portuguese with his visual descriptions. But his observation was accurate. Some of the older part of the city was plagued with seriously decaying apartment buildings as tall as five or six floors. A noticeably curious abundance of grass and ivy grew over the roof tops and from within the building's gut perforating through the outside walls and the wide-open windows, a perfect example of mother earth taking over her ground at all levels. Some apartment buildings had chains holding the front door closed and a sign, "Do not enter, danger," as an indication of being condemned. The cobblestone sidewalks were uneven or broken with huge sandy-like potholes from parked cars using the sidewalks versus the streets where they belonged. But in all fairness if the cars did park on the street, there would be no space for through traffic. The city was busting at the seams. I also had to keep an observant eye ahead of me if I did not want to step on dog feces or twist an ankle on a hole where cobblestones were missing. It was like nobody cared anymore. To Ralph everything looked typically foreign and charming. It also helped he had nothing to compare it with, since that was his first trip to Portugal.

Maybe what I remembered being perfect was an illusion I had created in my mind, as it related to my childhood.

It was fun watching Ralph enjoying the Portuguese cuisine. Actually, I enjoyed eating as much as him. Perhaps a bit too much, we were constantly bloated. My parents insisted we join them for all the meals, so we returned home for lunch and dinner because we did not want to offend them. But when we went out exploring the sites, we would stop at local taverns and bakeries and try whatever enticed us by the sense of smell or looks. It was the palate experience of a lifetime.

My younger brother José lived with my parents, and we only saw him when he sat with us at mealtimes. His medication was added to the soup he ate, otherwise he would not take the drugs he needed to control the schizophrenia. He used to be such a good-looking bright youngster, I could not make myself look at him, it was too creepy to see him smile and or talk to himself. He ate and then returned to his bedroom where he sat at his desk resolving geometrical problems until he was called for the next meal.

Papa took me aside one morning and whispered, "Verónica, it was very nice of you to send your mother the trophy. You know, the so-called 'Academy Award.'"

I had no intentions of breaking down. "Papa, it is a real Academy Award from the Simy Dinner Theatre Company. Mama deserved it for her lyric poem 'And the Black Panther Cried.'"

Papa winked at me and smiled. "Verónica, I'm not stupid. I know exactly what you did. You're a good daughter and you made Mama very happy when you sent her the trophy." He gave me a long hug.

That night Ralph decided to explore the Lisbon nightlife and I stayed home with my parents. They freaked me out over the dangers facing anyone daring to go out alone into the big ugly city full of sinners and killers roaming the streets at night. Ralph did not speak Portuguese. If he were to yell for help, nobody would understand him. I was extremely worried.

The television was in my parent's bedroom and by nine

they wanted to go to sleep. Mama drank a glass of warm milk, to which she attributed her youthful skin, and Papa ate a banana, which he believed helped him to sleep like a baby.

Once in my bedroom I sat by the window from which my two brothers and I had done the silly stupid things kids did, like spitting and throwing dirt on the pedestrians walking below. I closed my eyes to better listen to the city sounds of cars' engines, rolling tires over the cobblestones, horns blowing, people walking below my window talking, a radio in the distance playing the Fado, the scent of fish stew from a neighbor's kitchen. I took a deep lungful in and out through my mouth as my whole being absorbed each single particle of oxygen and I could not help smiling, it felt no different from twenty-eight years ago. When it got chilly I closed the window and laid in bed waiting for Ralph to come home. As I prayed for his safety, I did my best to push away the images of gypsies robbing and killing him.

I heard the front door open at two in the morning. I thanked God for Ralph's safe return and fell asleep in an instant.

This trip was quite different from the previous times where I visited my parents and remained seated with them in their room talking the whole time. After three days in Lisbon, Ralph and I took a bus to Faro, in the south of Portugal.

Ralph wanted to find the Esagui's roots, so that he could finish the family tree he had started years earlier. We already had the Wartenberg's tree from my father's side, but when it came to the Esagui's on my mother's side there was a bit of a mystery. His grandfather's parents were from Morocco, but what was their family connection to the south of Portugal? We were hoping to find out.

Before leaving to Faro, Mama told us that Ralph's grandfather was either second or third cousin to Nelly. But

Ralph did not want to settle with a guess, he needed to gather concrete evidence to properly put the family tree together. Mama informed us that the best place to start the investigation into our ancestry would be in Faro, at the Jewish cemetery. She also encouraged us to visit the cemetery in Tangier, Morocco. "In Tangier you'll be able to find my grandfather's tomb. He was a great man, a very famous rabbi. He started the first Jewish Temple in North Africa and was considered a holy man."

"And where is the cemetery in Tangier? Do you have the address?" I asked.

"It's easy to find," she said in a matter-of-fact. "When the ship arrives at the dock you'll see a large avenue bearing to the left side and going along the beach. That is the road you want to take. It's called the Principal Avenue or something like that. Within two or three blocks you'll see the cemetery on your right. You can't miss it." She wrote on a piece of paper the address and phone number of an aunt who lived in Tangier, and most likely would be glad to let us stay with her.

"I wish I could come with you, just to have some couscous," Papa said. "But I can't leave your mother, she needs me."

We promised to find our aunt, have couscous, and visit Mama's grandfather's tomb. Our intentions were then to travel through Spain and France before returning to Portugal.

Ralph and I left very excited with the promise of an adventure about to unfold. This was going to be the trip of a lifetime since we would be following the footsteps of our ancestors and discover the many missing links of the Esagui family tree.

When I lived in Lisbon I never had the opportunity or the reason to travel to the south of Portugal. I couldn't wait to finally see the cork and almond trees that had made that region so famous.

Our bus rode on the straightest road I had ever seen, through an endless flat terrain of arid, dusty land. I imagined Don Afonso Henriques, who became the first king of Portugal, riding his horse along with his men, in those dried fields. He would have worn the appropriate heavy armor of those days and carried the heavy tools of war to kill the moors and take over their castles. Attending school in Lisbon while growing up, I had read many books about Portuguese history and their bloody battles. I shared some of the more romantic stories with Ralph.

In Faro, we found a pensão, which was one notch above a hostel, for only ten dollars a night. The single beds had very thin mattresses and at night we ached all over from sleeping on top of metal springs. The bathroom was down the hallway, but we didn't mind since the price fitted our next-to-zero budget. The front desk girl told us the Jewish cemetery was up the hill only two or three blocks, from the pensão. Following her directions, we found a cemetery up the street. It was a Catholic cemetery.

"Excuse me sir, but can you tell me where the Jewish cemetery is?" I asked the guard at the gate.

Visibly appalled by my question he said, "Why the hell would you want to know where the Jews are?"

I was very quick to answer, since my *innate intelligence* told me, that I'd better come up with a good answer or he was going to tie us up and burn us at the stake.

"We're news reporters from the United States of America and we need to see very old graves, you know… history!"

"Why look at an old cemetery when you can look at this new one instead? Look over there," he pointed to an impressive large mausoleum. "Isn't it grand? Have you ever seen anything like it? This is the cemetery you should be writing about!" He puffed up his chest like a cock by the hen's house, in this case *his* cemetery.

"You're absolutely right," I said. "I can see those

mausoleums up there are a real work of art, very nice indeed. But we need to write about the ugly as well as the beautiful. If you can direct me to the old junky Jewish cemetery we'll start there, and then finish our American news investigation report here at this beautiful cemetery. How does that sound?"

He shrugged his shoulders and then brought them down as he let out a loud sigh, then looked up at the sky as if to ask God to give him some form of endurance. He murmured under his breath, "Dear Virgin Mary," and then pointed to his left, "Go up that street, and after passing the hospital make a right, across the way you'll find the damned place." He turned his back on us.

As we were walking I told Ralph about the prejudice I had encountered while growing up in Portugal. "Most of the Portuguese are Catholics and, in my days, they were constantly being reminded in church that the Jews killed Christ. Here in Faro during the fourteenth century the Jewish community was famous for their contribution toward education, the arts, and businesses making it a very successful city but that didn't save them when in 1496 the king of Portugal began expelling those who did not convert to Christianity. The story is that even the Pope tried to rid Europe of all Jews and Muslims since they did not follow the Catholic teachings. Spain and Portugal welcomed the Inquisition with open arms." I could tell Ralph was listening but he did not become aware of what I meant until we reached the hospital grounds and I asked two old ladies walking arm-in-arm. "Excuse me, but by any chance do you know where the Jewish cemetery is?"

They drew back as if the devil had jumped in front of them and crossed themselves at the same time. One cringed, "Jesus Christ!" and crossed herself again. The other followed like an echo, "Jesus Almighty!" Then the first one that had spoken proceeded to spit on the ground, right in front of us as they hurriedly walked away.

We looked at each other for a moment and without a word we kept on walking from one street to another, and twice around the hospital asking anyone that would stop to help us. Finally, a middle age man pointed across the street, "Right there. Right over there, can't you see the wall?"

Ralph and I stood motionless gazing at the thick, white-painted stone wall, so tall that it seemed to touch the sky, in front of the wall was a parking lot with rows and rows of cars tightly parked. The cemetery did exist but in a surrealistic manner, and its existence suddenly became part of The Walls of Flesh our senses. We ran across the street to touch it. Our ancestors were behind the white wall!

We ran along the wall eager to find its entrance. It faced the other side of the parking lot. An extremely tall, thick, black iron gate was locked tight with a thick metal chain and an impressive bulky lock, making it clear that no one was welcome. In the US there were no walls or doors like that around cemeteries. It was as if the dead were hiding from the living. Ralph thought he might be able to climb the metal gate, but the sharp edges on the top discouraged him. I asked someone going where was the closest firehouse. There was one only two blocks away. "Let's borrow a ladder from them." And then I added, "Okay, now, being newspaper reporters has not gotten us anywhere. We need a stronger, more dignified title."

I couldn't come up with anything. "Tell them we're archeologists, it might just do the trick," Ralph said.

"Yeah, good idea, and I'll speak English to give it more muscle."

"Excuse me," I paid extra attention to my pronunciation as I addressed the three handsome firemen seated behind a table, chatting. "We're archeologists from North America and need to borrow one of your ladders so that we can climb the wall into the Jewish cemetery."

"Oh, Americans," said the one most likely to be the fire chief since he was wearing a badge. "Sorry, but we can't lend you a latter. If one of you falls you'll sue us."

"I'm Portuguese," I proclaimed immediately. "See? I speak Portuguese, I was born in Lisbon, I'm one of you, you can trust me and as a Portuguese I'd never sue you. I'll climb the latter and have my son hold it. You can trust me."

"Oh, so now you can speak Portuguese huh?" he laughed. "Well, we still can't take a chance."

But he did allow me to use their telephone to call the local police station. I was told to wait until Monday morning and get the key to the cemetery directly from the city town hall. Ralph and I agreed; it was probably the best and safest path to follow. We were stuck in Faro until Monday morning.

When we arrived to the pensão, the front desk girl recommended a restaurant she liked, but neglected to inform us that it did not open for dinner until ten at night. We soon found that out, when the bus dropped us off at the restaurant and it was closed. It was a chilly, windy night and being off city limits we were in nowhere land with no place in sight to take refuge. We sat on the hard cobblestone steps in front of the restaurant and waited patiently for an hour with high expectations of a great dinner and entertainment.

The food was far from being Portuguese; it was made for foreigners, pre-made, frozen, and then defrosted. A young man with cerebral palsy played a couple of tedious songs on an organ and that was the extent of the entertainment. Ralph and I did a lot of talking. That was the best part of the evening. I had a lot of family stories to share with him and being a historical lover, I told him everything I still remembered about Faro's history and other famous Portuguese cities. We took our time walking back to our pensão. The next day it was Sunday and since everything was closed, we planned on sleeping late.

The next morning, we didn't get up until lunch. We ate half a dozen codfish cakes each and shared a large plate of freshly cut fried potatoes at a local tavern which got me sick of my stomach. Then we took a leisure walk around the historical town where not much of anything was happening. But we didn't need to be entertained and took the rest of the day as an opportunity to walk on the same cobblestone streets our ancestors had once walked on.

Monday morning, we were up early enough to have coffee and more than a share of pastries at a bakery and then we headed to the city hall's office. When the well-dressed man behind the desk asked me why I wanted the key to the Jewish cemetery, I thought that being in a government building where people were better educated we could tell the truth.

"We would like to borrow the key to the Jewish cemetery so that we can visit the tombs of our ancestors."

His face turned red with irritation as his voice went up a pitch higher, "You are Jewish?"

It was too late to back up, "Yes we are. We would like to see…"

He leaped from his chair and opened the door to the hallway yelling, "I don't deal with Jews!" The arteries in his neck stuck out as if ready to bust. "Get out of my office right now."

Ralph did not need me to translate his words to English. I was ashamed of my country and its people, and even though I knew that was the way some of the lower uneducated class had been indoctrinated when it came to blaming the Jews for killing Christ, I didn't expect a government official with some kind of education, to act so hatefully. We left the government building with our heads down and walked at least two blocks silently, once in a while glancing at each other. We held hands. Ralph finally spoke, "Mom, I'm stunned by what I've just witnessed."

"We're still surrounded by a world of narrow-mindedness people, but nothing is going to stop us, right?" I said. We decided to visit the local library.

Two young librarians went out of their way to help us, when we told them we were archeologists from North America and looking for old birth and death certificates of people that had lived in Faro. We were taken to a private room and they brought us local churches' registers among many old documents of births and deaths in Faro from the last one hundred and fifty years.

I asked timidly, "And…by any chance would you also have a list of who is buried in the Jewish cemetery?"

A true miracle then happened. They brought us three large books. They were written in Portuguese, and in one of them I recognized the original Ezaguy name. In the books were the names of many of my mother's side of the family including my great grandparents, birth and death dates and even pictures of the tombs with their Hebrew names translated to Portuguese underneath the photographs. This was even better than having climbed the wall. We would have been at a loss looking at old tombs' inscriptions since we did not read Hebrew. We made copies of all the pages and thanked the two librarians. We were ready to continue our pilgrimage to Spain and then to North Africa.

We boarded a bus to Spain but with all the stops made along the way we didn't get to cross the border until sundown. By the time we arrived to the Spanish city of Cadiz it was pitch black and we decided to spend the night there before continuing on to Algeciras where we would board a ship to Morocco. While we looked for a hostel for the night, we stopped to watch a Catholic procession, chanting in Latin. They walked at a very slow pace, and wore a black hooded cape, while holding a lit candle, close to their faces. The only light in that narrow, gray cobblestone street were from the lit candles. The eeriness of the situation, and what we had experienced already in Portugal, gave us an image of what an Inquisition procession must had been in those days; after all, it had started in Spain. Ralph and I did not need words to express our uneasiness.

The hostel we stayed that night for five dollars was a bargain except for the bed bugs. "Good night, sleep tight, don't let the bedbugs bite." Whoever came up with that had to be kidding. In the morning their little bite marks were everywhere on my body. Ralph was fine, which meant his bed was clean.

We boarded the morning ship to Morocco and stood on the top deck gazing at the calm waters around us with not much to see. The embalming heat and the soothing rocking of the ship invited me to look for a seat to take a nap. Luckily, I found a vacant wooden bench on the lower deck. I used my backpack for a pillow and quickly dropped into a comatose state of oblivion. Ralph woke me up to inform me that we were approaching land. From the distance, North Africa did not look much different than any other country. On the other hand, I had no idea of what to expect; I just thought it would be different.

Once the ship docked it open its bottom like a huge dinosaur's mouth and let out all the cars that had been carried in its inner guts. On the dock, waiting on the other side, were men dressed mostly in white or black and white stripped long robes. The urgency of the Arabic language, the characteristic men's attire, the very air told us we were definitely in Tangier, Morocco.

As we had finished going through the proper procedures of showing our passports and having our backpacks searched, a man dressed in an impeccable gray suit and tie, like an official might wear, approached us and with a perfect British accent demanded our attention. He told us he had been sent by the Moroccan government to stay with us and protect us from the riff raft waiting at the gate of the city ready to annoy and rob us.

I told Ralph to ignore him and that we were fine on our own. Mama had been very explicit with the directions; we were to take the main street ahead of us when we got off the dock. We could take care of ourselves. We exchanged one hundred dollars each at the exchange kiosk for Dirham currency. The man followed us like a fly on a horse's tail, but Ralph wasn't making it easy for him to leave us alone. Ralph had lots of questions concerning the city ahead of us. One thing about Ralph, he hardly ever went by feelings, when it came to making a life or death decision his engineering mind worked only with concrete evidence or proof. Ralph showed Mr. Amed, as he had introduced himself to us, my aunt's address that Mama had written on a piece of paper. Mr. Amed told us he knew exactly where our aunt lived and he would be delighted to take us to her house. I pulled on Ralph's arm and whispered, "We don't need a guide, we know from my mother's directions where to go and besides, I don't trust him."

"Mom, we're in a foreign country. It makes sense that we hire him to guide us to your aunt's house. You need to stop being so skeptical."

Ralph agreed to hire him, and Amed asked what I considered to be a small fortune, but after I did my Portuguese bargaining, he agreed to cut the fee in half.

Instead of following the flat wide avenue to our left like my mother had advised us to do, Amed pointed to the right side where a fortress wall stood. "It's still early in the morning, let me show you around the Kasbah, then I'll personally take you to your aunt's house."

Ralph said okay and once again against my intuition I went along with it. This was the part of me that still made me angry. I lacked the assertiveness to make myself heard. Amed took us through a small entry archway which led to very narrow streets weaving into each other like an intricate labyrinth. We would go up a street and then we were facing a small dark tunnel between the houses that could turn right or left and then into another narrow street. There were no sidewalks. It made sense; the roads were too narrow to have a car drive through. The small narrow buildings mostly between one and two floor levels high gave the impression they had melted into each other with peeling wall layers showing the vestiges of previous colors, a drastic variance of wash-down blues, greens and yellow showing years of serious neglect, with narrow short wooden doors and small windows with metal bars possibly for protection from robbers. They must have been built around the same time and by the same architect. After twenty minutes of walking Amed turned to us, "I want you to meet my family. My cousin is a good man and he would like you to have tea with him."

"We don't drink tea." I looked at Ralph to see if he was going to back me up.

Before Ralph could say anything Amed pointed at a store with lots of carpets hanging outside. "I'm tired of walking and you must be too. Let's drink tea with my cousin and rest."

It was bigger than I thought inside and it was covered with carpets of all sizes and colors. We were asked to sit on stools covered with carpet strips and a man dressed in a white robe and sandals served us a very hot sweet tea with peppermint. We spent an hour being pressured by Amed's cousin, as he had introduced him to us; to buy one of the carpets.

If a car salesman ever wanted to polish his expertise at selling cars, he should sign up for a carpet apprenticeship in Tangier. Talk about carpet salesmanship! Moroccan carpet salesmen were the true kings of forcefulness with all the annoying, pushy, selling techniques that were enough to make a saint commit suicide. It didn't matter that I told him we had no money, and we were on a tight budget. It didn't matter that all the rooms in our house were already carpeted wall to wall; their museum quality carpets could go on the walls and over our poor American quality wall-to-wall carpets. It didn't matter we hated carpets. No one left his cousin's carpet store without a carpet! It was their policy, legal Moroccan, North African policy.

I stood from the carpeted stool and announced impatiently, "We have to go." Ralph followed me outside. Amed came running after us. We had offended his cousin after he had spent so much time with us and had gone through the effort of making us tea. Ralph and I went through the whole list of why we didn't need a carpet and the only reason for being in Tangier was to find our aunt. "You said you knew where our aunt lives," Ralph said politely. "How about you take us there now, as promised?"

"Okay, okay as you wish," Amed said curtsying to us with a dry smile. "I'll take you to your aunt's house. But first, let me show you something you'll fully enjoy. It's still very early and you can't come to Tangier and miss the true flavor of the Kasbah. Let's go." He knew how to manipulate Ralph, and that's what I had become aware of from the first time he approached us.

We followed Amed like sheep and climbed one narrow, broken down cobblestone street after another until he stretched his hands out toward an old open building, "Here, we are. In this market you'll find everything you could possibly need, take a good look around, enjoy."

Dead chickens hang from hooks in the open air and the flies were the only things moving. Large burlap bags and wood bins were filled to the brims with a large variety of beans and spices being sold by weight. Ralph bought saffron from one of the vendors even though I told him I doubted the yellow painted dried grass was saffron. Old bikes, purses, clothing and tires mingled indiscriminately inside and outside the building. There were lots of vendors on the street selling silver and gold chains. Children buzzed around us pulling on our clothes with their hands extended begging for money. Amed yelled at them in Arab and I bet he was saying, "You little rats get the heck out of here or I'm going to beat you to death. These suckers are mine, do you hear?" They immediately scattered away as if the devil had spoken to them.

The array of fresh vegetables and fish and flowers for sale produced a melting pot of scents which in many ways reminded me of the farmer's market in Lisbon. One merchant sold corroded scrap metal, from the back of his bike cart and a shoemaker was busy hammering nails into a men's old shoe heel. A toothless old lady dressed in black except for the light blue shawl over her hair and draping around her shoulders stood from her chair when she saw us walking by. She tried to hand me a roll of brown and yellow cotton cloth making gestures for me to touch it and said something I took for, "This material is perfect to making yourself a beautiful dress."

Fried food and flat bread was being sold and served on plastic dishes, and tea and soda was also available in see-through plastic cups. "It looks like the tentacles of civilization have spread even into the depth of Kasbah," I said. Ralph flashed one of his approving smiles.

The market looked like an old fort and possessed the same labyrinth feeling as the tortuous streets outside. We were completely dependent on our guide. Mr. Amed, pointed to the "divine" blind men standing on the street corners begging. After seeing Mecca, they no longer wanted to see anything else and poked their eyes out to show their religious devotion. They were holly men. He told us we were lucky that he was our guide, since he was a good Muslim. The bad Muslims killed the foreigners without giving it a second thought.

I had no doubt that Amed was using a lot of psychology to scare us into trusting him, but to me it rubbed me the wrong way. He also told Ralph the American shows on television were spoiling their women by brainwashing them into wanting more freedom than they already had. According to him, women should only go out of their house to go to the market to buy food for their families, or to use the facilities in the community bathhouses.

This would explain why we only found men everywhere we walked. The coffee houses, or I should say tea houses, were filled with men of all ages mostly older and dressed in their robe-like attire sitting inside and outside in small groups and sipping on tall glasses of tea with peppermint. He told us that Muslims didn't drink alcohol, it was against their religion.

"Why do men have more than one wife?" Ralph asked him. "Are they that rich?"

"No, quite the contrary," Amed told him. "The poorer you are, the more reasons to have more wives. You can have up to four wives, and that way you have more children preferably boys so they can work."

It was three in the afternoon when Amed met another cousin in the street. After talking to him in Arabic, he said to us, "My cousin Mohamed is a good man, you can trust him. I gave him the address you gave me and he's going to take you to your aunt's house. I have to go home to see my family. But don't worry; we'll see each other again." He was gone before we even had a chance to thank him. We couldn't believe that we were finally on the way to my aunt's house.

We followed Mohamed as he took us from one street to another. He would say, "I believe she lives here, let's see," and he would knock at somebody's door, exchange a few words with the occupants and then translate to us, "No, your aunt doesn't live here." Two hours later we were still going from door to door and Ralph and I came to the conclusion that Amed's cousin was as lost as we were.

"No, not allowed, forbidden," said Mohamed when I pulled my camera out of my backpack ready to shoot a picture. When he had his back to us I raised my camera and took a quick shot of a woman with a ragged brown dress and without shoes filling a plastic bucket from a dilapidated water fountain. She had her back turned toward us.

Suddenly Amed showed up around the corner. He sent

his cousin away and looked at his wristwatch. "Hum, it's getting late. We'll start to look for your aunt's address early tomorrow morning. I'm going to leave you at a very nice but inexpensive hotel that my uncle owns. Tomorrow morning, let's say seven; I come by to get you. I promise to personally take you to your aunt's house."

We were too tired and hungry to argue back and followed him like puppy dogs. The hotel had an austere but clean lobby, and the room the clerk showed us had two beds and a sink. The bathroom was situated on the floor below us. We didn't need luxury to be happy. We left our backpacks in the room, and since the sun was still out we felt comfortable enough to leave on our own and search for a place where we could have couscous for dinner.

We didn't have to go far, across the street from our hotel there was what looked a lot like a Portuguese tavern with reasonable prices advertised outside. The couscous tasted like boiled grainy rice and the stewed chicken was too greasy for my taste. "I'm kind of concerned with their sanitary conditions," I looked at the chicken breast on my plate.

"Mom, it's a poor country, what do you expect?" Ralph was either very hungry or he liked the food a lot because he didn't leave a single morsel on his plate. I gave him the rest of my couscous and the chicken.

After our meal, we walked into a small shop nearby with lots of household items hanging from the ceilings and an array of smoking pipes. The salesman was no different from the carpet vendor and he would not leave us alone, insisting that Ralph needed to buy one of the pipes for smoking hashish. It did not matter if we smoked it or not, he was going to sell us one anyway.

We decided not to look into shops anymore since it was a lot of work to get out of them without having an argument with the salesperson. We opted to explore the streets and see what was out there. Accidentally we found ourselves out of the Kasbah. The streets were wider and the buildings were taller and a lot more modern, cars going by and trees graced the wider sidewalks. We were back to civilization.

"Wouldn't it be amazing if we were close to my great grandfather's temple?"

"It's a big city," Ralph said. "I doubt that."

A cop was busy directing traffic at a crossroad. "Let's ask him," I said. He spoke a little French and Portuguese and was very polite. "There's only one Jewish Temple I know around here." He pointed to an old building across from where we stood. "That one," he said.

We could not be more exhilarated than at that moment. We opened the tall, wide, walnut wooden door slowly and walked in with an intense feeling of reverence. We sat quietly on the only wooden bench available in the half-moon shaped lobby. The chanting sound of men praying in Hebrew resonated like a chorus through the closed door, just a few feet from us. We waited patiently for them to finish praying and hopefully they would talk to us.

They came out and surrounded us, some still wearing the tallit (prayer shawl). They were as curious about us as we were about them. They spoke several languages and finally we settled down to English, "Who are you? Where did you come from? Are you Americans? What is your family name?"

"Ezaguy." Ralph said. They looked at us a bit strange so I added with an exaggerated attitude. "We are the Ezaguys!"

The response was a buzz of oohs and aahs as they all wanted to shake Ralph's hands. We were the descendants of Rabbi Ezaguy, the one that had gathered their community to build the temple where we stood.

One of them introduced himself as the Portuguese Ambassador to Morocco. He was married to an Ezaguy, and that made him automatically a member of our family. He gave us his calling card and offered his house in

Marrakech where we were welcome to stay as long as we wanted. We thanked him but had to decline since our plans were to meet my aunt the next morning, and see Mama's grandfather's tomb at the cemetery, and then continue our travels through Spain and France.

Our backpacks were at our hotel. Still remembering partially, the way back into the Kasbah, we thought we could find the hotel on our own, but it was pitch dark now and the narrow, deserted streets became a lot more threatening than they had been during the day. We seemed to be going around in circles and the small shops seemed to be synchronized at rolling down their louver like metal door gates. We found a mini spice store still open but the guy could only speak Arabic. Ralph told me to stay put while he would go around the corner to find someone to help us. A young man dressed in a dark suit noticed me standing on the doorway of the shop and stopped about five feet from me. "Parlez-vous français?" he asked.

I figured that if I ignored him, he would go away. He reminded me of a gipsy.

"If you are not French you must be an American," he said in a mocking tone.

I shook my head.

Just then Ralph came from around the corner. "It's so frustrating," he complained. "I can't find anyone to give me directions."

"I knew it. So, you are both Americans! You in luck, I speak English. For a fee I'll take you there. What's the address you're looking for?"

Ralph showed him the hotel's calling card. We had no choice but walk behind the dark shadow of the man who was going to take us back to our hotel or ambush us. Ralph and I held hands and his hand shook as much as mine.

Our guide looked back at us momentarily and remarked with a snake's smile, "You two are frightened I can tell. I could take advantage of you if I really wanted. But don't worry; I'm only a poor student looking to make a couple of bucks."

I couldn't recall how long we walked in the dark, and narrow deserted streets. Then, there we were in front of our hotel. We gladly paid what he asked for.

We went directly to the hotel's front desk; luckily the new employee could speak Portuguese. I gave him my aunt's address and phone number and he called her on the phone. I gave her a summary of what had happened to us and our quest to find her. "Oh, dear," she sounded alarmed. "The Kasbah is not a safe place to stay. I live on the other side of the city, and your guide most likely knows that by the address you gave him." We had been taken. The decision to leave was not even a question, and I told her we would be back again someday in the future, but for now, we were ready to go back to Spain, the next morning. Tangier wasn't a friendly city, and the people were too far-out in their culture. For us it was difficult to feel even remotely comfortable.

Ralph agreed with me, we could not trust Amed who had lied to us by acting like he was helping us to find our aunt's house. We needed to get out of Morocco as soon as possible, but it was late at night, and we were better off waiting until daylight to make our escape.

I didn't sleep much, and when I did there were images of Ralph and I being taken to the desert by Amed. No matter how much I screamed and cried, he and his cousins killed Ralph and I was kept as a sex slave for the purpose of making bread for the tribe and giving birth to baby girls. The babies were put into boxes and kept until their ripe age of being sold as brides for dowry.

I awoke at five in the morning. Ralph was sleeping in the bed next to mine. I shook his shoulder to wake him up. "Ralph, get dressed. Amed is coming back to get us," I told him. "Let's get out of here now."

We gave the hotel manager an envelope with half the

money we had promised to Amed. Even though he had taken advantage of us, Ralph felt we should pay him something since Amed had shown us the Kasbah and a way of life we did not know existed.

The question was how to leave the Kasbah and find the dock. "We're up on a hill; all we have to do is go down, no matter how many turns or twists," I told Ralph.

We walked at a fast pace. When we spotted the shore in the distance where the ships were docked, I got hold of Ralph's hand and proclaimed joyfully, "We're going home."

We entered the terminal ready to purchase our tickets and a well-dressed man looking like an official — very much like Amed—said in perfect English, "Passports, passports." He snapped his fingers at us to show urgency.

"Thank you," Ralph couldn't be any politer. "We take care of our passports and tickets ourselves." We had learned from our previous experience and were too smart to fall for it again.

The man looked straight at Ralph. "I'm not here to make money. I work here. Now… give me the money to cover the cost of the tickets and your passports so I can expedite the process."

Ralph gave him our passports and the money needed to purchase the tickets.

About ten minutes later, the man returned, "Here are the tickets and your passports. It's ten dollars for my services."

He had lied and Ralph refused to pay him. But the guy argued back, and would not leave us alone. Concerned with the man's voicing getting angrier and louder that we were trying to rob him, I pulled a dollar bill from my pants' pocket and gave it to him. When he argued about the amount I told him, "It's better than nothing." He walked away disgruntledly, but at least he was gone.

Ralph got mad at me for giving in, even if it was only one dollar. He was right, but I just wanted to be free of all the hustling.

While waiting to board the ship, I noticed near the dock a pulling cart full of mini souvenirs, mostly stuffed camels. I told Ralph I would be right back and ran outside. I couldn't leave Tangier without a keepsake. I bargained and bargained for a ten-inch stuffed camel and finally the guy gave it to me in exchange for all my dirham change and my wristwatch.

What a joke going through customs. One of the security guards opened my backpack before Ralph's and when he saw my green silk pajamas on the very top he remarked scornfully, "Americans! Just go!" And he signaled us to move forward and board the ship.

"If I'd known it would be that easy, I would have bought the pipe and the hashish," Ralph laughed.

Once in the ship we voted to return to Portugal. The original plan of going to France and possibly Italy no longer made any sense considering how little time we had left. It was a lot more logic for us to tour Portugal and enjoying our time there.

While traveling back from Spain by bus, Ralph came down with a severe cold and no tissues available. It was horrible to watch him dripping from his nose without stopping. We sat on separate seats in the back of the bus and away from each other and took his dripping condition as a sign that returning to Portugal was definitely a better idea since we were burned-out from our experience in Morocco. I also became aware of the most important item needed when traveling in foreign countries: toilet paper. There was no toilet paper or any type of tissue available inside public bathrooms. A few had a small size booth appropriately located by the entrance where a middle age woman usually with an attitude of take or leave it, sold thin square pieces of toilet paper, for a quarter each.

We were walking from the bus station in Lisbon to my parents' house when I saw an advertisement on the window of a restaurant. "Papasorda, today's lunch special." I hated it when I was a kid, but a perverse nostalgia, made it very appealing.

Papasorda was the Portuguese poor-man's regional dish. I had eaten a lot of it while growing up in Portugal, when my parents were experiencing financial difficulties. Papasorda was made of boiled and then mashed old bread, fresh minced garlic, cilantro, salt, and pepper. If you needed to stretch it out a little further, you added more water. The result was papasorda soup. Now if you could afford to buy an egg, the soup was a lot more acceptable with a poached egg.

The papasorda served at the restaurant was the pasty kind, just as nasty as I remembered. Ralph didn't like it either.

Mama and Papa were extremely happy to see us return early from our trip. When Mama heard that we had papasorda at a restaurant, she was hurt that I hadn't told her how much I missed it. She immediately called her employee and asked her to make it for dinner. I told her I hated that dish as a child, and even more now as a grown up, but if the employee was willing to make green soup, and white beans with cow's feet, I would be open to it.

The next day I led Ralph, to the São Jorge castle at the top of one of the hills in the center of Lisbon. We walked all around the castle enjoying the striking view of the city and the river Tejo. I bought a hand-made mandala with attractive purple stones from a young French craftsman. He said it would bring me luck.

We were walking back from the castle down the steep and narrow cobblestone streets when the smell of delicious food from a tavern nearby crawled up our nostrils like fishing hooks. Ralph went ahead and ordered a glass of beer and a couple of Portuguese pastries filled with seafood. The narrow tavern was packed with people standing while eating and drinking. Taverns were the best place to get real Portuguese food. When I heard what Ralph was being charged, I raised my voice to the bartender behind the counter, "Hey, what're you doing, overcharging my son?"

"Oh, I thought he was a tourist. He didn't speak Portuguese to me."

I crossed my arms and stared hard at him. "He's my son, and you're not going to rob him."

The bartender was visibly embarrassed. "I'm sorry, I'm very sorry." Then he added, "We always charge more to tourists. They can afford it."

Ralph and I made a pact, from that moment on if we bought anything, I did the talking.

The next day Ralph and I rode the local bus to the main Jewish cemetery in Lisbon, on Rua Afonso III. It was my way of introducing him to some of our family members that I had known while growing up. Before going in we filled our pockets with cobblestones since it was customary in the Jewish religion to leave a stone on the tomb you visited. As a kid I remembered asking my mother, why did we use stones instead of flowers and she said, "Flowers die, but stones last forever."

"But flowers are prettier," I said.

"Yes, they are. But stones symbolize the permanence of memory." And she put two stones on her mother's tomb, one from her and the other from me.

Founded in 1868 some of the older stone markers in the cemetery were ineligible. We began to look for Aunt Heydee's among the newest zone—where I anticipated her being buried. We looked and looked, but her stone marker was nowhere in sight. I inquired with the caretaker who remembered Aunt Heydee with fondness. "Every month she came to visit her parents. She brought a picnic basket and sat by their stone markers and talked to them. Nice lady, she always gave me a piece of fruit." He smiled with delight as he led us to her place of rest.

Aunt Heydee had made plans before she died to have her spot as close to the entrance gate as possible. Anyone entering the cemetery would see her stone first. We didn't expect her there. But at the same time, we were not surprised, only moved by her tenacity. She had managed to literally squeeze herself into the already overfilled old burial ground. I cried, and then laughed with joy. Aunt Heydee, even after dying, was still Napoleon Number One—as we fondly used to call her when she outdid herself.

The best way to explore Portugal was to rent a car for the five days we had left, instead of relying on their happy-go-lucky bus transportation.

The salesman at the car rental wanted to charge us for insurance but we voted on not getting it. "I swear to you," he put his right hand over his heart. "You're going to need it because driving in Portugal is an accomplishment that not many foreigners can boast of."

"Don't worry about it," I said. "My son and I are used to driving in New York City, and nothing can be more challenging or dangerous than that."

None of their cars had automatic transmission and since I had not driven a stick shift for twenty-five years, Ralph offered to drive. His first Portuguese lesson on the protocols of driving, threw him for a loop, when on one narrow road a car drove head-on at us. I stretched my legs out, tightened my jaw and put my hands out, ready for the impact. He drove off the road stopping adjacent to a cliff. He shouted, "Freaking crazy driver was he out of his mind?"

When the next car did the same we had another emotional breakdown, with some added heavy-duty curse words, and then we sat in silence.

"I think I know what's happening here," Ralph spoke quietly as if letting out his thoughts, "I bet they expect us to move slightly off to the side to give them enough space to go by." And as it happened again and again along the way, Ralph was delighted to have caught up on the Portuguese rules of the road and felt a lot more secure, but he said, "This would never happen in the US."

He drove while I played navigator. I wanted him to see Eiriceira my favorite beach in the whole world, but first we stopped in the magical town of Sintra, known for numerous castles and palaces. We explored the Castle of the Moors built high on a steep hill by the Arabs during the eighth century by North African Moors until it fell in the hands of the Christians crusaders with the conquest of Portugal. We also toured The Pena National Palace a nineteenth century Romanticist castle of colorful combinations of architectural Neo-Gothic, Renaissance and Islamic styles. I had been to Sintra with my family several times while growing up, so for me there were no surprises, but for Ralph everything was a discovery of the senses.

The next stop north was Eiriceira, and by the time we got there it was nine in the evening, but fortunately, we found a charming hotel for the night. The front desk person who was also the hotel owner teased us when I told him we were mother and son and needed two beds. I did look young for my age, and at the time Ralph insisted on wearing a small goatee, which he thought it made him look good, but it also aged him five or ten years more.

Dinner in Portugal was usually served until eleven; it was nine when we found a busy seafood restaurant overseeing the Atlantic Ocean. Being that it was Saturday night we felt like celebrating our return to Portugal, with a banquet of fresh seafood delicacies. Ralph ordered a bottle of white wine to which I warned him, "I don't know if I should drink any, you know what happens with me."

"Mom, don't worry if you get silly. Let's just enjoy it."

Half a glass of wine later, I found the restaurant's elaborate menu as the most hilarious thing I had ever read. I stood, faced the dinning crowd with the menu in my hands and after reading the top three courses I added a little of my creative juices, "Sardines, freshly caught this morning just for you, yes ladies and gentlemen, these sardines are so fresh that they might bite you back." I chuckled and went on. "Oh, oh, now this is a good one, fresh, steamed young whole lobster, hum young and a bit shy I guess the reason for their pink blush so, don't be too rough on them when you pull their legs off, oh yeah the snails cooked in their own juices with bits of garlic and cilantro they are always delicious, and don't worry they are dead so go ahead and use the pins to pull them out by their little heads and…" I raised my voice, "Enjoy your meal." Nobody applauded. I sat and laughed until my cheeks hurt. Ralph was cool, and I was very happy that we were the best of friends. After dinner, the waiter removed from our table covered with white paper as our table cloth, now stained with a mess of empty shells and oceanic debris, the empty wine bottle, the glasses, the two mini wooden blocks and mini hammers we had been using to smash open, brown and pinkish red crabs and lobsters, and the pins used to pull out the snails from their shells and the dishes wiped clean from the stew we had shared of goose barnacles, and other delicious crustaceans. Then he returned and proceeded to write, with a large black magic marker, our total bill on the paper covering our table. To our embarrassment the restaurant only accepted cash or Visa and we only carried American Express, and when it came to cash we didn't have any except for small coins. The term, "banking hours" was part of the Portuguese way of life, and on weekends the banks were closed. I asked to speak to the owner who was busy overseeing the cooking in the kitchen.

"I'm very sorry, but we only have American Express and no cash," I told him in Portuguese. "But my son and I will help you with the work in the kitchen, tonight and tomorrow, and on Monday morning we'll go to the bank and pay you for our dinner."

"Are you kidding?" he laughed wholeheartedly. "Take a good look at all those tourists eating. I'll be making more than enough money on them. You and your son just go on home, you don't owe me anything."

Ralph was stunned. "This would never happen in the US."

Funny, but Al had said the same thing when he first came to Portugal to marry me and the train made a special stop so that someone could bring me a glass of water, since there was none on board.

The next morning, we walked to the main square, a quarter of the size of any other town square, but Eiriceira's hot spot for people gathering. Families and the elderly sat on park benches talking and children played hopscotch and jump rope. The streets were long and narrow flanked on both sides with white painted brick houses with one door and one or two windows, a lot like in Tangier, but here the houses were freshly painted, the streets were clean, people smiled and said hello and there were no hagglers to contend with.

The imposing stone wall that kept the ocean away from the town and wrapped around the fishermen's beach, was still there the way I remembered. We stood by the wall watching the fishermen below smoking their pipes or cigarettes while mending the holes in their fishing nets and others sanding or painting the bottom of their boats. Bathers didn't walk on that beach, it belonged to the fishermen and the sand gave out an unpleasant odor of burned oil, old fish, paint fumes like those of a car exhaust, sea salt and dirty looks from the fishermen daring you to step on their territory.

Then we walked to my beach. I sat on the sand like in the old days gazing at the ocean spraying over the rocks and caressed the warm finely textured sand in my hands. Ralph stood staring at the ocean. Before we left I showed him the abandoned run-down one floor stone house barely holding itself for dear life at the edge of the cliff, where my family and I had lived during the summer months some thirty-six years ago. A watery glaze over my eyes didn't last long. I thanked God for giving me the opportunity to share with my son a little of the past while knowing that the present was all that really mattered.

The next morning Ralph and I were back on the road and on our way to the city of Coimbra when the familiar woody sweet smell of eucalyptus told us we were surrounded on both sides by huge fields of eucalyptus. When I asked him to stop the car he immediately pulled over. I ran into the forest with Ralph. One tree with her lower branches weighing down from the hundreds of leaves, lured me to rub them in my hands. The leaves crunched like potato chips in my hands and I opened my palms to show them to Ralph. "Here, smell. What do you think?"

"Wow, what an amazing scent, I love it," he said. And he walked over to the next tree and pulled toward his face another branch. Some people liked to make angels in the snow; I made them amid the ground covered with dried eucalyptus leaves.

The eucalyptus forest had taken on a complete new meaning to me; I had someone to share it with. I watched Ralph going up to the trees to touch them, picking up the leaves and smelling them and I was happy. He came up with the idea of taking a couple of branches with us. They were going into our luggage and we were taking them with us, to America!

I didn't worry about asking Ralph to stop the car whenever I caught a glimpse of something interesting to explore, because I knew he felt the same way as I did. There was only one thing I was seriously concerned about, the speed at which he drove. I had earned the moniker of Roadrunner in New Jersey, yet by my standards on safety I was scared we were going to wind up at the bottom of a ravine. When I complained about his speed around the curves he remarked, "Mom, when you drive in Europe, you have to drive like a European in order to get the full experience."

The more he drove like a European the more I disagreed with his tourist like philosophy. By the time we arrived to the city of Coimbra I knew I better brush up on my stick-shift technique or we were going to die on one of the steep curves we had encountered on the way there. So, after taking the car to a garage when one of the tires was going flat, I announced, "You drove north and now it's only fair that I drive south."

Later I would thank God for my insight, because on the way back, we got lost on a narrow dusty country road. I was sure that all the locals knew about it and that was all that mattered to them since no one drove on their roads, they didn't post any warnings.

Luckily for us, I was driving about 15 mph and paying extra attention along with Ralph as we searched for an exit of some kind. The road kept going up and up the mountain and it was getting narrower and narrower. "It might be a figment of my imagination," I brought my head forward and squinted. "But it doesn't look like there's any more road up ahead, what do you think?"

He raised his upper body and lifted his head higher. He hit his hands flat on the dashboard and his legs went straight out bracing for impact as he screamed, "Stop the car!"

I slammed on the brakes causing a loud screech until we came to a stop only six feet from dropping straight down into a ravine. We remained in the car unable to utter a word. "There were no warning signs. What kind of a country is this?" he asked.

My voice trembled, "The highways are good."

When we calmed down, we walked around the car to evaluate the situation on how we were going to maneuver the car to make a U-turn on such narrow space. Ralph's engineering mind concluded that since the car was smaller by three feet on each side of the road, and five feet in front of us, there was a good chance we could do it. I was to be behind the wheel and he would stay outside giving the instructions.

Literally one foot at a time back and forth and back and forth we finally turned the car around, and down the hill we went.

We couldn't find the main highway to Lisbon and when we reached a little village, I drove up the sidewalk to get directions from a policeman standing by a store talking to some people.

Ralph cringed back in his seat, and yelled out, "No, you can't drive on the sidewalk! Are you out of your mind?"

To which I was proud to say, "This is the norm in Portugal. You don't yell at a cop from your car and bother him asking for directions. You show him respect by driving up to him."

The cop gave us directions and we drove away as Ralph repeated, "This would never happen in the US." Of course not, each country had a different approach concerning legalities. A good example of that took place after we returned our rental car and took a leisure walk back to my parents' apartment. We came upon a good size hole in the middle of the street where two men were working about six or seven feet below.

"This is incredible, I wish I had brought my camera," Ralph said. "There are no caution signs, someone could fall into it. Aren't they even worried? Ask them, what happens if that happens?"

"Excuse me," I raised my voice so the workers at the bottom of the hole could hear me. They looked up. I waved my hands at them, "Good morning." They waved back. I had their complete attention. "Excuse me for bothering you but, aren't you worried about someone falling in and getting hurt?"

One of the workers yelled back, "Who wants to know?"

I pointed to Ralph. "My son, he's an American and he's very curious. There are no warning signs up here."

They laughed. Then one of them said, "Well, tell your son that if he falls inside here, tomorrow he can read the headline in the newspaper, 'Stupid American fell into a large hole in the street.'"

I almost forgot to mention that when we returned the car to the rental place the salesman wanted to charge us $150 for a missing hubcap. I finally convinced them to call the garage affiliated with their company in Coimbra. The mechanic in Coimbra was honest enough to tell him that after fixing our left front tire, he had forgotten to put the hubcap back. I learned from that experience that anytime I had to rent a car in a foreign country, I should always remove the hubcaps and then put them back when returning the car. It was a miracle we didn't lose all the hubcaps upon hitting so many potholes in Lisbon and on the backroads.

Every parent should take a vacation with their child, preferably when they are no longer teens, as adults there's a more balanced relationship and the bonding will likely remain for the rest of their lives. My intentions were to do the same with Steve in the future.

The only downer to our trip was that all the soap bars I bought to give as gifts must have been confiscated, because of the two dozen I had enclosed in the luggage, there were only three. But the eucalyptus branches survived the trip.

Steve told me that while I was gone Michael's mom had called twice at the music center. I drove over and found Michael painting their kitchen after which he planned to remove the cement steps from the front of his house and replace them with wood. I offered to come by and help him whenever I had free time.

They had officially put their house up for sale and were

planning to go live in South Carolina. Besides all that, Michael had broken up with his girlfriend and she was moving out at the end of the month.

Someone from a framing company called the Howell Music Center to tell me they laminated and framed news articles, and that they had done mine from the March /April issue of Monmouth County Business Today. I'd forgotten about that interview. They wanted to drop it off for me to take a look, and if I liked it, I could have it for twenty-five dollars.

I told my friend Joe, the owner of Crazy Joe furniture store across from Howell Music Center, what happened to Ralph and me in Morocco, and how we had been basically kidnapped and taken into the Kasbah. "I'm not surprised," he said. "If you had told me that you were going to Morocco, I would have warned you not to go." He had been there a year ago with a tour group, and a young girl with extremely tight jeans had been robbed. Until today he couldn't figure out how someone had insert their hand into her pocket and taken the money out without her even feeling it.
    Joe's wife was funny. She always threw me a kiss from behind her desk and say, "We have to do lunch one of these days."
    We had known each other for over five years and I had no idea how tall she was.

I was busy all weekend putting the set up for "Bell, Book, and Candle," and on Monday I sent out press releases to all the newspapers about holding auditions for our next production, "Bedroom Farce," even though the director had most of the cast picked.
    I had to agree with Al and Steve; the laminated presentation of my interview with the Monmouth County Business Today looked very nice even though I looked like

a nerd. There I was under entrepreneurs, "Ronnie Esagui, Energy in Action." I put the plaque up on one of the back walls of the Howell Music Center.

"Bell, Book, and Candle," received raving reviews. Sandi Van Dyke, the director, did a great job, and our patrons left the theatre with a smile on their faces. Michael was busy renovating his house, and I had no intentions of bothering him with the theatre unless it was absolutely necessary. Through the years I had gathered a dependable stage crew that made my job as producer a lot easier.

I used my free time to visit Michael and help him paint, but when we got together he'd rather sit in his cellar talking while he drank a beer and smoked a cigarette. I admired the way he was able to balance a lit cigarette between his lips, but I guess it was no different from me being able to apply lipstick without a mirror. On and off his mom would invite me to come up from the cellar and have tea with her. She was good at telling stories, and lately mostly gossip about Michael's soon to be gone, ex-girlfriend.

Last Monday, she said in her usual jovial tone, "Not official yet. Not until she leaves this weekend, can we say his ex." And she laughed while coughing at the same time. She coughed a lot; Michael did too but not as much as his mother. I told Ralph about it and he thinks she might have emphysema from smoking most of her life.

Malcolm one of our customers at the Howell Music Center told me he was a janitor and could use extra work. He charged five dollars an hour. I hired him on the spot to clean the store on Fridays. He was very shy and hardly spoke but did a great job. After one month of working, he didn't show up Friday morning and I figured he was sick or something. He called that evening. "This is Malcom, I like you a lot, that's why I wanted to work there, I wanted to see you. Will you go out with me?"

Stunned momentarily I surprised myself when I responded that I was happily married, and please not to come back. A few years back I would have gotten flustered and given the phone to Al. I felt proud of my inner strength. I was finally growing up. I had just proved that I could take on any task no matter how difficult to handle.

Ralph bragged so much about Kobe's delicious rolled eel, that I tried it yesterday for lunch. An hour later after I got home, I was on my knees facing the toilet covered in cold sweats, quivering and groaning. To describe how I felt the first time I experienced food poisoning many years ago was to say I fell off a train and broke all the bones in my body. To depict how I felt this time, I would have to add that after falling off the train and breaking all my bones, I got dumped into an active volcano. I truly believed that it was going to be my last day on earth. I had no doubts that if I had been any older, my heart would not have been able to take it.

The next morning, I told Katie, the hostess at the Kobe, what had happened and she passed it on to Mr. Ounuma. He took it very personally and said emphatically, "No, no, Ronnie, everything in my restaurant is very fresh. It's impossible. You got sick from eating something else, outside my restaurant."

Later that day, Mandy, one of the Japanese waitresses, came upstairs to the theatre and took me to the side of the room. "I heard what happened to you," she whispered. "This is just between you and me, okay? Never eat eel here, at the Kobe, they get it frozen from Japan. If the eel is spoiled, the poison comes alive with the cooking."

I promised myself never to eat eel again, not at the Kobe or anyplace else.

Tracey gave me a two months' notice to find someone else to do the props for the theatre, she no longer could be my theatre partner. "I'm too busy being a grandma, and besides, my mother died at my age and I want to enjoy the time I have left with my family."

She was fifty-eight and suffered from high blood pressure, she felt the odds were against her. I didn't see her dying anytime soon. It was definitely a psychological thing with her.

Since the theatre had not been doing so well lately with attendance; it was more like a blessing that Tracey was leaving. I gave it full consideration and decided that I could do the props myself and did not need another partner.

Summer of 1990

Al's leg healed perfectly and it was up to him whether to leave the screws in or take them out. Al told his doctor that he saw the bill for the surgery and since the screws had costed a small fortune he wanted them back. Afterward, he gave them to me thinking I could use them in the theatre to hold the sets up. I showed them to Barney who said they were special screws, and very expensive. If he were still in practice he would have bought them from me.

I was so impressed with their value that I kept them in a plastic bag and for a while I showed them to everyone I knew as if they were precious diamonds.

How many times did I have to do something I knew was not good for me before I learned my lesson? I pondered that question over and over again, later one evening, after suffering the consequences of my stubbornness.

The temperature outside was in the high 90's but I had no intentions of waiting for the evening to cool off. Oh no, not me. I stood on top of a tall metal ladder holding a box of sign letters under one arm while clinging to the Kobe's billboard and began changing the letters for the upcoming play. I was used to doing that type of balancing act for every production without a problem. I also refused to admit failure just because my maximum capability of standing in scorching heat was no more than ten minutes. I envied people that sweated! I believed I had been born without sweat glands and as such I was unable to cool down. Halfway done inserting the letters into the billboard I began to shake. *What an odd feeling,* I thought. *Usually I feel flushed, dizzy and then pass out. I better go in right now.* I dragged myself into the Kobe Restaurant where Mrs. Ounuma saw my red-bug-eyed face and went to get Mr. Ounuma. Concerned with my overheated look he handed me a tall glass of cold plum wine. Did I tell Mr. Ounuma that I couldn't drink wine because it made me sick and act weird? Nope, I wasn't going to offend him. Besides, I had never drunk plum wine. I took a tiny sip. It tasted like fruit juice and I was very thirsty. I drank fast as if I was stranded in the middle of a desert. Three large gulps. He brought me another glass full. Yummy, yummy, refreshingly sweet and...*Oh my God! Help!* My lips moved but no sound came out. My heart was racing like a ticking bomb ready to go off and the room was spinning just as fast. My head felt too heavy to hold up and since I was seated at the sushi bar I let it drop on the counter. I had no idea how long I remained in that position. I only knew that suddenly I became a lot more aware of the Kobe being in dire need of something more exciting than that constant Japanese music; ding-a-ling ding, ding ding ding... over and over again. I knew exactly what I was doing but had no control as I started singing "This land is your land. This land is my land, from California to the New York Island..."

Mr. and Mrs. Ounuma seized my arms and helped me upstairs to the theatre and then laid me on the couch backstage.

I awoke to the familiar sounds of patrons arriving and dinner being served at the restaurant downstairs. I stood slowly. My head felt twice its weight. When I walked down the steps I noticed through the large glass window that the sun had gone down. Mr. Ounuma took a quick glance at his wristwatch. "You slept three hours." He smiled. "You should not work outside when it's too hot," he shook his head. "Not good for you." Mrs. Ounuma joined us and said to her husband, "No more plum wine to Ronnie."

I loved Mr. and Mrs. Ounuma. I wished I were a Japanese child so that I could adopt them as my parents.

No matter how much Steve or I talked to Al, concerning our declining economy, he remained in denial. "Everything is fine," he said. "You two need to stop worrying so much." We barely made enough to pay the rent and utilities but to Al owing money just meant paying the bare minimum on our charges as he was used to doing all his life.

Steve and I were aware of our predicament when someone would sell us a used Fender electric guitar for $10, but when we tried selling it for $50 no one could afford it, even though the instrument was a bargain at $800.

It didn't feel like we were in a recession like the news wanted us to think. If anything, it was more like being in the midst of a depression. Of the seven stores in our mall there were only two stores still open besides ours. The meat market and oddly enough the karate school at the end of the mall.

I called the landlord and asked him to reconsider not hitting us with the extra-added cost for the problems he was having with the sewage. If anything, he should consider giving us a break until we were back on our feet. He said that was not his problem.

I brought up the idea of consolidation to Al and Steve, which was another way of pulling all our resources together and they agreed.

We closed the Marlboro Music Center and moved all the instruments and equipment back into the Howell Music Center.

Once in a while I was challenged with a problem on my hands concerning one of the actors. Larry had an obnoxious attitude and no regard for anybody's feelings. Even though his wife was always with him and did a pretty good job at keeping him calm, she could only do so much. Larry was a very good actor but the tension was too much for everyone working with him. Then, one evening Larry made the mistake of using his nasty attitude on Ben, the bartender hired to work upstairs during the shows. Ben took upon himself to get even with Larry by replacing the cup of tea he was supposed to drink on stage, with whiskey. That night Larry was on stage acting his part and thank God, he only touched the drink to his lips, because according to his wife, he was highly allergic to alcohol and it could have been fatal. Larry's wife wanted to sue the bartender for trying to kill her husband.

Mr. Ounuma fired Ben.

A member from the Howell Cultural Arts Committee called to ask if I'd consider joining them again. "I heard about all the good work you did as a member and the committee has voted to have you back."

"I don't know if you guys really want me to return. I have no problem attending the meetings, but I'll be delegating the work to every member, and that means everybody will be very busy working." I put full emphasis on, *very busy working.* "Maybe you should talk to them about that and then let me know."

She said she would pass the message to the group.

I called several mental institutions for a straitjacket we could borrow as a prop for our next production, but to my dismay I was told, they no longer used them. I was about to give up when an actor suggested I call the psychiatric hospital in Morris Plains. A Dr. Seine answered the phone and to my surprise she was more than happy to help me out. She gave me directions to the hospital, and the building number where she worked as the head of the department. I made an appointment to meet with her the following Thursday morning at ten.

I asked Al to come with me by enticing him with a ride into the countryside followed by lunch. "Great," he said. "I always wanted to visit a mental hospital."

Except for what I had seen in the movie "One Flew Over the Cuckoo's Nest," I had no idea of what to expect. It was worse than I imagined. The hospital consisted of a gloomy conglomeration of heavy massive brick buildings with jaillike narrow windows with black metal bars. The humongous property had one entrance, a double black metal gate, which gave the buildings the austere look of a top-security prison. "This place must have been something else in its old days," Al said, as he drove around the property looking for Dr. Seine's building number. We finally found the building after passing it several times, it was raining and the building numbers were hard to read.

We found the front door locked but after ringing the bell several times a strikingly tall severe-looking young woman with thick eyeglasses and wearing a short grey smock opened the door. It was raining a lot heavier now but she said that due to security reasons, we had to wait outside until Dr. Seine arrived. We stood with our backs flat against the door and the porch overhang above us was large enough to kept us dry that way. Al complained about the long trip, wasting his time waiting for the doctor when he could be home relaxing and that I was a nut case to even be there. An hour later I was ready to agree with him about my lack of mental faculties when a short skinny brown hair woman wearing a long black raincoat, black rubber boots and an oversized black purse came rushing up the steps with a serious frown on her face. When she reached the top I asked, "By any chance, are you Dr. Seine?"

She tilted her head slightly to the side and narrowed her

Awakening the Woman Within

already beady eyes at us suspiciously, "Yes I am. And who are you, are you here to inquire on a family member?"

"No. My name is Ronnie Esagui and this is my husband Al. I spoke to you three days ago, concerning the borrowing of a straightjacket for a play I'm producing in Howell." She gave me a suspicious look and I said, "Dr. Seine, we made an appointment for this morning to pick it up, don't you remember?"

"I never spoke to you. Something is wrong here." She reached into her raincoat pockets. "Let me find my key and then you two follow me into my office,". She mumbled a few words under her breath and got on her knees to hastily empty all the contents from her large purse on the ground. Her eyelids flickered and her hands shook as she searched among make-up items, a hair brush, two eyeglass cases, a bunch of papers that looked like bills including small note books, pens and pencils an overfilled wallet and a cosmetic type of bag. *She is on the edge of a nervous breakdown,* I thought. Al looked at me and made a face like what the heck is the matter with her. "Why don't you ring the doorbell?" Al said.

"Good idea," she put all the stuff back into her handbag. The same young woman opened the door and we walked into a large foyer naked of furnishings except for a small desk where the woman immediately took her place behind it and got busy reading a novel. Dr. Seine found her key chain inside the zipped pocket of her purse. Dr. Seine's office had no windows; it reminded me of a large closet. Lots of books piled in corners and plenty of diplomas hanging on the walls. She asked us to have a seat. When she looked at me with a blank look on her face I reminded her again, "Dr. Seine, I spoke with you on the phone three days ago and I'm here to borrow the straitjacket for the play I'm producing."

She had no recollection of talking to me. But since we were already there she would call a storage staff member at building #4 and maybe they had an old one in storage. We were to drive over and someone would be waiting for us.

Al didn't say anything while in her office. But as soon as we left the building, he remarked, "That was a psychiatrist? I'd hate to see her patients!"
I nodded in agreement.

When we got to building #4, Al told me not to take too long as he was going to wait in the car, at the front door. I ran in. The large reception room was empty and there was no one behind the reception counter either. I rang the counter bell and called out, "Is anybody home?"

I tapped my fingers on the counter and waited what I felt had been a respectful amount of time and then noticing a door behind the counter; I walked around to it and turned the knob. I was happy to find it unlocked. The hallway was empty with not a sound around except for my voice, "Hello, is anybody home?"

A woman dressed in a nurse's outfit showed up at the end of the hallway and walked hurriedly toward me.

"Hi, I'm so glad to see you," I said joyfully. "I'm here to pick up the straitjacket."

The woman didn't smile back. "How did you get into this hallway?"

"I used that door over there." I pointed to it.

"That's completely impossible. That door is always locked!"

Oops, I'm in a mental hospital, I better respond calmly. "Look, that door was open; otherwise I would not be walking in this hallway, now would I?" Keeping my tone soft while sticking to the reason I was there in the first place, I added, "So, do you have the straitjacket? Dr. Seine called here not even ten minutes ago."
She seized my hands firmly, "Show me your wrists!"

Was she thinking that I was a mental patient trying to escape? I immediately showed her my wrists but it didn't help much, she made me walk in front of her as she lead me into a room that looked like a pantry and locked the door behind her.

She pointed to a chair. "You, sit there, while I check with Dr. Seine. It's strange that she didn't call me." She picked up the phone and dialed.

Dr. Seine was not in her office, and to make things worse, nurse Watters wouldn't believe the reason I was there, no matter how many times I kept repeating that I had a dinner theatre and needed a white straitjacket as a prop for our next show.

She argued back, "Straitjackets are no longer being used!" She grabbed my arm forcefully, adding, "Stop talking nonsense. You come with me and don't make a fuss."

She didn't let go of my arm as she led me back to the hallway. Was she going to throw me in a cell and lock me up? I was getting increasingly nervous and tried to reason with her, "My husband is waiting for me in our car by the front door. You can take a look if you don't believe me. If I don't come out of this building right now he's going to come in looking for me, and believe me, you don't want that to happen. Now let go of my arm!" I pulled my arm away. We were standing by the front glass door, and she saw Al in the car. "Okay, you can go," she said. I ran out.

Al wanted to know what had taken me so long, where was the straitjacket, and not to count on him anymore to look for props for the theatre. I didn't share with him that I had come very close to being a hospital inmate and if it hadn't been for him.

We didn't have enough money to pay the rent for the Howell Music Center. I called the landlord once again to see if he would charge us less just for a couple of months so that we could get back on our feet.

He laughed before he hung up.

Al heard me on the phone. "It is bad all around," he said.

"Even Ronnie's Music Den is doing terrible. I sit there all day and nobody is buying. It's not worth keeping it open. Let's close it."

"Let's sell it. It's a business."

"You always come up with the craziest ideas." He waved his hand in the air as he always did when conveying his intolerance for stupidity. "Only a jerk would buy a tiny shop of five by ten feet with barely anything but a couple of cheap acoustic guitars and some picks."

I reasoned that I had nothing to lose and put an ad in the Asbury Park Press. "You're wasting your time," he persisted.

Two potential buyers called the day after the ad went in the newspaper.

I sold Ronnie's Music Den to the one that showed up with the $10,000 check. Too bad I didn't think of doing the same with the Marlboro Music Center. But it was too late, and it didn't do me any good to cry over spilled milk.

I showed Ralph our bills and the store's records. He was very direct; we needed to go bankrupt like he had done a year prior. We were deep in debt.

We held a family meeting to discuss our options, but besides bankruptcy there were none. We made plans to start selling everything below cost and as fast as we could. We needed money to get started someplace else.

I drove to see Crazy Joe at his furniture store across the street. I wanted to know how he was doing with his business. He was sitting with his feet up on a chair and reading the newspaper. "I'm not worried about the recession," he said. "True, our business has dropped considerably, but we have enough money saved that we can wait indefinitely for things to go back to normal."

I was impressed with his indefinite savings.

Autumn of 1990

Al and I made an appointment to visit a bankruptcy lawyer. Except for Crazy Joe, New Jersey's businesses were a goner and the whole state was going berserk. The latest in bumper stickers said it all, "The last person leaving New Jersey, turn off the lights."

I racked my brain thinking of ideas on how to save our music center but nothing seemed feasible. According to Ralph, when he looked over the books, we were $250,000 in debt.

Al and I turned in our Life Insurance and put the money aside along with the $10,000 we made from selling Ronnie's Music Den at Collingswood Flea Market. We were going to need every penny to survive our downfall.

Michael and his mom moved to South Carolina. The house as it stood wasn't ready to go on the market but their real state lady told them to do it anyway. He promised to call when back in New Jersey.

I'm too busy to think about him, I told myself as I drove to the music center, after we hugged and said goodbye. *I still love him but I'm more mature now, and I realize that life is what it is and there's nothing I can do to change it.*

Most of the directors at The Simy Dinner Theatre had a group of actors they used for just about all their plays because they were extremely talented, easy to work with and reliable. But we still held auditions. It was our way of finding more talent to add to our already awesome group of performers. The theatre was still my escape, and I had to be on vacation or pretty sick to miss a show or rehearsal, but without Michael, the theatre had lost its charm. I just went through the mechanics of running it. Setting up a set with Al's help always turned into a battle, we simply didn't get along. I counted my lucky stars whenever Barney was available to help, since some high school students were unreliable, and even dishonest.

This morning I received in the mail a copy of the checks for the month, and to my surprise one was made out to Joel a high school student, for $500 with my falsified signature. The checks I had made to Joel and the other two boys helping to build the new set had been for $50 each.

Before I dared to accuse him, I drove to the bank and the bank teller in charge showed me Joel, on video camera wearing a hooded jacket, cashing the check at the outside window. I called him and he denied having done it. I told him the bank had a video of him cashing the check and he had until the end of the week to bring the $500 in cash to the Howell Music Center. I expected the money by nine on Friday morning, or I would call the police. He came Thursday morning and handed me the cash. He didn't even say he was sorry; instead he blamed me for giving him a blank check, it had been too much of a temptation not to take advantage of my carelessness.

I finally understood what Papa had once told me, that the majority of crooks and criminals in jail blamed their victims. Joel was no different; he must have thought that what he did was not a big deal, because he asked me not to fire him since he loved working with me. I bet he did. But I had one rule in business I didn't work with thieves.

A day didn't go by without thinking about Michael. I wondered how he was doing out there in the boondocks, as he described the place where he and his mother had moved to.

When the teachers at the Howell Music Center heard of our financial predicament, all nine teachers got together and unanimously offered to work for free until we could get out of debt. We were moved, by their more than kind offer, but we were too far gone to be rescued.

That night it was hard to fall asleep, thinking about their

future, and what they were going to do to make a living when we closed our music center forever.

I received a letter from Mama, telling me that Alice, her new employee, had been trying to convince her and Papa to allow her two young daughters, who were prostitutes, to come live with them. Mama and Papa were not comfortable having the girls living with them because it was a way of life they didn't find respectable. Alice was mad at her for not allowing it.

A week later I received another letter from Mama, Alice was engaged to a guy who had been in jail for ten years but when he got out in a year more or less, they were getting married. "Verónica, this means that I'm going to lose Alice. I don't know how I'm going to manage without her; she's the best employee I ever had."

I wrote back advising Mama to look for another employee, because it sounded like too much trouble brewing ahead.

After going from one beauty shop to another to borrow the beauty equipment, we needed for the next play; miracle of miracles, Barbara came to our rescue. She made a deal with the owner of the beauty shop she frequented. In exchange for advertisement in the playbill, they offered her all the beauty shop props we needed for "Steel Magnolias," including four old, beat-up professional beauty chairs with the hairdryers included. They were the perfect props for an old town beauty shop.

A warm fuzzy feeling came over me, thinking about the end result of "Steel Magnolias," with Barbara as the director.

Joe, the owner of Crazy Joe Furniture was our theatre patron saint. I first met him after I moved all the props out of the chicken coop and into a regular storage unit, which turned out to have limited space to store larger pieces of furniture. I walked into his furniture store to ask for his patronage and he took me under his wing.

In exchange for a full-page advertisement in the playbill, and two theatre tickets with Hibachi dinner included, any furniture we needed could be borrowed for the duration of each production.

The beauty about borrowing furniture from Crazy Joe was that I could select the furniture style we needed, and at the end of the run I just returned everything back to his store.

I no longer had any need for extra storage space. Two larger props, a fireplace, and a bar and stools, that didn't fit into the small rental unit, became part of our living room décor. Al complained that our apartment looked like a consignment shop, but it wasn't that bad.

The fireplace looked real and it gave a warmth feeling to our living room and the African wooden bar with three matching stools covered with leopard skin, the envy and desire of everyone that saw them on stage, gave our apartment a certain party flare. The front of the bar was carved with three African-like masks and the front of the stools had the same matching masks, but a lot smaller. More than on one occasion I had been approached by a theatre patron who either wanted to buy the bar and stools or wanted to know where I bought them. They had been donated to the theatre so long ago that I didn't even recall who gave them to me. But I do remember Michael being impressed when he saw them, "Ronnie, as always, you have outdone yourself."

Ralph strained his back from lifting a television set. The chiropractor he used after having a car accident, a while back had helped him a lot but was not available and supposedly his assistant who was still attending chiropractic college, popped his back so hard that he suffered a back injury from it. I would have to be dying to allow myself to be treated by a quack. Just the thought of it gave me the willies.

I received a very disturbing letter from Laurie, our beloved stage manager of two years. She had moved to Georgia with her family and her high school teacher saw her speaking to a black student and told her that in the south, white girls were not allowed to speak to black boys unless they wanted to jeopardize their own lives. I was shocked to learn about that as if we were still living back in the darkness of the '50's or '60's.

I always felt that people from different religions had it bad when it came to prejudice but having your skin a different color had to be the worst curse one could have when it came to having a normal life among a bunch of ignorant white people. I would never be able to live in the south under such conditions; how Michael could stand to live in South Carolina, was beyond me. He couldn't possibly be happy there.

Barbara was inflexible. "The pin for "Steel Magnolias" has to be exactly three inches in diameter!" It wasn't easy to be a prop person. Every bug pin I bought didn't fit Barbara's standards.

After two weeks of looking into every jewelry store as far as Ocean County and way north in Woodbridge, I found a golden spider with fake diamond toes and green eyes for fifty dollars, of all the places, at the Freehold mall. The mall gave me the heebie-jeebies. Half the stores were closed, and there was nobody shopping. It looked like a ghost town. Obviously, businesses were doing badly everywhere. The theatre was still going; when it came to eating great food and enjoying excellent entertainment people were still willing to spend.

I presented the spider pin to Barbara during rehearsals last night. She must have liked it because she said, "It will have to do."

I planned on keeping the pin after the run of the show.

The critics raved about Barbara Shiavonne's production being flawless and many of our theater patrons said the play was better than the movie.

Every time Rosanna and I got together which was at least once a week, she would tell me about her dream of being a television talk show host. I hated listening to people telling me their hopes and dreams and never doing anything about it and one morning on the bus to Chinatown, New York City, to go dim sum hopping as her guest, she brought up the topic again. I told her if she wanted to do it that badly I would help her out even though I had no idea of what was involved. She said she needed time to think about it.

I had never eaten dim sum. I loved the small bite-sized delicacies of steamed and fried savory dumplings served on small plates that we shared, except for chicken feet and other oddities like duck tongue that she wanted me to try. I felt quite adventurous when it came to food, but certain animal parts I had my limits.

On the way back from New York, Rosanna said, "Okay, I thought about it and with you as my helper I know I can do it. I'm ready to start my first television production. It will be a talk show for singles and then later on I'd also like to do a community talk show about local events and interesting people. Do you think you can be my cameraperson and do the screen editing?"

"As long as I get some kind of training I don't see why not," I said overjoyed with the idea of working in a television station even if it was only a local cable station.

Saturday morning, two stagehands carrying the couch downstairs to my van bumped into Mrs. Ounuma's favorite glass vase arrangement of silk maroon flowers sitting pretty on the red-lacquered mantelpiece downstairs. The vase hit the floor like a firecracker and broke into a million pieces. Thank God there was no one else in the restaurant except the three of us. I used a broom to gather all the broken glass and put it in a paper bag to throw in the trashcan outside. Then I carefully put the silk flowers inside a clean garbage bag.

Knowing how much Mrs. Ounuma loved her silk flowers, I couldn't possibly throw them away. It would be a criminal act. But if I left them on the counter, she would know that I was guilty of not paying attention while guiding the guys with the couch down the staircase. My only option was to take them home.

"My God, those are the ugliest fake flowers I have ever seen," Al said. "Don't you even dare think of using them to decorate our home. Forget it."

I knew my limits and I wrapped them in a towel and hid them under our bed like a dead body.

The New Year's Eve show "Adults Only" was sold out by mid-November. I had finally mastered enough experience to know what titles attracted audiences. "You are the best thing that ever happened to us," Mr. Ounuma said. "Times are very hard now and we don't want to go out of business, it would mean having to go back to Japan. Not good."

I advised him to advertise the restaurant with coupons in the newspapers, and that worked well but at the same time he would get upset when they brought in the coupons. He called those customers "cheapskates."

Meanwhile, we were busy trying to sell as much and as quick as possible by lowering everything in our music center below our cost. Luckily, we had Christmas at our doorstep, and it helped us a lot since there were still some people buying for the holidays even if they couldn't afford it. With the low prices we were offering, they would be fools not to take advantage of our downfall.

In about two months according to our lawyer the papers for bankruptcy would be finalized.

Winter of 1991

Every time Al went to the Kobe restaurant and spoke to Mr. Ounuma I already knew nothing positive would come of it. Al always came up with a comment that was either derogatory or dumb. Either way it was trouble for me. It had taken me months to convince Mr. Ounuma to share with me the cost of advertising his restaurant and my theater in the newspapers. Mr. Ounuma was making small talk with Al and told him he was hoping the newspaper advertisement that month would continue to bring new customers to the restaurant. "What a waste of money!" was Al's immediate response. "Nobody is going to even look at the ad."

By the time Al finished telling Mr. Ounuma all the reasons for not advertising, Mr. Ounuma cancelled all future ads. In five minutes Al destroyed everything I had worked so hard for.

Katie called me at the Music Center and asked me if I could get to Kobe two hours before "Move Over, Mrs. Markam" was to go on. Katie, Mrs. Ounuma, and Hiroko, my favorite Japanese waitress, had a mischievous look on their faces when they insisted that I follow them upstairs to the theatre's dressing room. I trusted them enough that when asked to undress down to my underwear I did it while giggling along with them. First, they had me slide into an embroidered white chemise that had to be worn in a very specific way so it could fit just right under the beautiful green cotton kimono with flying white geese pattern. Mrs. Ounuma apologized for using a cotton summer kimono, to which Katie said that she had an extra winter kimono and the following week she would give it to me as a present. They spent extra time making sure the white chemise showing in back of my neck was properly displayed since in Japan that was the sexiest part of a woman's body. A black silk sachet was tied around my waist and a black silk pocket called the hump was hooked to the back of my waist and a white doughnut shaped plastic piece wrapped in a green scarf got inserted into the hump and then tied securely with another black scarf. Then they used black and light green silk ropes to tie around my waist. By the time they were finished, I was so tightly bound that I couldn't take a deep breath. Then I was fitted into a pair of odd white socks they called tabi, where the big toe was separated from the other toes and handed me a pair of slip on black sandals. Hiroko proceeded to comb my long hair up into a double bun and inserted three silvery ornamental hairpins into it.

Mrs. Ounuma smiled along with the others and then she said, "My husband and I appreciate everything you do for us."

Katie said, "This is our way of saying thank you. You are our sister."

Hiroko said, "Everything you have on is a present from us." They bowed and I bowed back.

After the show the cast and crew left in a hurry, it was snowing. I had nothing to worry about; my van was equipped with snow tires. I hung out at the bar downstairs talking to Jerry, the bartender, and a middle age couple who were not concerned about the snowstorm either. I told Debbie and her husband Dan, the couple at the bar, that I was having trouble locating a double-sided desk for the next show. They had no idea what I was looking for.

They kept asking Jerry and me, "What is a dexk?" And Jerry kept raising his shoulders like, don't ask me.

"You know, a dexk, where you put the typewriter, and

do your typing?" And I acted the part of seating at a dexk with a typewriter.

"Oh, you mean a desk? No wonder, we couldn't understand you," Dan laughed. "You're pronouncing it with an x, instead of an s."

"Yeah, that's what I said, dexk," I insisted, still unable to hear the difference. Debbie stood from her chair and using both hands on my face she gently made me look straight at her. "Look at my lips, listen to the word desk with an s and then with an x."

As luck would have it Debbie taught English at the Howell high school. She and her husband took their time to show me how to place my tongue in back of my front teeth when saying desk and then took turns saying desk so I could repeat each time. I knew I had it when with a beaming smile of accomplishment, they said in unison, "Perfect."

I gave them each a hug and thanked them. I asked Jerry to put their last drink on my account. It was snowing heavily, and when I walked to my van the fluffy snow covered me up to my ankles, but I was too delighted to worry about my cold feet when I had just learned to say a word in perfect English, that could be added with pride to my vocabulary. I turned the heat on and drove off as I kept repeating desk, desk, desk. It had such a nice ring to it. My van rode as far as three blocks when the swooshing flapping sound coming from a tire warned me to stop. I had a flat tire. I knew there was a gas station just around the corner and it didn't seem to be much of a walk. But wrapped up tight in my kimono, I could only take mini steps, while guarding forward so I would not be thrown backwards. The snowy gusty winds didn't help and if anything had pushed the snow to about two feet high along the pathway to the gas station. I was shivering from head to toes, when I opened the glass door to the building where two attendants sat on plastic crates, drinking from mugs by the lit stove. They looked me up and down and remained silent without a hint of emotion.

"I work in a Japanese restaurant." I gave them a faint timid smile.

They looked at each other then back at me, as if asking, so what do you want. "My van is just a block away from here and I need someone to fix the tire."

"Mam, this is a gas station, not a garage!" said the older one.

"I know, but can you help me to change the tire, anyway? I have a spare in my van."

They wouldn't budge but let me use their phone to call Al.

When Al and I got to the top steps of the courthouse on Monday morning, we wondered where to go from there.

A guard came up to us. "The bankruptcy courtroom is on the third floor." And he pointed to the elevator.

"We were just going to ask you where to go, how did you know?"

"Lately, that's what everyone is coming in looking for." He didn't even smile

The courtroom was packed with people overflowing into the hallway waiting to be called in.

Our bankruptcy lawyer had told us that the landlord had to give us one-week notice, but he never did. January 15th, the Howell Music Center, our Alamo last stand, was taken over by an unconcerned landlord who grinned at Steve while putting his hands on the only piano we had left in the store. "This black baby grand is going to look great in my living room."

Poor Steve was by himself when the landlord with the court papers in hand asked him to leave the premises. We all knew that was going to happen, we just didn't know when. Thank God that a week before, I had taken home the *toolbox* where I kept all the cash we had been saving. Except for small musical accessories, the baby grand and three guitars, our music center was basically bare.

Al, Steve and I talked once again about moving to Florida and start a new music center. We felt it was a lot more practical than remaining in New Jersey where there was no future. It helped our decision by recalling what a great time we had many years prior when we went to Florida on vacation. We began feeling optimistic about our move. When one door closed another opened; that was my philosophy.

The money saved in the toolbox from our life insurance, what we sold in the last few months, and from the sale of Ronnie's Music Den, was divided equally between Al, Steve, and me.

I made it clear to Al that no matter what happened, the money saved should be considered nonexistent, and it belonged to our future. What future I didn't know, but I had no intentions of using my share buying junk and I encouraged him to do the same. I told him and Steve, "If all our cash is gone, we'll have absolutely nothing to fall back on. We're all healthy so that's very good. But, we need to get a job to keep us going without touching our savings, until we decide what to do next. Meanwhile with what I make at the Kobe it will keep us going if we are thrifty."

I heard from our neighbor upstairs that a fast food restaurant in Freehold gave away fresh chicken gizzards to farmers to feed their animals. I drove to the restaurant and asked the manager if I could have some to feed my family. She asked me how many buckets of gizzards I needed.

One full bucket was definitely more than enough for a month of cooking!

Rosanna went live on Monmouth Cablevision Public Access with her first fun and exciting talk show. At first it was challenging, because as the director I had to learn to enter the data in the computer, and when it came to being computer savvy I could only compare my knowledge to that of a two-year being able to read a book. But the people working at the station were very patient and I finally learned the procedure including running the two cameras in the studio.

I enjoyed seeing Rosanna happy.

"Veronica's Room" was set to start February 15th. Did I agree to produce it because it had my name on the title? It did help my decision. Besides, Barbara would be playing the psychotic main character, and the rest of the cast were in the same caliber of professionalism.

"Et tu, Brutus?" I understood exactly how Caesar must have felt when he got knifed by his so called trusted friend. The same feeling came over me except that I didn't have to die.

The Spring Lake Theatre had gone ahead of us and put on "Veronica's Room." How did that happen? Hum, let's see. One of the actors in our present production was also a member of the Spring Lake Theatre and he told me that while present at one of their board meetings he overheard from our supposed friend and director of one of our past productions, telling the Spring Lake Theatre group, "Let's beat the Simy Dinner Theatre by producing "Veronica's Room" before they do it." Our traitor knew we were planning on that production for February, because I had shared my plans with her.

I was devastated, and so were the actors. We were already two weeks into practice. To rub salt into the wound, the critic for the Asbury Park Press buried the Spring Lake Theatre production alive to say the least. I was sure that when the general public read such terrible review they would have no desire to see our production.

I called a meeting with the actors and director. After some debate, we agreed that if we didn't do that play the other theatre would have us under their thumb.

Why did she do that? Malice or jealousy was the only answer; it didn't even matter anymore. One thing was for sure, it would stay in her conscience, and God had already paid them back by turning the critics against them. Oops, my father would not agree with my thinking, so I fixed it immediately. God had nothing to do with their show being terrible. The only ones to blame were them for putting on a lousy production. I shared my thoughts with the group and they voted on, let's do it!

I sent an invitation to Yolanda the critic for the Asbury Park Press. She called to inform me that she couldn't come; it would be pure agony to see the same play again.

I told Yolanda about my first experience with "The Pirates of Penzance," at the Lakewood Theatre, and what happened when I saw the same production directed and performed by another theatre in Massachusetts. It had been like night and day. I begged her to give us a chance to prove ourselves and promised her that she would not be disappointed. I added, "I'm not exaggerating about our cast, if you can't attend you'll be missing an outstanding performance. Let me put it this way, have dinner at the restaurant and if you don't like our production, you are my guest and I also don't expect you to do a review of the play."

"Okay, I'll come to see the show," she said. "But if it is as good as you say, I'll pay for my own dinner."

Even though we had a standing ovation on opening night of "Veronica's Room," Yolanda had not changed her mind about the subject of the play, but agreed that the quality of the production was, without a doubt, way above what she had been exposed to at the other theatre. She kept her promise and paid for her dinner, but she also said that she would have to be true to her readers.

Yolanda's review raved about the quality of the production, but true to her word she also mentioned how strong she felt against the subject of incest and murder. Such review only demonstrated how much people were attracted to violence and sex. We were sold out every night and had to extend the production two more weekends.

One evening one of our patrons had to be held back as he tried to climb on stage to save Katie Grau from being murdered. And when Barbara Shiavonne cried in the end of the last act, she brought cold chills down every patron's spine, and I had to hold my own tears back because I knew her anguish on stage was not an act. After the first performance I offered to replace her with another actress, but she swore that she was fine and if anything, it helped her come to terms with her own emotions and what she had gone through as a child, being physically abused by her mother.

I got a great deal on plane tickets, and all of us, including Ralph, went to Florida to see what might be available to start a new life down there.

The trip proved to me that when you go anywhere with plenty of money in your pocket it can give you the impression of an idyllic situation. But it was a completely different story when on a budget. The car we rented to drive around from town to town was small and had enough ants living inside to fill a stadium. For five days we stayed at the cheapest motels and ate our meals at McDonalds. We didn't go to Disney, and there was no leisure time cooling off at the pool. Where we stayed there were no pools. It was hot, and humid, and worst of all we had no idea in what direction to go. We drove randomly through several towns, and cities, but there were music stores everywhere we went, and we came to the conclusion that Florida was saturated with them. Our trip had been a great disappointment but we knew it was just a question of time before we moved out of New Jersey in quest of a better life.

Following Rosanna with the video camera took me to places that I'd otherwise never have the opportunity to experience, like the day when she was covering a party at a golf course in Rumson and the featured guest was no other than Geraldo Rivera. While we were waiting for him to show up, Rosanna got sick to her stomach and we had to leave before he arrived. I began taking the equipment back to her car, but on the way out I couldn't help grabbing a puffy cream-cake from one of the dessert trays in the lounge. When I got to the middle of the parking lot a chauffeured black limousine pulled in, and to my surprise Geraldo himself—and what looked like his family—had stepped out of the vehicle.

I walked up to him like a robot, "You're one of my favorite television stars. Can I shake your hand?"

I was holding the camera over my shoulder with the left hand and the cake with the right. In order to shake his hand, I quickly stuffed my mouth with the cake. He smiled, said thank you for the compliment, and shook my hand laden with whip cream, and kept his smile as he joined his family.

I remained frozen on the spot, my hand still outstretched. It was my first one-on-one encounter with a famous person.

Rosanna came walking in my direction and asked me what was wrong. "You won't believe this but Geraldo Rivera just shook my dirty hand." I said gazing at it.

I become very creative with cooking rice with chicken livers, sandwiches with liver pâté spread, stewing rice and chicken hearts, and our favorite old-timer, chicken soup. We had meat every day at our table and plenty of rice to keep us full, a roof over our head and I was able to draw a check each month from our theatre at Kobe. I felt we were very fortunate but Al and I needed a good paying reliable job.

Steve wanted to see what a television studio looked like, so he met me at Monmouth Cablevision Public Access, in Jackson. Rosanna's show was about singles looking for a mate, she interviewed them and if someone watching television liked what they saw they could call the number at the studio and make a date to meet that person. After entering all the required information into the computer, I ran the cameras in the studio.

After the singles show was over, Steve went into the studio to look at the cameras more up-close. Rosanna's guest a woman in her mid-forties stopped me outside in the hallway, "Did you see that young man in the hallway? He looked at me and I almost dropped to my knees! Do you know his name? Can you get me his phone number?"

Rosanna tried to control her laughter as she introduced me, "This is Ronnie my television producer and director. By the way, Ronnie is *his mother."*

Rosanna's guest didn't even blink; she pulled a calling card from her purse and handed it to me. "If he's not married, please tell him to call me."

I didn't give Steve her card. He already had a girlfriend.

This morning Al and I left the Welfare department very disappointed. We decided never to return to their headquarters. Besides, Al was worried someone we knew might see us there.

A woman without any sense of humor told us to come back when we no longer had a car, and then she would talk about us getting food stamps. As long as we still had a car we were not entitled to any financial help.

"And how do we get here, if we don't have transportation?" I asked. "We're already here, so why can't you process the food stamps?"

The woman answered annoyed, "Take a taxi." "We can't afford to pay for a taxi!"

"Bring the bill and the Welfare Department will pay for it." And she asked us to leave since she couldn't help us until our car was gone.

No wonder the government was losing money, their employees lacked common sense. We were there already, why didn't she give us the food stamps?

Good thing that Ralph had advised us not to put our condo into the bankruptcy statement. We still had a mortgage payment to make but without the apartment we had no place to live.

Two days later our business van was taken away. But Al's car was still in our possession for another week. I told Mr. Ounuma about our predicament, and that Al and I planned to move out of state as soon as we figured out where to go. "Don't worry," I told him. "I promise to find someone to take over the theater so it doesn't have to close." Mr. Ounuma asked me to sit down at one of the dining tables. His wife brought me dinner and he asked me to eat and wait until all the customers had left.

Once the restaurant had lost its momentum and was getting ready to close, Mr. Ounuma sat at my table while Mrs. Ounuma stood next to him looking down at her clasped hands. "Please don't go," she said softly. "Please stay."

"How much money do you need per month, to pay your bills?" Mr. Ounuma asked, and then like his wife, his voice softened. "We don't want you to leave us. Our restaurant depends on the theatre crowd to survive."

"If I were to stick to an indispensable amount, we would need $250 a week to help with our basic monthly bills. Lately what I make with the theatre is very unpredictable, and having lost our income from the music stores, has put us in a serious financial jam. We were thinking of moving to Florida, but now we are not sure."

Mr. and Mrs. Ounuma spoke to each other in Japanese and then he said, "My wife and I are prepared to give you $250 a week, no questions asked, and for as long as you need our help."

My eyes filled with tears. "The only way I can accept your offer is if I can help out at the restaurant and my husband for sure will want to do the same."

Mr. and Mrs. Ounuma spoke to each other briefly and then smiled at me. "Can you come and open the restaurant in the morning and take reservations so I don't have to be in so early?" he asked timidly. Mrs. Ounuma said something to him in Japanese and he added, "Your husband can do some handyman work, yes?"

I assured him that Al and I would be more than glad to help them with anything they needed.

Al agreed to work at the Kobe helping with painting and any other building maintenance as long as he didn't have to climb a ladder to fix the roof.

Al and I needed to find regular jobs, so we didn't have to depend on charity. It was also imperative that we have a car to look for a job and to go back and forth to work. Living out of the city limits put us in the predicament of not being able to get anywhere without transportation. Local buses went by where we lived, but there were no bus stops.

Mrs. Swan our neighbor and I were checking our mailboxes and as always, she kept me informed on the latest goings at our apartment complex. "Our good for nothing maintenance man has been fired and the property management company is presently on the lookout for another handyman to do the job. I hope the new hired hand is more dependable." My mind was racing at the speed of lighting and that was how fast I got back to Al. It took me all day to convince him that he should apply for the job. His opinion was that no one in their right mind would hire him without prior experience. I wrote a letter stating that my husband Al was an amazingly good handyman with lots of experience working at the Kobe Japanese Restaurant and I his wife was also very handy at carpentry and he would be ideal for the job.

    My letter did well. The manager at the main office liked the idea that Al had a wife as his assistant. The good news was that Al would be well paid, and as soon as the maintenance man left his apartment in two weeks, we could move into it. I put an ad in the Asbury Park Press about our condo being available for rent. The rent would go to pay the monthly dues on our mortgage.

~ *Chapter Four* ~

THE CHIROPRACTIC MIRACLE

1991

Spring of 1991

    Buddy, Ralph's friend, who was a car salesman, sold me a used car for $200. I had to use a stick shift, and the car was very small, but its striking green color made it highly visible on the road.

    On the first day I drove it from Buddy's used car lot, the side mirror fell off. The next day the handle on my driver's side door came off in my hand, the only way in and out was through the passenger side. The outside didn't have a single dent and its green crispy color was the admiration of everyone. It also ran well except for when having to stop for a red light or at a stop sign. Then I had to keep turning the key over and over again until it caught on.

    Michael sent me a letter wanting to know how I was doing, I wrote back describing all the tribulations with my car and finished the letter by adding that I had run over a squirrel on Route 9 but since I didn't stop, the car had made it home.

    Ever since we had gone bankrupt Ralph and I had been

talking about going into business together. He was doing well at Bell Core, had a good salary and his name was in several books he had edited for a couple of physicists that worked with him, but he was ready to start another career a little more challenging and fulfilling. I could see that he was a little like me in the sense that once I became successful, I was ready to try something new. We talked about opening a Portuguese Restaurant and what main courses we would be serving. I even drew an artsy menu I called *Comida a Portuguesa.* But it took more than having a menu to open a restaurant. We started to look for a building and came to the conclusion that if Ralph was to take a loan to match the $20,000 that Al and I had saved, it still wouldn't cover a down payment on a broken-down shack in the middle of nowhere.

I could not have been any angrier than when Al parked his new car in front of our apartment. He had just blown his ten thousand dollars. Steve was not that far away from him, he had spent most of his share too. It was down to Ralph and me to start a business. We came up with a great idea, a fish farm. I still had my ten thousand dollars, we could rent space in an empty lot, dig a couple of pools, fill them with water, add some fish eggs and just wait for the fish to hatch. How difficult could that be?

    Al had been right to buy himself a new car. Like he always said, when you buy a used car you inherit someone else's problems. While driving on a busy intersection in Manhattan, I stopped for a light. No matter how many times I turned the key, the car wasn't budging. Since the car was next to a sidewalk Tracey and I felt safer standing on the sidewalk next to the car versus sitting inside and get rearended. We waited patiently for someone to help us get the car started. A street person stopped and looked under the hood. "For five dollars I can fix the problem, but I need a paper clip," he said. "Do you have a paperclip?"

I stayed by the car while Tracey went to find a store that sold paper clips. She brought us a couple and the man stuck one of them somewhere in the engine and when I turned the key the engine started. He told us not to stop the car until we got home. I gave him the well-deserved five dollars, and he gave us a copy of a letter he had written about the world blowing up at the end of that month. Then, to make us feel better, he said, "Don't worry, the paper clip will keep the car running until then."

Al and I moved into the apartment where the maintenance man and his wife used to live. Life couldn't be better. Our new apartment had an extra bedroom—which we used to store Al's maintenance tools and the theatre props I had kept in the living room, were now out of sight. Luckily, we found a renter for our old place, so our mortgage was taken care of, while we lived rent free in our new larger apartment.

I did meet the old maintenance man once. He came over to our old apartment to check a water leak in the toilet. I remembered him because he told Al and me that his wife had gained a lot of weight since they had gotten married a year before, and to him that meant she was satisfied with her new life. I wondered if food had become her real source of happiness.

Ralph did a lot of research on fish farming and came to the conclusion that it was not an easy business. A lot more went into raising fish than we had thought at first. The water had to be constantly treated and there were all kinds of diseases that could kill the fish all in one shot if we didn't really know what we were doing—and we didn't know what we were doing. Fish farming became too much of a gamble for us to get into. He decided to continue working at Bell Core and in the meantime, we would keep our eyes open for other business opportunities that might come along.

Mr. Raster, the owner from Westwood Greens, an independent senior facility where I had applied for a job called. He wanted to meet me the next day, May 7 which happened to be my birthday.

I was hired as activity director! I couldn't imagine a better birthday present from the Gods. But there was one prerequisite; in order to work there, I was to become their croupier with blackjack, poker, five-card stud and craps. I told him I didn't even know how to shuffle. He gave me a package of playing cards and encouraged me to start practicing.

Westwood Greens was only a ten-minute drive from our apartment—if my car broke down, I could always walk.

I gave the good news to Mr. Ounuma. Al and I no longer needed financial aid. We were doing fine on our own now. I had to work at Westwood Greens, Monday through Fridays from nine to three-thirty but he could still count on me to help at the Kobe to answer the phones, on weekends whenever possible. Mr. Ounuma accepted the offer gladly. It was the least I could do.

My job at Westwood Greens couldn't be more perfect but it also gave me anxiety attacks. I knew it was something to do with anxiety because my heart would flutter and I experienced difficulty breathing, even before I left the kitchen with the fruit cart, to dispense a piece of fruit to each of the residents. I was not allowed to give each more than one piece of fruit but they fought over the bananas or if an apple was too small they wanted two apples, without regard for the other folks. As I tried to get away, they would run after me like spoiled bratty children. Mr. Raster called me into his office and reprimanded me for my lack of control over the seniors. There were complaints from the cleaning staff about fruit flies in some of the rooms. Like, what could I do, scream at them? Run them over with the fruit cart? Smack them on the hands like children if they grabbed the fruit? I truly loved my job but only until three, before the fruit zombies attack.

The next day I tried a new method, I waited behind the kitchen doors, until three, before coming out. But as I looked in the peep hole of the kitchen door, I knew I was in deep trouble, their eyes were transfixed with excitement waiting for me to come out. As soon as I entered the lounge with the cart, the ones that could get up on their own—and that meant about half of them—stood and came shuffling toward me as fast as their feet could move. I immediately turned the cart around and into the kitchen where I hid behind the doors, my heart pounding steadily like a grandfather's clock. I waited a good two minutes before sticking my head out to take a peek. To my horror they were right there clustered next to the doors waiting for me. Mr. Raster came out of his office yelling at them, "Back, back into your seats. Ronnie will dispense the fruit, and if I hear of anyone grabbing an extra piece, that person better answer to me, and there will be no fruit for a whole week."

Wow, I mumbled to myself. *Nothing like a father figure screaming his head off to make them settle down.*

Last Wednesday I got turned in by one of the seniors, for speeding at 55 miles per hour in a 50-speed zone. But it wasn't my fault, every time I took them shopping, there was always one or two that disappeared. By the time I found them I had to rush back or the poor starving seniors complained to Mr. Raster about their fruit not being distributed at their much-expected time of three o'clock.

Now the good things at Westwood Greens, as the entertainment director I got to pick the activities and drive the facility's van to take them on fun trips twice a week.

I started sending money to my parents. It was only $50 a week, but I intended to increase it when I made more. The pension check Papa received from the German government was not enough to live on. But luckily our cousins from England were helping my parents financially. According to Papa, if it weren't for his family in England, he and Mama would be destitute.

Theresa, one of my favorite residents at Westwood Greens, saw me in the hallway and took hold of my arm. She whispered excitedly in my ear, "My high school sweetheart is coming to take me away next week and we're getting married on Friday. Would you like to come to my wedding?"

"Of course, I do," I said just as excited. "Congratulations! What time is the wedding and where, here?"

She wore a beaming smile. "Yes, right here in the lobby, at eleven in the morning."

I made sure I announced the happy event to the others seated in the lounge, "Did you hear the good news? Theresa is getting married Friday, to her high school sweetheart."

Sofia put on her typical smirk. "Theresa? Who would marry her, just look at her. She's ugly and older than Grandma Moses."

The average age at Westwood Greens was 80, which was Sofia's age. How much older could Theresa be? And when it came to being ugly, my goodness, Theresa was an adorable petite lady with an enormous positive attitude matched by big brown eyes with thick long eyelashes. If anything, Theresa was going to be a beautiful bride.

I gave the wedding news to Pat the women at the front desk. She circled her forefinger next to her temple. "Theresa is not well up here," she said.

I was heartbroken. Theresa seemed so normal so happy. When I saw her across the lobby I called out, "I'll see you this Friday, at your wedding." She stopped, gave me a joyful smile and then running toward me with the brightness of a young girl in love, she gave me a long hug. "Thank you for being my friend," she said. "Friday, is going to be the happiest day of my life." And she walked away humming a tune.

Friday, Theresa came up to me and told me as if she was giving me the news for the first time, "My high school sweetheart is coming to take me away next week and we're getting married on Friday. Will you come to my wedding?" Theresa had been in foster homes since she had been born and now she spent the rest of her life at Westwood Greens. People, much like pets were either lucky or not. Some dogs died tied to a post outside in the elements and or barely fed. Others were loved and cherished dearly by their owners, like in Portugal where there was a cemetery in the Lisbon zoo where pet owners paid a small fortune just to have their little pooch happily buried, their name and a short but loving description of what had made them special, engraved on their headstone.

I had two high school teenagers helping me with building the sets, but sometimes they didn't show up and I was forced to do it on my own, even when it involved lifting which made my lower back horribly sore. Still I preferred not to ask Al to help me. While working on the last set alone, a door resting against the stage wall fell on top of my head, when I let go to grab a screw that fell on the stage floor. I understood the meaning of seeing stars, and stars I did see.

Barney was no longer with us; he simply stopped coming in with his wife Patricia. All of that coinciding with what happened with "Veronica's Room." Like the song says, "Nothing lasts forever but the earth and sky."

With the ups and downs of the economy, the theatre had become a bit unpredictable; occasionally the numbers were low. Every now and then I sat upstairs, staring into the darkness, dreaming about the old days when Michael was an important part of the theatre and my life. I missed working with him, our talks, the hugs and kisses. I kept busy, and was always surrounded by people, but I felt very lonely. One could be in a crowd and still be alone. I was one of them.

Mr. Raster came up with the idea of taking the seniors to see a baseball game at the New York Stadium. He and another staff member joined me and that was great because between the three of us I didn't have to worry about losing anyone in the stadium. I still had no idea what baseball was about, but I was too embarrassed to ask anyone to explain. I liked football a lot better. Probably because in Portugal it was the most popular sport and I had grown with it.

Mr. and Mrs. Walter, a couple at Westwood Greens were an outstanding personification of the Duke and Duchess of Windsor. They never mingled with the other residents and dressed everyday as if the Queen of England herself was joining them for tea. Robert showed up for breakfast in a dark brown suit and a white silk scarf around his neck and his salt and pepper hair parted in the center with greasy pomade which made him look like he belonged to the 20's era. His wife Jocelyn sported a tailored dark brown outfit with matching purse, hat and gloves. They stood out like sore thumbs among the meagerly dressed residents.

All the seniors that signed up for having lunch on Wednesday at a restaurant knew they had to pay me five dollars each, to cover the cost of their food and tip. The Windsor couple came along for the first time and insisted on eating at a separate table from everyone else. When they finished their meal, they walked out and went to stand by the van outside, waiting to be taken back to Westwood Greens. I had no problems collecting the money from everybody, but when I went outside to collect the ten dollars for their meals, they refused.

I told Mr. Raster, what happened. He refunded me the money and then I suggested that the front desk collect for the lunches prior to taking the residents out. It worked like magic.

I awoke with the right eye pink and gooey and had to go to an eye doctor. He said I had "pink eye," and perhaps I'd picked it up from one of the seniors, since it was highly contagious. The prescribed eye drops felt more like burning acid than medicine. I called their clinic just to make sure they had not given me the wrong prescription. With my luck with doctors and medicine I would not have been surprised if they had given me sulfuric acid by accident. But they said that was the way it was supposed to feel. Later in life, many years later, I learned that a drop of baby shampoo and warm water was just as good to wash the eyes and a lot less painful.

I was getting stamps at the post office in Lakewood when the postman behind the counter stared at me with disbelief. "You're Mrs. Esagui, aren't you?"

"How do you know my name?"

"You don't remember me, but I was the one that drove the ambulance when you and your husband took your little boy out of Fitkins Hospital and to the hospital in New York. He was two years old and had meningitis if I remember correctly. Did he live? I always wanted to know what happened to your son."

It had been the winter of 1965. This man had risked his own life driving amidst a major snow storm after Al and I kidnapped Ralph from the hospital where he had been misdiagnosed and dying.

His eyes swelled with tears when I told him that Ralph was not only well and healthy, but he was twenty-eight years old!

One of the stories at Westwood Greens was about Mr. Mafioso, as everyone called Frank, one of the seniors. Supposedly he had been involved in organized crime in but when he became too old and hard to reason with, he had been put away into the retirement home.

I saw him in the hallway yesterday and had to ask, "They say you used to be part of the Mafia, is that true?"

As soon as I said it I knew I had made a big blunder. He looked at me with his knife-like dark beady eyes and retorted, "I was the boss. I killed many with my own hands." Then he drew a finger across his throat as if he was using a knife and said in his raspy voice, "For one dollar, I'd even kill you."

That did it; he had been a Mafia member or he was crazy, probably both.

On Thursdays, Frank paid a visit to the game room even though he never played. He walked around the room hovering over like a vulture and mumbling offensive words while I dealt the seniors their poker cards. He seemed to take pleasure watching me fuddle. One morning, while doing my best to shuffle the cards without bending them, they went flying off my hands. Frank who stood against a wall gazing at me yelled out, "You need to get rid of her. She can't play cards for shit."

After such demonstration of hate, I paid a visit to Mr. Raster's office. "I'll do anything to make the residents happy, except be a card dealer. They get hot tempered and smoke and yell and the atmosphere is very negative in the game room. It's stressing me out." I didn't tell him about Mr. Mafioso.

Mr. Raster had received multiple complaints and had just taken care of the issue. One of the staff members would play cards with the seniors on Thursdays since I couldn't shuffle cards even if my life depended on it. He was very delicate about it.

Working with the old folks gave me a new leaf on life when it came to understanding that being old only meant the parts were slowing down or in need of repairs, but they were no different from me or anyone else younger. Except for giving them their daily fruit, which was still a hard one to handle I had bonded with most of them.

We were having our usual Wednesday lunch at a restaurant when Marcy, one of the residents, pulled her underarm deodorant out from her purse, unbuttoned her shirt, and proceeded to apply the deodorant stick under her armpits. A young couple seated at the table next to us whispered to each other and shook their heads in our direction.

I turned to them with a serious frown on my face, "What're you looking at?"

Marcy had lived in New York City as a renowned artist, until the day she was rear-ended in a car accident and flew through the windshield. The brain concussion and what happened to her body had been serious enough to leave her dependent on others. After a year in the hospital, her family admitted her to Westwood Greens. Marcy was the youngest; only fifty-one years old. She had a weak bladder and couldn't go more than half-hour before she had to rush to the bathroom. She wore diapers but preferred to use the bathroom like everybody else. If I knew a trip took longer than half-hour drive, Marcy couldn't come with us.

Yesterday I drove eight seniors to Shop-Rite a supermarket nearby. Luckily, I caught Rose — who was eighty-five and suffered from dementia — from leaving the supermarket arm in arm with another older lady from a different retirement home. When I asked Rose to come with me, she pushed me away. "No, I want to go with my new friend."

They locked themselves into a tight embrace and neither was willing to let go of the other. I couldn't pull them apart. The caretaker for the other home was a stocky woman that seemed to be used to that type of situation — she told me to move out of her way and then using her hands like pulleys, she succeeded in separating them.

I shared with Rosanna some of the delicate issues that came along with getting old, like those among the seniors living at Westwood Greens. She made me swear that I would let her know as soon as I noticed she was developing the first signs of dementia.

I asked her to do the same for me.

John Fraraccio had played in several of our productions, "Don't Drink the Water" in 1988, "The Nerd" in 1989, and "Bell, Book, and Candle" in 1990. When he mentioned he would love to direct "The Playboy of the Western World," an old Irish play written in 1907 by Synge, I told him the month of August was available.

It would be his first directing job, but after producing theatre for so many years, I knew by gut feeling when someone had the potential to be exceptional and I looked forward to John's production.

Summer of 1991

"Talk Radio" a 1987 Pulitzer Prize-nominated play was another very successful theatre production at the Kobe. It was directed and performed by Carlo Durland, the personification of a radio talk-show host-with-the-most. He kept the audience in the palm of his hands, and we had pretty large crowds.

Michael would have loved the play. His house was still in the market. It felt like ages since I had last seen him.

John Fraraccio held auditions for "Playboy of the Western World" and instructed the cast to start practicing their lines preferably with an Irish accent.

He also introduced me to Katherine a friend of his who

knew a lot about the Irish culture and the wardrobe style of the early 1900s. Katherine volunteered her time to design the wardrobe for the play with the help of Susan—the stage manager, who just happened to have a sewing machine. They boasted of being able to create a true all-Irish wardrobe by the time the production went up.

I sewed a long black cape made of glittering material for Steve to use while performing solo one Friday night during one of my original weekend musicals. I called the production, "Friday Night Live."
    Not very original name but it drew a nice crowd. I used a smoke machine for the first time, and Steve put on a very theatrical entrance. He sang and played one of his original tunes on my red electric Yamaha guitar. I had given it to him a couple of years prior when he played with his band at the Freehold High School Battle of the Bands and won second place. I blamed school politics that he and his band didn't win first place.

We were having rehearsals for "Playboy of the Western World" when Katherine, informed me that she couldn't be at the Kobe the following Monday, she had an appointment to see her chiropractic doctor that afternoon.
    "What's wrong?" I asked.
    "Nothing, that's why I get adjusted by my chiropractic doctor once a month, to maintain my health," she said.
    She had nothing wrong with her health but she went to see a chiropractor. I had never heard anything so bizarre in my life.

Since the first day I started working at Westwood Greens I had noticed three sweet ladies that always sat together on the lounge's larger couch. When I got to work at eight in the morning, they were already sitting on *their* couch. They always smiled at me, and I hug them one at a time and then they would say things like, "Oh, you're so young," or "Oh, you're so pretty," or "Oh, you have such a lovely smile," I liked them from the very start—and also because they never ran after the fruit cart.

Sitting there all day like frogs on a pond, they only stood to go to the dining room for lunch, and then returned to the couch until diner. That was the extent of their daily physical activity.

One morning I squeezed myself between two of them. "I have a secret to share with the three of you," I said. "But first I must ask you, can you keep a secret?"

"Of course, we can." Joan was the speaker for the threesome.

Wearing my trustworthy expression, I lowered my voice as I said to them, "What I'm about to tell you is going to shock you. As a matter of fact, you might not believe me and I understand completely if you feel that way." I waited a little for impact, as they pulled themselves toward me eagerly. "Okay, here it goes," I said. "I'm not as young as I look. I know, I know I look young. Are you ready?" They nodded their heads in unison.

"I'm older than you. I'm more than one hundred years old." I expect them to start laughing, and they did quite raucously.

I waited for them to quiet down and then went on with my secretive tone of voice, "Fifty years ago, on May 7th to be exact, I turned one hundred years old, and that's when I decided to become more active. And then guess what?" They shrugged their shoulders in unison, their eyes widened by curiosity. "My age started to reverse itself." I waited for them to laugh their heads off again, but to my surprise I had their attention. "I'm forty-seven years old (besides my birthday date, the only thing that was true), and I'm still reversing my aging process because of the way I live."

Joan spoke for the other two ladies, "I'm ninety-two,

and Martha and Susanne are eighty-nine years old. Tell us what to do; we're getting pretty close to one hundred."

They were where I wanted them, and I continued to talk in the same secretive manner, "In order to reverse the aging process, you need to do exciting and adventurous things you never did before. Now, this is a very important question, what would you all like to do, and remember it has to be something special that you never did before."

They talked among themselves. Then Joan said with a twinkle in her eyes, "We've never been to a racetrack. Does that count?"

"I'll be right back," and I ran to Mr. Raster's office to clear my plans for that Wednesday. "If you want to take them to the racetrack, that's fine with me," he said. "But I want the wooden massage roller I've seen you use on their backs. My wife is pregnant and I know that she would love it."

"They sell them for ten dollars at Britts, in Freehold."
"Honey, just give it to me." He motioned with his hands. "I'm not asking you for the moon."

I made the mistake of telling Al about Mr. Raster request. "Why did you take it to your work? He said. "That roller felt good on my back when you used it on me. He clearly stole it from you. You should have told him to go buy his own or at least to pay you for it. I'm not surprised. You always let people take advantage of your good nature. What's the matter with you?"

Even though I agreed with Al, about Mr. Raster being too lazy of a bastard to buy his own massage roller and taken advantage of me for having no backbone to tell him to go jump in the lake, after a good half-hour of listening to Al's objections over and over again, I left the apartment under the pretense of having to buy cereal for breakfast.

Ten people signed up for the Wednesday trip. I drove to the Monmouth Park Racetrack, with everyone singing along with me, "99 bottles of beer on the wall…"

Before everyone left the van, I explained that we needed to stay close together, and it would even be a good idea to hold on to each other's arms because the Monmouth Park Racetrack was not the place to get lost. Finding one of them among the crowd would be as difficult as finding a needle in a haystack.

I got them seated in the lower bleachers. The race was about to start, but they wanted refreshments. I wrote down their orders and reminded them to stay in their seats until I came back with their drinks. When I returned I counted heads and found that Joan was missing. Nobody had noticed her leave, not even her two closest buddies. The race had started but I wasn't going to wait until it was over to look for Joan. With the nine seniors trailing behind me, we checked the bathrooms, and stopped to ask people if they had seen an old lady with short white hair. Nobody, including myself remembered what she was wearing. We could hear the roaring crowd outside, as the horses raced around the track. Taking a more serious measure on my own, I called security. I couldn't return with one resident missing. I would lose my job.

The race was over when we spotted Joan in the distance, waving at us. She boasted a beaming smile as she walked toward us, holding on to the arms of two racetrack policemen.

"These two good-looking young men were kind enough to escort me down to the promenade. What more can I ask for?"

She had taken the elevator to the bleachers way on the top, and from there she had watched the race. She couldn't wait to brag about her mischievous escapade to her family and the old folks at the home. She'd had the time of her life and couldn't wait for more adventures.

The racetrack story grew to delicious disproportions and Joan found herself surrounded daily by the other residents who wanted to know exactly what happened to her. If you hang out with Ronnie you are guaranteed to reverse the aging process, became the latest word around Westwood Greens.

I did a lot of research before designing the set for "The Playboy of the Western World," and if I ever was to go to Ireland, I knew exactly what to expect in an old country Irish tavern. Katherine did an amazing job with the wardrobe design, following to a T the time period. The set couldn't be any closer to authenticity and John Fraraccio, bought real Irish antique pottery and an antique table. The table lasted until the very last show when the actors became rambunctious. During the fistfight, two actors took it upon themselves to fall on top of the table. The legs on the old table gave way and collapsed under their weight. The audience clapped during the dramatic scene. The interesting thing about the play was that it brought in a large crowd every night, most under the impression that the play had something to do with the Playboy magazine. Still, no one left unimpressed with our production.
    James Gardner from the Asbury Park Press wrote "… The Simy Dinner Theatre Company does poetic justice to this great play, which ages like the finest wines in the Western world…this production is vintage Synge, and very much worth tasting."
    "The Playboy of the Western World," fooled everyone into believing that the cast had been imported directly from Ireland. This was one of our proudest moments in the history of our dinner theatre company.

When one of the kitchen helpers at Westwood Greens called in sick with the flu, Mr. Raster asked me to help in the kitchen during lunch time, just for two days.
    It was gross, what went on behind the scenes. One of the cooks was recovering from a cold, and he would wipe his

nose on his sleeves and then mix the potato salad with his hands. The heat in the kitchen seemed to affect the other cook sweating over the soup pan on top of the stove.

Except for the Kobe Restaurant, where the staff was very particular with the food preparation, at least from what I had observed—I promised myself not to eat out anywhere else.

In preparation for each week at Westwood Greens, I used the weekends to come up with fun things to do with my seniors. As their activity director, I had an obligation to keep them entertained. I didn't put on the home activity calendar where we were going on Wednesday after lunch, I wrote, Destination? SURPRISE!

In the old days I used to take my two sons to the Lakewood Park every summer. The sparkly clean lake was perfect for a cool swim and we always enjoyed a picnic on the man-made sandy beach surrounded by tall branchy trees that provided a blessed shade and a slight breeze. I had no plans to have the seniors swim in the lake and had no picnic basket with me; I just wanted to share with them, the panoramic view of the lake and put a little physical action into their lives.

But when I pulled the van into my old favorite spot in the park, all I could see was asphalt. Black asphalt had taken the place of the sandy beach and the trees had been cut back. I didn't share with them my disappointment; instead I drove back to the main road around the lake. No way in heaven were they going home to complain about my SURPRISE after lunch. On the other side of the lake, I found a large enough grassy plateau shaded by pine trees next to the water. Not perfect but good enough to create perfection of the spirit. I set my battery-operated tape recorder on the grass and pressed the play button to the sound of a waltz.

"Okay folks, grab your partner and let's dance." They

looked at me as if I had lost my mind, but by then they should have known me better. "Feel the music; breathe in life, the fresh air, and the beautiful surroundings. My friends, life is to be felt with each ticking second of our lives." Mr. Phillips, a sweet man in his mid-80's, offered me his hand. "I know exactly what you mean. Ronnie. Will you dance with me?" Once they saw us dance, everyone followed. A contagious laughter took over and when the music stopped, they clapped. Mr. Phillips hugged me, and they took turns saying thank you, and Mrs. Olivia a very old but jovial lady, said, "You're definitely a bit unusual and possibly whacky but I'm willing to do anything you say, as long as I'm getting younger."

I looked up at the blue skies and said thank you to my Aunt Heydee my mentor while growing up. She was right there with me, still the guiding light of my life. The next tune on my cassette was *Aloha Hawaii* and I showed them a few hip movements. That didn't go well, but they found it hilarious.

Sunday evening, I prepared a large pan of lasagna, big enough to freeze for eight individual meals.

Our kitchen was very narrow, and when I inserted something into the oven I always had to bend sideways. As I twisted to put the lasagna pan into the oven I felt a pop on my lower back and couldn't stand due to a sharp radiating pain down my right leg. Bent over and holding on to the walls I made it to the living room floor where I laid curled up in a fetal position waiting for the pain to go away.

Steve had broken up with his girlfriend and lived with us. Lucky for me, Al and Steve got home at the same time. I told them what happened and that I needed them to stretch me out so I could stand. Al lifted and pulled my arms and Steve did the same to my legs. It seemed to help because I could stand, but oddly enough I couldn't sit or lie down without hurting more.

I spent the night standing against the bedroom wall, and taking turns sitting on a chair. The next morning, I still planned on going to work. Taking small painful steps, I made it to my car, but it wouldn't start. Being at a stage in life where I refused to allow futilities like pain stop me from going about my usual activities and feeling sure that if I didn't pay attention to it I would recover soon enough, I had no intentions of wasting precious time trying to walk around our apartment complex to look for Al to drive me to work. Instead, I used each valuable step to walk off our parking lot. How I was going to walk close to three miles amid traffic, didn't enter my mind. I walked as far as the end of the block on my street before the pain nearly took me down on my knees. I couldn't take another step and I knew it in my guts that, just like my old jalopy, I was breaking down and needed to get back home. I took one small step and stopped. Then another step and stopped again. One step at a time I made it back when I saw Al coming out from the building adjacent to ours where he had fixed a kitchen faucet. I asked him to drive me to Westwood Greens. I planned on standing while attending to my seniors. I was able to get into his car, but when it came time to get out, I couldn't. "So weird, I don't feel my feet." I touched them. "I hate to ask you, but can you take me to see Dr. Lehman, the orthopedic surgeon?" He had fixed my back when I got hurt working at a bakery many years ago. The pain as I remembered wasn't as debilitating as now.

I couldn't climb the five steps to Dr. Lehman's office. Al had to push on my backside upwards.

Dr. Lehman asked me to bend over and touch my toes, but any movement made me shriek. He told me I needed to go to the hospital immediately.

"No, I can't, I'll lose my job." And I cried. "Why do I have to go to the hospital? Why can't you fix my back here, in your office?"

"You're a very hard-headed woman. I'm your doctor

and you need to listen to me. You have to go to the hospital, right now."

If I went to the hospital I would be as good as dead. I asked Al to drive me back to work and assured him that by the time I got there I would be fine.

When Al pulled his car by the curve at Westwood Greens, I couldn't lift my feet to get out. "This is plain ridiculous," I complained to Al. "One day I'm fine, and the next day I'm paralyzed." One never knew what could happen from one day to another, another reason why we should always give thanks to God for each blissful minute of the day. Man, did we complain about so much junk, having legs that worked, should be part of our daily thanks.

The idea of getting fired from my job was too much for me to bear; but I had run out of options other than to agree to be taken to the hospital. I asked Al to call my boss later and tell him I would be back the next day.

When I got to the emergency room I couldn't lie down, but they gave me a shot in the rear-end that knocked me out instantly into the land of darkness. I awoke on my back inside a plastic white tube, when I heard someone ask repeatedly if I was awake. "Yes, I am now, but I have to go back to sleep my eyes feel heavy and keep closing."

"No," insisted the same female voice. "You must remain awake. Try to stay awake and don't move. "

"Okay, okay, I'll try." I could tell by her voice that it was important for me to remain conscious. I kept alert by doing basic multiplications in my head.

I awoke in a hospital room. A piece of plywood had been put over the mattress to keep me straight and flat on my back and weights had been tied to my ankles. Dr. Lehman came to visit me the next morning and said the plastic tube I mentioned, was called an MRI machine and it showed I had a herniated disc between L4 and L5. I had no idea what that meant but sounded more like I had a broken back since he didn't want me to turn or move in any direction. The apparatus he had me in was called, spinal traction. After three days of lying flat on the plywood I was suffering from severe muscle spasms, but Dr. Lehman still remembered how I reacted when he gave me drugs for pain control and he would not prescribe any medication.

Mr. and Mrs. Ounuma sent me a huge flower arrangement of exotic, colorful plants. The nurse placed it right across from me, on a table underneath the television. I awoke in the morning looking forward to seeing the flowers.

I had always believed it was cruel to cut flowers and put them in a jar with water just for our own decorative purposes, but I no longer felt that way. I had changed a lot in that aspect. They reminded me of the beautiful colorful world out there and reinforced my belief that I needed to get the heck out of the hospital as soon as possible if I was going to live. Staying in a hospital was contradictory to that happening. I cried a lot.

Dr. Lehman came to see me one early morning, and I noticed he limped and used a cane for support. He yelled at the nurses for not following his instructions. They had attached the heavier weight on the wrong side. When he sat next to my bed, I asked him what was wrong with his legs and he said he had a bad hip.

"Oh, I'm so sorry," I said. "Maybe you should have surgery and have it fixed."

"My colleagues have offered to do the surgery at no cost, but I'm no fool. At my age, it's too much of a chance. I'm afraid the surgery would kill me."

I liked him, he was such a nice doctor. He treated me like a fellow human being. I appreciated that he shared his fear of surgery or, as they said in Portugal, going under the knife.

I had just finished the lunch on my tray, a cup of tomato soup, a turkey sandwich with potato chips and for dessert a cup of fruit cocktail, when a neurologist came in and asked me to wiggle my toes. "You're not moving them," he said impatiently.

"Yes I am."

"You know you're not. Now, try harder." Then he ran some pins over my legs and under my feet but I couldn't feel them. He left mumbling to himself.

What an idiot! Like I loved not to feel my toes and be stuck in a bed day after day like a prisoner while missing days from work and the theatre. Then, everything became beautiful again when an older lady wearing a pink top and a pink ribbon holding back her curly thick white hair came into my room. "I'm a volunteer," she said. "And I like bringing a little joy to those stuck in here. Would you like to have your fingernails painted pink?"

It was a nice feeling to be pampered and to have someone hold my hands.

Later that day a young man wearing a white jacket came to visit me. "Hi, my name is John Johnson, but you can call me Jay. I'm a physical therapist and I'm here to show you some exercises to help you get stronger."

"Exercises?" I panicked. "I don't want to have muscles like a man."

He must have thought I was joking, and because he laughed, I felt I should explain, "I meant that I'm happy with the way I am, soft."

"No, no you don't have to worry about developing muscles like a man. That's silly." He laughed again. "The exercises I'm going to show you will help you tone your muscles so that your back can get strong again."

I still didn't understand what that had to do with my back hurting but I did what he asked me to do. He took the weights off my ankles and had me lifting my back up and tightening my stomach inwards. It made my back hurt even more. I was far from happy.

He returned the next morning and pushed my bed down the hallway, and into an elevator that took us to the basement. Jay and a nurse put me into what looked like a leather harness and they lowered me slowly into a large metal tub filled with hot water jets.

The hot water felt great, except for the hospital gown that came up to the top of the water like a balloon. "Do you mind if I take this stupid thing off?" I asked them.

They consulted with each other and then she said, "We agree with you. But most of our patients are too embarrassed to be naked. That's why we provide you with a gown."

"I have nothing to hide and I'm in too much pain to worry about that."

She took my gown off. I let myself relax. When the nurse left the room, Jay walked over and said, "You're very beautiful."

I didn't answer; who cared what I looked like. I was nothing but a cripple, an invalid. If being naked made him happy, then I was glad for him. I understood Aunt Heydee's philosophy about bringing happiness to those less fortunate, like the time we went to a movie theatre in Lisbon, and the man sitting behind us slipped one of his hands between the seats and rested it gently over one of her breasts. She felt so sorry for his obvious loneliness that she didn't do anything about it.

Jay came by my room that evening. He placed me in a wheelchair and said he wanted to take me out for a little ride down the hallway. Then he set me up in front of one of the windows and standing behind my wheelchair he put his hand on one of my shoulders. "It's raining outside, isn't it romantic?"

"Romantic?" I protested. "It's windy, cold and it's pouring out there!" He annoyed me to no end. I could tell that he was lonely, but romance was the furthest thing from my mind. Also, the thought that I might never be able to walk and would have to sit in a wheelchair stuck at home for the rest of my life with Al, drove me crazy. I was better off dead.

I awoke with a cough, most likely from sleeping all night with what started as heating pads until I awoke with cold dripping wet pads on my back. I had used the push button several times during the night for one of the nurses to take them away, but no one came. It did cross my mind to take the pads and wet towels and throw them on the floor, but I couldn't get enough courage to do something so childish.

The next morning Dr. Lehman came by and said he was thinking about giving me an injection into the spine, and if that didn't help then surgery was to be considered; after all, I had been in the hospital for two weeks and I was showing no improvement.

I waited for him to leave, and then I called home. I wanted to get out of the hospital as soon as possible. Al couldn't come until later in the afternoon and Steve was nowhere to be found. Ralph offered to pick me up. I couldn't stand the idea of shots or surgery on my back. My instincts told me that drugs or surgery would be a mistake; besides, being in the hospital and getting shots of any kind had me scared.

Ralph used a wheelchair to take me out of the hospital, and on the way home he stopped at a Chinese restaurant and helped me out of the car. I walked in, dragging my feet like a broken down old lady, while gripping on to Ralph's arm. I was able to sit but kept complaining during lunch about my life being over.

"Mom, this is the way it is, and nothing more can be done to make you better again. You have to get used to the reality of the situation and accept it."

Accept it? Never! I told myself.

I spent the next two days lying on my back flat in bed, pondering about the end of my life. I came to the conclusion that I was cursed with a high degree of pain tolerance because I worried about being called a crybaby. I liked being a superwoman except for when I no longer could take the hurt and had reached the end of the rope, then I paid the price.

Dr. Lehman called to ask me how I was doing. "Not good." I cried. "I can't get out of bed, without hurting and when I do I can't walk."

"Back surgery is really the only option you have, my dear." He called me every day to find out how I was doing, and I loved him dearly, but surgery sounded like a death sentence.

There has to be a solution, I told myself as I rolled over in bed to find a position where the pain would be less unbearable. I prayed, *Dear God, please help me. I can't stay this way. There's got to be something that can be done to restore my life back to normal.* And then to myself, *this is America, nothing is impossible in America. In America there's a cure for everything, I just need to find it.* I covered my head with the blanket while trying to remain still not to aggravate the radiating pain down both legs.

Mr. Raster called that evening. He wanted to know how much longer I needed to be off work. "I have been in the hospital with a herniated disk of my lower back," I told him. "And now I'm home, but I still can't walk because of the pain."

He cut me off, "Jesus Christ, I thought you had the flu. Call my chiropractor, Dr. Peruzzi, right now. Go see him today and then come back to work Monday. The residents miss you, and I need you here."

When Ralph heard about my boss's advice, he reminded me that the first one that treated his back when he suffered a car accident had helped him a lot but the one he went to see later for a strained back after lifting a television set, had seriously messed up his mid back, and he was still suffering from pain in that area. He encouraged me to stick with my orthopedic surgeon. Al stated that only a fool would go to a *quack* and have their neck twisted and broken. They concurred that a lot of people had either died or become paralyzed for life after being "cracked" by a chiropractor.

I called Dr. Peruzzi. The way I saw it, Ralph had gotten a lot of pain relief from the first chiropractor that treated him. True, the second one had hurt his back, but so what, with every profession there were good and bad ones. I was the living proof of all the medical screw-ups that had been done throughout my life, but I still went to see them. Desperate enough to try anything I rationalized, *so I'm already paralyzed from living my life; the worse that can happen is Dr. Peruzzi breaks my neck and I die. Oh, well, we all have to die sooner or later, and I guess in my case it might be sooner.* This and many other negative thoughts crossed my mind as Al helped me to climb the two front steps to Dr. Peruzzi's chiropractic office. While seated in the waiting room Al incorporated extra fear into my psyche, "I hope you're not going to be sorry for allowing a quack to treat you."

Dr. Peruzzi was very old, probably in his mid-seventies but he looked like he worked out. Even though his face had a lot of wrinkles, and he had snow white hair, he also had a great physique. He wore a white doctor's jacket, which struck me as funny since he was a chiropractor and not a medical doctor. His handshake was very strong, and that made me even more scared. He sat behind a large desk, and he showed me a plastic spine and told me all kinds of nonsense about the nerves from the spine going through the body and that once I had my spine adjusted I would be back to normal. I didn't believe one word he said. He asked me to follow him to the adjusting room where I assumed the torture would soon begin.

"Dr. Peruzzi," I brought my hands together as if praying and gazed at him with what I considered a pathetic look of fear in my eyes. "Whatever you do, please, don't touch me, my back hurts too much already."

He put his hands on his hips, shook his head, and after a loud sigh, he exclaimed partially annoyed, "I have to use my hands to adjust your spine, there's no other way." Then he added a little more compassionately, "But don't worry; I'm not going to hurt you."

I asked myself what the heck I was doing seeing a chiropractor, but it was too late to turn around and leave. It surprised me that the exam consisted of gently touching my back everywhere except where it hurt, and that made me relax a little. He asked me to lie down sideways on a low table, breath in and out and let go of my anxiety. Then he punched me hard on the left side of my neck, very close to my ear. It hurt really bad as my brain flew out of my head and after hitting a wall bounced back, much like in one of those cartoons I used to see with my children on television, a long time ago. But when he asked me to get up and walk, my pain was not only gone but I could feel both my feet. I lost all sense of pride and jumped on his lap, my legs around his waist and my arms around his neck, "This is a miracle! Anything you want just ask me, I'm your slave forever." Tears ran down my face.

Dr. Peruzzi smiled self-righteously and said with a certain amount of passion, "Witnessing my patients getting better like this is all I live for."

Al had been watching the whole thing and was just as surprised with my sudden recovery. He thought that maybe I had been hypnotized, nothing else made sense to him.

"I can feel my feet, my legs, I can walk," I announced out loud to the Universe outside as I made my way to the car and got in without a problem. I was so high on happiness that as soon as I got home I called Dr. Lehman's office to share the good news with him.

"You were lucky he didn't kill you," he said. "Please, listen to me, whatever you do, don't go back to see him."

His response was not what I expected and I felt that there was some kind of jealousy between the two professions since Dr. Peruzzi had helped me more in one single visit than he had in the two weeks I had been stranded in the hospital and then at home.

"Oh, okay, I won't go back to the chiropractor." I did not want to hurt Dr. Lehman's feelings but I had no intentions of returning to his office.

Later in the evening my lower back started to hurt again, but not as bad, and I could still feel my feet. To me that was a really good recovery.

That night I slept like a baby, and when I awoke the next morning I wondered, what would take for me to be a chiropractor just like Dr. Peruzzi. It couldn't be that difficult, if all I had to do was to learn to punch people on the neck to get them out of pain. I awoke Al to share with him my thoughts. He laughed and called me nuts.

I called Dr. Peruzzi before I left in the morning to go to work and made an appointment to see him afterward.

"Dr. Peruzzi," I said as soon as I walked into his office. "I want to be a chiropractor like you. Do I have to go to school to learn to be a chiropractor? How long will it take for me to learn everything you know?"

"Hey, take it easy, one question at a time. I don't mean to discourage you, but it is a long process. Pre-meds and then chiropractic college. I say about five or six years in school." He sighed. "I must tell you this…what a waste of time studying anatomy, and chemistry and whatever more they're coming up with these days, when all you need is to learn to adjust the spine properly." And he went on talking about the nervous system, and how through spinal adjustments we could all be healthy, and there was no illness in the world that could not be treated by getting the spine adjusted.

At that point, it scared me that he blamed all illnesses on the lack of spinal adjustments and decided that I was better off getting out of there as soon as possible before he killed me with his so-called adjustment. Even though I wasn't completely recovered I had no intention of letting him know that, he might want to twist my neck and my back and I may not be as lucky as the first time.

I looked at my wristwatch to show some urgency and stood ready to leave. "Well, thank you for your time, Dr. Peruzzi." I stretched my hand out to shake his. "Now I have to go, and by the way my back doesn't hurt any more..."

Not letting go of my hand he pulled me forward, over his desk and toward him. I fell flat on my chest on top of his desk. He finally let go of my hand, but he was angry, he waved his hands above his head, the same way Al did when he was frustrated. "What do you mean you have to go?" he yelled out. "You're not leaving without getting your spine adjusted! Have you not learned anything from what I have been telling you all along?"

Shit, he had no medical education, he only believed in cracking bones. Luckily, I survived the first adjustment, but one could not push their luck twice in a row. These and other terrifying thoughts crawled into my mind at the speed of lightning. *If I say anything it will get him more upset than he is already. Oh my God, he's going to break my neck for sure! This is the end of me, I'm done for good.* I followed him, as if I had been sentenced to sit on the electric chair. He led me into the adjusting room and once again he had me lying on the same low table as before and he punched my neck. He called the adjusting technique, Toggle. It surprised me that the adjustment didn't hurt like the first time.

"You told me you wanted to be my slave, now you want to be a chiropractor, humm?" He sounded sarcastic.

I was tongue-tied for a few seconds. "I want to be like you and help people," then I asked the most important question burning in my mind, "Is there a chiropractic school close by?"

He told me his favorite was Life Chiropractic College in

Georgia, but he had heard of another college in Pennsylvania that had a strong chiropractic philosophy and should be getting accredited soon. No, there were no chiropractic colleges in New Jersey.

"When you put your mind to doing something, there's no stopping you," Al said. "If that's what you want to do, go ahead, it's fine with me even though I think that, at your age, you're wasting your time going to school."

Al could have stopped me right then and there but he was a very kind and supportive husband. He was my best friend.

Dr. Peruzzi no longer intimidated me as a chiropractic doctor. I only had one goal in mind, to learn as much as possible from him about chiropractic and went to see him three times a week like he told me I should, to get my spine adjusted. He said that since I would be his colleague in the near future, he no longer would charge me for my adjustments.

He was my chiropractor, but he was also my friend now, and he showed me a secret door, which was covered with an ugly brown curtain at the end of the hallway. To my utmost surprise it was the direct entrance from his meager looking chiropractic office to his lavish residence.

I couldn't help staring at the white living room with wall to wall white plush carpet and a large chandelier hanging over a white baby grant. When he returned from the kitchen with two glasses of water, I was still standing on the same spot. "You like it?" he said. "Behind you is my gym where I work out every morning before I start seeing patients." His gym was a large greenhouse with healthy and vibrant tropical plants and stocked with several gym machines. A long red couch took the full length of the living room, along with three square glass coffee tables each with a crystal vase with a fresh red rose. It was right out of a glamour house magazine. There was so much to admire inside as well as outside. A wall to wall bay window overlooked an amazingly manicured backyard, making me feel like Captain Nemo in Jules Verne's, 20,000 Leagues under the Sea; if fish had swum by I would not have been surprised.

I convinced Al to come with me one evening and he must have been impressed because he didn't say anything derogatory. Dr. Peruzzi had all kinds of surprises to share with us that day. A brand-new karaoke machine had been connected to a large screen television in the living room and he sang for us several mind-numbing tunes from Frank Sinatra's repertoire.

Eight seniors signed up for a shopping spree to the Ocean County Mall, but they were only interested in one store, K-Mart. Once in K-Mart they took off in all directions except Sandra, who never let go of my arm when we went out. She was the personification of a depressive mentality, and sometimes her negative thoughts, got the best of me. That morning she was complaining about her age and how being ninety-one years old sucked. I wanted to say, stop complaining so much and give me a break, when the perfect opportunity came along. A young man dribbling at the mouth and seated in a wheelchair was being pushed into the store, by a middle-aged woman, maybe his mother.

"Sandra, how old do you think is that young boy in the wheelchair?"

"I guess about twenty."

"How would you like to change places with him and be young again? I bet he would love to trade places with you."

"Oh no, that's a terrible way to live."

"You bet. And here we are taking for granted that we are getting old and yet we can walk anywhere we want. How about us being happy from now on, what do you say?"

I had spoken from personal experience. She said she understood my point and then miracle of miracles she let go of my arm, walked over to him and after saying something I couldn't hear, she gave him a hug.

I owed much of my positive philosophy to Aunt Heydee but there was nothing like the ups and down that life brought along to appreciate the simple gifts we all took for granted. I would always thank God, for allowing me to walk again.

"Sleuth," was a gift from the gods. The director offered to build the set and to get all the props. I scarcely had anything do with the production. Even the lights were being run by a friend of his. During the week I drove to the theatre to oversee the evening rehearsals for the next show "What the Butler Saw." I wrote during my free time and spent more time at the Howell Music Center.

Katherine was a six feet tall, healthy looking slim senior who sat quietly on the closest chair to the entrance door at Westwood Greens. Every time I walked by she nodded and smiled as if she knew me and then her attention went back to staring at the front door. There were four other chairs next to hers always taken by other seniors, but they stared at the wall in front of them. One morning, I noticed a vacant seat and sat next to her. "Are you waiting for someone special?" I asked her.

"No, dear I don't expect anyone." She maintained her gaze.

"Every time I walk by you are staring at the front door."

"I wish I could take a walk outside." She sighed. "But, no one will take me."

"Really? Well, I'll go with you."

"You, you will do that?" Her eyes brightened.

"You bet. Let's go now, before they stop us." I stood.

She hoisted herself swiftly and holding her shoulders back and her chest out with perfect posture, she held my arm as we walked out and into the parking lot. She took two steps and stopped. She closed her eyes and took a deep breath in and out. Then she opened her eyes with a smile and we walked a few more steps as she looked appreciatively from side to side and then up at the perfectly blue sky.

"Would you mind if I take off these slippers?" she asked. "I know it's a parking lot but I would love to feel the earth under my feet."

"What a great idea, I'll take off my sandals too."

It was only a ten-minute walk but she was thrilled. She had been living there for two years and except for being driven for a doctor's appointment no one was available to take her for a walk. She had no family. I promised to take her out every day.

Mr. Raster called me into his office the next morning. Someone had snitched on me for taking Katherine out for a walk during my working hours. Mr. Raster said I could do whatever I wanted when I was off, but not while being paid to work for him.

So, I began taking Katherine out after I was done for the day. She waited patiently by the front door, and her smile always made my day.

She had been born in New York City and she was ninety-four years old. She had been one of the very first women allowed to work in the N.Y.C. Fire department. She showed me her picture in uniform, next to other firemen. She had been happily married twice but had no children. She loved being physically active and walking was one of the things she most missed. I understood that feeling completely.

Katherine and I believed that Sofia was the one that turned us in, she was always ready to rattle on others for any small infraction. Sofia was a spy for Mr. Raster. I bet that Sofia was mean even before she became old. The skin wrinkled with age but souls didn't change texture.

Inspired by the lady who had done my nails at the hospital, I bought a little heart-shaped straw basket and filled it with different colored nail polish bottles, nail polish remover, cotton balls, and a nail file.

The reason I picked Sofia as the first one to be pampered was that I hoped she would break down and become a kind person, by realizing that not everybody was out to screw her, as she constantly proclaimed. I sat next to her and offered to do her nails.

She looked at me for a moment like what do you want? Then remarked, "You must be kidding, if you think I'm going to fall for it. You're not getting a dime from me."

"Good because I'm not charging you anything anyway."

"Nobody does anything for free. I'll give you a dollar."

I was not going to give up that easily. "Sofia, I can't accept your dollar. I'll do your nails only if you don't pay me. Now, tell me, what color would you like?"

"Well, if you're that dumb, go ahead and work for nothing." She picked the ruby-red polish.

I knew I had touched her heart when after I finished painting her nails she forced a smile and said, "Okay, thank you. I like it, it looks nice." Then the haughtily side of her came bursting out, "But if you're smart, you'll charge the others."

I wondered what she did for a living when she was young, if she had been married, if she had a family. I should have asked.

Once in a while my back felt weak and hurt as if it was going to give in. Just the idea of not being able to walk again became a reality check reminding me to visit Dr. Peruzzi more often. I tried my best not to lift anything heavy at the theatre, but it was hard to stop old habits. Besides, admitting that I no longer could lift was like saying I was defective, falling apart at the seams, a shadow of what I used to be. I couldn't accept it and went into denial every time I faced a situation where lifting could put me down for good. I became dependent on Dr. Peruzzi to fix me, every time I hurt myself.

Poor Dr. Peruzzi suffered from serious depression mixed with anger issues and would get very emotional as tears walled up in his eyes. "I regret each day of my life that I was not a chiropractor because I could have saved my mother from dying of cancer." He really believed that adjusting the spine cured every disease known to mankind, but it was hard for me to believe that.

I drove to Brookdale Community College to inquire what pre-requisite classes I needed to make me eligible to enter chiropractic college. My records at the college showed I had accrued plenty of art credits but I still needed science courses such us, biochemistry, organic and inorganic chemistry, anatomy, biology and physics I and II. But I wasn't worried, because when it came to taking subjects with an aura of difficulty, I simply recalled people I knew, like my dentist, my gynecologist and others who had made it through college and didn't came across as being any smarter than me.

We were having dinner at home when I mentioned to Ralph that since he had witnessed my recovery with chiropractic adjustments, he might like to be a chiropractor like me, and we could go to college together. "I'm intrigued by the profession," he admitted. "You really have made a miraculous recovery with your back. I might consider it since as you know I no longer find my job exciting." He paused and put his fork down on his plate. I stopped eating too and waited to hear the magic words, *okay, I'll quit my job and join you.* But he was just thinking aloud, "I have reached as high as I can go in engineering and there are no more challenges, it has become a boring job. It's probably a good idea to change career at this point, while I'm still young." He chuckled. "The health profession is very appealing to me, but I need to look a little more into it. I'll let you know."

I crossed my fingers that he would favor chiropractic versus medical.

Tracey and I enjoyed going to New York City several times a year and had started taking the bus from downtown Lakewood, into the Port of Authority just a little over an hour ride and no headaches about tending to traffic or where to park. Being that Tracey was an artist and taught art classes, I learned a lot from her when we visited the Metropolitan Museum of Art and the Museum of Modern Art and some fancy art galleries. The time period had a lot to do with the technique used, but I also became aware of successful artists getting away with just about anything as long as their name was on it. At one prestigious gallery in SoHo, a piece of cardboard hanged on one of their walls, with a price tag of twelve hundred dollars.

Once in a while her son Kirk, who lived in New York City, came to meet us at the Port Authority Terminal and took us around the city. He was an actor, singer and a model. Pictures of Kirk's body were used all over the billboards, except his head. His body was cut to perfection but his eyes were too small and far apart, his nose slanted to one side probably the result of a strong punch and he had flat cheeks and no upper lip. But he had a great sense of humor like his mom and it was fun hanging out with him as he knew all the hot spots to take us.

Kirk met us last Saturday morning at the bus terminal. We were walking on 42nd Street when Tracey said, "Wouldn't it be fun to go to one of those sex shops and see what goes on inside?"

I had always wondered about that, but never had the courage to peek inside. It would be the same as incriminating myself as being curiously depraved.

"Okay, girls," Kirk pointed across the street. "Just follow me. We're going inside that shop and upstairs where the girls wait for their customers."

Tracey and I couldn't be more excited. The three of us walked through an adult sex store with all kind of sex magazines and pornographic material including plastic penises of all sizes, and blow-up plastic dolls. This was my first time inside a sex shop, and I wanted to stop and look but Kirk told us, "Don't touch anything and just follow me closely." He walked briskly ahead of us, and we went up a narrow flight of steps into a badly-lit hallway on the first floor where three girls in skimpy clothes stood by rooms with no doors just flowery cloth curtains hanging from a rod above the doorways. One of them a tall black girl with a blonde wig must have read my curious mind and she pulled the curtain to the side so I could take a glimpse inside as we walked by. Her space was the size of a narrow closet with a single bed covered by a white sheet. They all said hello and we answered hello back but we didn't stop to chat. We followed Kirk out to the other side of the hallway and down the steps, and hurriedly crossed the sex shop, as we exited laughing and giggling like juveniles.

It took me a while to fall asleep that night. I could hear the lamenting sound of "The House of the Rising Sun." The images of the living dead above the sex shop haunted me.

I didn't share with Al, my outing with Tracey and her son.

Classes at Brookdale Community College were starting the following month; and I had to stop working at Westwood Greens if I was going to devote myself to studying. I gave Mr. Raster one month's notice to find another activity director. The courses I signed up for were all brain-busters, and I needed all the free time to study. The theatre was not a problem; it basically ran on its own except for changing the set every six weeks, for the next play. When my low back started to hurt, I paid a visit to Dr. Peruzzi who yelled at me for not coming in regularly for maintenance instead of when in pain. He always got me out of pain but it didn't last too long. I began losing my patience with the on and off backache. Feeling guilty as hell I made an appointment to see a different chiropractor in the hopes that he could do better than Dr. Peruzzi and cure me once and for all.

Dr. Holdman performed an exam and to my dismay his opinion was not what I hoped to hear. "Honey, I'll be honest with you. You're going to need chiropractic care for the rest of your life. Your lower back is trashed and if you insist on lifting stuff that's more than ten pounds, I can promise you'll have a relapse of the herniated disc."

For some unexplainable reason, I believed he knew more about chiropractic than Dr. Peruzzi, and on my third visit that week I asked him what kind of advice he could give me so that I could be a good doctor, like him.

He whispered in my ear as if giving me the secret of life and death, "Your intention is the key to your success."

"My intention? What does that mean?"

He put his right hand on his chest. "Your intention comes from here, your heart. This is all you need in order to become a good doctor."

I didn't have the courage to tell him that I still didn't understand what he meant by intention and what did that have to do with the scientific technique of adjusting the spine.

Every day I wondered how to ask Al for a divorce without hurting his feelings. We slept together, but there was no physical contact. I loved him as the father of my children, but there was nothing else keeping us connected. Since we didn't see anything eye to eye on any topic, I stopped speaking to him except for the usual polite exchange of words like, hello, see you later, have a good day and goodnight.

Considering the subject on how to pay for my future chiropractic college, I told myself, things always work themselves out. First things first, were my motto. I needed to concentrate on getting financial aid for the prerequisites' classes and I refused to use the money I had saved for a rainy day. Brookdale College wanted me to bring records of how much Al and I had earned in the last year. If below what they considered a normal amount to live on, I would be eligible for financial aid.

It was kind of ironic that Mr. Raster had been the one that encouraged me to see a chiropractor, and now I would be making a serious career change.

There was no doubt in my mind that we were all connected to each other in one way or another. Even a stranger walking across the street from us could make a change in our lives, very much like a ripple in the ocean. I was a *Twilight Zone* believer. Things happened that made no sense, but later they did. Like being stuck in traffic and getting home late, perhaps that was what had saved our lives. Everything on earth had its own fate, like the fuzzy warm blanket I kept in the back of my store van for years and years in case I should get stranded somewhere in the bitter cold.

Then, two winters ago while driving my Howell Music Center van on route 9 in Lakewood an accident happened ahead of me. It was snowing heavily, and a young bicyclist had been run over by a car. He was lying on the icy cold, snow-covered road, bleeding from his head and shivering. I took my blanket from the back of the van and laid it on top of his body. When the ambulance arrived, the paramedics put him on a stretcher and I told them that he could keep the blanket.

The blanket had been bought and kept in my van all those years just for that man.

I was walking in the hallway when Mrs. Thompson saw me

as she was coming out of her bedroom. She came up to me, grabbed my arm, and led me into her room. She closed the door behind us and proceeded to pull from under her bed a large plastic blue container, where she kept a multitude of news clippings and awards, a reminiscence of her past good deeds. She wanted me to see how vital she had been in her community, and how much she had done for those "ungrateful bastards," as she called them. Mrs. Thompson, had just reinforced my belief that all the appreciation letters I had received from the Mayors in Howell, Freehold and Jackson, and the newspaper interviews I had collected over the years, were merely pieces of paper and as time went by, they would turn yellow and finally into dust.

She was far from reality; awards were thank you notes, nothing more. She may have worked hard in her community but she had missed the most important factor for complete happiness, one should never help others while expecting something in return, otherwise there was no value in what we had done.

"Now that I'm old, and no longer of any use, nobody calls or comes to visit me to thank me for all the work I did. Instead, I have been put away, discarded by my ungrateful family and phony friends." She put her hands on my shoulders shaking me and would not let go. "Please don't leave me. I apologize if I have been cranky and mean to you in the past. I promise to behave from now on."

"Mrs. Thompson, your behavior has nothing to do with why I'm leaving." I gave her a kiss on the forehead and she let go of my shoulders. "I'm going back to school," I didn't expect her to jump up and down with joy, but it would have been nice. "And in order for me to do that," I said. "I have to stop working here."

She said she understood and changed the topic to Nathan one of the residents, who had been her companion for the last six months. She and Nathan had been a couple until sleazy Pamela, as she called the newcomer, had arrived at the home. A week ago, she had found them talking to each other very closely-seated, and it was obvious that they were more than just friends. She immediately broke up with Nathan.

I was in the middle of a teenage love triangle but I was not surprised; just because you were old didn't mean you no longer had feelings. There were plenty of love affairs, at Westwood Greens and emotions ran high among the residents. Mrs. Thompson had too much of a despondent attitude, one bad attribute, especially when one considered the calm softness Pamela radiated.

Ralph was still busy researching the medical profession versus chiropractic. He wanted to see which career would be the most gratifying in helping people get better and still afford him the time to spend with his own family—which he hoped to have someday. During his investigation he spoke to several medical doctors including two anesthesiologists, and except for two single doctors the others confided that they were not happy with their demanding career because it had a negative impact on their families.

Meanwhile I bought an anatomical bones' chart at the college bookstore and every day I memorized two bones. My idea was that by the time I took anatomy I would be able to name all the bones in the body.

I went to Westwood Greens to say goodbye. I made Katherine promise me that she would never walk outside by herself. Marilyn, who always wore pink and had been a ballerina, asked me not to leave, but when I told her I was going to school to be a chiropractor, she said, "Oh, that's wonderful," she clapped her hands joyfully. "When you get done, promise me that you come back and fix my back so I can dance again."

I thought I had said goodbye to everyone, but when I

was getting into my car I heard Mr. Phillips calling, "Wait Ronnie, wait, don't go yet."

I met him halfway across the parking lot. "Please, let me hug you before you leave," he said. "I'm going to miss you a lot."

We hugged and then waved goodbye.

Katherine, the costume designer and I had become good friends since the production of "The Playboy of the Western World," and when she asked me if I could give her a hand with moving, I was more than happy to help out. She and her husband had sold their house and were moving to Florida in two months.

She gave me a tour of her three-story mansion by the sea which was more like an old palace and beautifully furnished. "Let me know if you see anything you like," she said. "We're downsizing and I would like to get rid of a lot of stuff."

I loved everything, but those were her belongings and there was no way I was going to ask for anything. After two days of helping with packing, she said we needed a break and she led me to her attic where—a sight to behold—presented before my eyes, brand new rolls of fabric, paintings, furniture, large old-fashioned trunks—like those seen in pirate movies— and a world of crowded antiques and treasures that I never thought possible to exist except in Aladdin's hidden cave. She caught my look of amazement, and said, "I confess, I have a passion for buying beautiful things, but as you see I ran out of space where to put them. I just wanted to show you how much stuff I have up here." She chuckled and pointed to the rolls and rolls of fabric stacked high on one corner. "Textures appeal to my senses. Let's not worry about the attic. I'm having the moving company pack everything."

As we were leaving the attic I pointed to an extremely elegant umbrella. "That is so exquisite!" I was only voicing my opinion but she picked it up and handed it to me. "Good taste," she said. "It's an antique British umbrella. It's yours, and here, let me give you this long skirt of glittering gold and browns. I never used it. I bought it because I was attracted to the fabric, and the way it drapes." I followed her down the steps and in the second floor as we were going by a bedroom; I noticed a colorful table lamp on a side table. "That's a gorgeous lamp," I said.

"It's a real Tiffany lamp, and very rare. I can't part with it." And she kept walking.

I went outside to put the umbrella and the skirt in the back seat of my car. When I got back Katherine was busy by the kitchen sink, making lunch, I offered to help, but she said she had everything under control.

She sliced a fresh tomato, scooped out the seeds and the juicy pulp, and threw it into the garbage disposal. Then she used the same scooping technique with a cucumber and cut it into small chunks adding them to the tomato pieces. I figured I had never learned how to properly slice tomatoes or cucumbers for a salad, but at the same time I was glad I didn't, since I loved veggies' guts. A salt and pepper glass shaker on the kitchen windowsill caught my attention. One was red and the other green, they hanged from a tiny ornate black stand. I held them up so the light could play off the colors. "They're so cute," I said. "They look like mini glass lanterns."

"They are antique and priceless," she said.

I put them back carefully.

"No, no. You like them, they're yours, enjoy them."

Besides the salad she also made a platter of mini tuna sandwiches and a pitcher of fresh lemonade and we sat on super comfortable cushioned seats in the backyard, eating and talking. Afterward, she wanted me to see her kitchen tea pantry. It was like walking into a fancy tea shop, several tea sets and tea boxes were neatly displayed on open shelves for easy access. Katherine collected teas from all over the world, particularly England and India. I thanked her for the offer but I didn't drink tea and didn't need a tea set either. But she insisted on giving me a set of four English tea dishes with an indentation just big enough to set the matching teacup on it thus keeping it from slipping off the dish. I had never seen anything so clever.

Then she handed me two serving trays with duck designs and two beautiful Japanese serving trays as she declared that there were never enough trays in a household. I had never used a tray in my life, but I figured that I could always use them for display since they were all very striking to look at.

"I have three bathrooms each decorated in its own style. Take a look on the first and second floor and then let me know which one you like the most," she said. One bathroom had a white bear rug, and other hunting paraphernalia, the other all kinds of antiques reminding me of the 20's and the other bathroom on the first floor was mostly duck décor. I thought she was just asking for my opinion considering the decoration. "Of all three bathrooms I love the bathroom with the ducks," I said.

"I knew you were going to pick that one." she said. "Please do me a favor and take everything. It's all yours."

Mama mia! Lush, quality towel sets with duck designs, a see-through shower curtain except for the colorful ducks, duck soap dishes, duck planters, duck tissue holder. She brought up a couple of empty boxes and I promptly filled them up. I was never so excited in my life as when I placed the boxes into my car.

I returned Saturday morning and Katherine encouraged me to take whatever I found in the hallway closet downstairs by the front door. A wood mini-alligator box with big teeth, and a children's puzzle box caught my eye. After that, I felt like I had enough stuff and every time she offered me something I said, "I already have one of those at home. Thanks."

The following day Katherine and her husband invited me to join them for a walk to the park close to their house. We sat on a park bench talking, and then to my surprise she handed me a sealed envelope. They told me that they had appreciated my help and wished they could pay me more than they were giving me. I opened the envelope; enclosed were three one hundred-dollar bills inside the thank you card. I told them I didn't want the money, but when I handed it back, they would not take it. Friends were not supposed to pay for help. I hid my hurt feelings behind a smile when I left them, but I was feeling down, and non-worthy. The presents Katherine had given me had been more than generous on her part and there was no need to pay me as if they were my bosses and not my friends.

Today I realize that I'm not good at receiving, only at giving and I need to work on that issue.

Autumn of 1991

I couldn't believe my ears when I was told at Brookdale College that I had been granted financial help. I signed up for the full-time schedule and bought a small pull-cart to carry the books back and forth between classes and to the car. Dr. Lehman was kind enough to give me a handicapped sticker so that I didn't have to walk too far to get to my classrooms He called me his doomed patient, because I was being treated by a chiropractor.

I took turns getting adjusted by Dr. Peruzzi and Dr. Holdman. I figured between the two of them I had a better chance to get well.

Mrs. Lawson, the anatomy instructor was a super cool person. Before we took a written test, she insisted that all students smile at each other. "Smiles cause a release of good chemicals from the brain," she told us. "Which help us to relax and think more clearly." The first time we followed her advice, our smiles were forced but slowly they melted down into contagious laughter. Smiling became my tool to engaging my memory bank into gear just prior to taking an exam.

I was very focused on doing well in college, but it was hard for my brain to suddenly switch gears from theatre and music to science. My head hurt from thinking so deeply.

Amazing how many future doctors and nurses were attending biology class with me. I found biology interesting but difficult. I joined a study group, but they were too fast for me. I needed to study at my own pace. At home I did all my studying lying flat on my back with a pillow under my knees. At the theater I delegated the heavy work to the hired hands, since my weakness which I now called my Achilles, was lifting heavy stuff.

I needed to get mentally and emotionally prepared for doing human dissection once in chiropractic college and I bought a dissection book with very graphic images, at Brookdale College. I made myself look at one dreadful page a day. At Brookdale I was told not to worry, their dissection labs consisted of using cats and rats, only when attending chiropractic college then I would be required to cut up human bodies—or, as they were officially called, cadavers. As if the name changed anything, it was still naked, dead people and the idea terrified me. I couldn't even conceive having to open someone's chest to look at the heart by cutting and pulling away the bones and muscles. That was the only thing I was concerned about not being able handle in chiropractic college.

I had only seen two dead people in my whole life. When Joe's father-in-law died, Al tried to stop me from going into the wake room at the funeral home. Good thing that I was curious enough at the time to insist on viewing the body. He didn't look alive or dead. He looked like a mannequin covered with make-up and wearing a white suit.

Also, when my friend Maryanne's teenage son died in a car accident she had him dressed in his jeans and favorite leather jacket, to make her son look alive. But the boy looked unreal, and I felt such thing called a "wake ceremony" should be made illegal. It was hard for me to comprehend how they could put the dead through such cruel display and say they were paying them respect, after mummifying them with toxic chemicals.

My first dissection specimen at Brookdale was a rat. I guessed he had been gassed because he had the expression of "Oh, no!" His eyes were closed tight as if he was protecting them from the burning fumes. His arms were extended out, and his little paws were clenched tight. We followed the teacher's instructions on how to open the rat's chest. "Oh my God," I told myself, my hands trembling as I faced the tiny lungs and heart, not much different from a human being, just smaller.

That night I couldn't sleep thinking about the little creature in the lab that had given his life for science. Most people would say, big deal it was just a rat. Not to me, a rat was still a living creature, just like man. Where was God, when the rat cried out for his last breath, or when a child was being abused, or when man murdered other men, women and children, and killed the animals in the wild, just for sport, where was God? *I need an answer,* I told myself before falling asleep.

I woke in the middle of the night, with what felt like a light had cleared my path to see the beginning of life on Earth. I let go of all preconceived ideas and allowed myself to look into the abyss of my mind and learned that once upon a long time ago, on another planet too far away from us to even conceive the idea of distance was where God lived. Yes, it was a planet of good beings, and it was called Hu. There was no war or greed, only love and understanding. Then, for a reason that no one knew, including God who pondered on what could have gone awry — possibly a gene that went wild, or something like a virus that entered the planet while crossing the universe and decided to stay — an epidemic of nasty symptoms took over some of the beings in Hu. Just to name a few of the symptoms: greed, hate and jealousy. God had to intervene immediately and in its infinite wisdom, God gathered those that had become infected with the virus, along with many of the animal species from their world, so they would not feel lonely without all the creatures they had grown accustomed to, and transported them all to a planet called Earth, which was on the other side of the Universe. God would not punish or try to make his people change their minds. Instead, he gave them the power of choice, and God called them Hu-man as he hoped someday the good would take over the man and they could return home to Hu, once again.

It wasn't that I loved rodents, but by cutting up the innocent rat—a victim of science and men's quest for more knowledge — I had found the explanation to why there was so much cruelty and also so much kindness on earth. Our ancestors were from Hu! This was the reason why some of us believed in changing the world for the better and living in harmony, and others were robbers and murderers. It was a constant inner battle between Hu and Man in all human beings. Until we could overcome the Man, in all of us, I was sure we would never have peace on earth and we would never be able to return to God's planet where we had originated.

Whenever I shared this finding with friends, which was clear-as-a-bell to me, they got very quiet.

My next specimen with dissection was a cat. Unfortunately, I was given a housecat and it was very difficult to identify each muscle. Housecats had blubbery tissue no real muscles to speak of. They were far from being toned, probably due to their lack of physical activity. I felt a bit jealous of the student next to me who was working on a street cat, or as everyone called them, alley-cats. Those cats were well-defined which explained why people that led an inactive life style disintegrated, and people that were physically active stayed in form and were healthier. The anatomy lab had become an intense learning experience. I wondered, if the seniors at Westwood Greens were to become more physically active, instead of sitting all day, would they be healthier, not only physically but also mentally? I believed in the old proverb, "If you don't use it, you lose it."

Pietro, one of the students in the Anatomy class, got along great. With English being our second language, we had a lot in common. Pietro, whom everyone called Peter, had been born in Italy and moved over here with his family when he was only twelve years old. We were standing by one of the lab tables checking out the labels on human bones of all sizes, and I said, "I can't wait to be a chiropractor and help people to get rid of pain without drugs or surgery. And you?"

"I want to be a medical doctor," he said vehemently. "And I'm planning on charging very little for my services to patients that can't afford medical care."

"Me too, I can't wait," I said.

Josh another student next to us remarked, "Well, I'm going to be a medical doctor, but at least I'm honest enough to tell you that I'm doing it for one main reason, to make money. Being rich is my goal."

Pietro said, "A doctor's main duty should be to help and care for the sick not to get rich."

"Yeah," I backed him up.

"Oh yeah? Well, you're either jerks, or freaking liars." And he walked out.

That incident brought Pietro and me closer. We made plans to study together but after the second time we met I found myself playing counselor and decided to study on my own.

Poor Pietro had fallen in love with one of the girls in the anatomy class. She was forty-five years old, married, and the mother of a twelve-year-old. She had confided in him that she was not happy and wanted a divorce. He hoped she would see him as a man and not as a kid. He was twenty-four years old but he would like to marry her. He wanted my advice, but when it came to the love department I was clueless.

I knew from years earlier, that formaldehyde fumes made me sick. I had a health issue when traveling in our new motorhome and later on in the modular house in Freehold. But it was worse now; the specimens in the dissection lab were freshly impregnated with formaldehyde.

Even though my body was not exposed and my arms were covered with long sleeves, the formaldehyde fumes penetrated through my clothes, and my skin took on the vivid color of a boiled lobster with sores, that looked a lot like second degree burns.

I showed my chest and arms to the anatomy teacher, who was so horrified that she excused me from dissection lab. She arranged for me to continue dissection studies along with two pregnant women in a different room where there were no formaldehyde fumes. The cats were presented inside a glass wall box, and we used thick rubber gloves to reach inside and cut their muscles and ligaments and pull their organs out. I hated dissection!

My little green car expired for good. The paper clip must have fallen off the engine, but the world was still turning on its axis, thank God!

Every car I got from Buddy, the car dealer and Ralph's good friend it fell apart soon after I drove it. Sometimes they didn't even make it off his parking lot. Buddy told me that he had no idea what was wrong with his cars, he bought them used and in bulk. The good news was that, since I was Ralph's mom, he was happy to keep exchanging the cars as they broke down. Buddy only charged me for the first car he sold me, the green car. The others were free for the exchange. Still, I never knew when they were going to break down and find myself stuck on the highway with my thumb up.

I bought a light folding cart to carry my schoolbooks, that way I didn't strain my back carrying them between classes.

During play rehearsals and even during the shows at the Simy Dinner Theatre, I studied behind the bar. There was a lot to memorize, and every minute was precious. I began playing with ways of storing information in my brain and then being able to withdraw it when needed for exams. Doodling on a piece of paper while taking a test, jotted my memory. I called the technique the doodle association method. I had tried word association and riddles, but all that did was mess me up even more because I couldn't remember what the associated word was. Smiling helped me to relax before a test and doodling helped with sparking my memory bank.

I was used to receiving A's with high honors in all my classes prior to taking my pre-meds to enter chiropractic college, but the science courses were doing a number on me. I didn't correlate well with abstracts, painful numbers, atoms, and protons, but I had made up my mind to remain focused on my mission. I was going to be a chiropractor no matter how hard the road ahead.

"Driving Miss Daisy" was cancelled due to illness of the main character. With live theatre, one had to deal with what life brought along, and I had learned that when one show couldn't go on, another one would pop up from the woodwork. I had noticed that from a chaotic situation, a masterpiece soon would take its place. It happened that way every time. And so, it did, a theatre company had lost their playhouse and was thrilled to go on with their already rehearsed and ready comedy show.

I signed up to continue my pre-requisites in January at the Ocean County College. I felt like a traitor leaving Brookdale, but it was so much closer to home that I would have to be a fool not to do it. Not that I could walk to Ocean County College, but it made a lot more sense in the winter to be closer to home. I had to make my life easier; I already contended with English being my second language, and my hearing loss, which made it hard to hear the teachers unless I found a seat on the first row. I did not need to have extra stress in my life, wondering if my car would get me to classes in the morning during a snow storm.

Winter of 1992

I won't mention the actor's name, since what he said was absolutely ridiculous, "The reason you're so successful with your dinner theatre is because it's in a Japanese restaurant!"

"Yes, that must be the reason," I was amused at his lack of perception. If the Simy Dinner Theatre had been located in an American greasy restaurant, we would be a lot more successful. Our audience's average age was between thirty-five and fifty years old. We missed out on the senior crowd and we had to struggle with the prejudice of the older folks nearby who refused to go to a Japanese restaurant even if it was to see a famous Broadway play, written by an American playwright.

Public Speaking class turned out to be the perfect venue of creativity. It helped me to mellow out between science courses. But the first time I spoke I came pretty close to croaking. *Great,* I thought *I'm going to pass out in front of everybody and get a head concussion when I hit the ground.* I could not control my hands and my legs from shaking, bringing to my mind Mr. Johnson an old customer at Howell Music Center who had Parkinson's. I held myself against the podium for body support and gazed back at the students. Soon they would be in my shoes trying to utter a word, without fainting in front of the rest of the class. I felt sorry for them. I smiled at the first row of anguished faces and let go of my own fears.

The teacher's advice to everyone at the beginning of the term had been, "You need to start your speech with an exciting topic to draw the audience's attention and keep them in the palm of your hands until the very end, where you must finish with a good punch line. The topic should be original if possible, and being controversial helps a lot, too."

I did my first speech following the teacher's recommendations to the letter. I showed the class a couple of handmade birthday cards. I explained that I had started making them after my father told me that he hated birthday cards unless they were handmade, only then did they mean something special to him. Then I told the class what made sense to write in a card if it was addressed to a family member or a good friend, and how you should always be honest when wishing your best to the ones you loved. "This is an example of what to write on a birthday card," I held the handmade card up for everyone to see and read to the class, "Happy Birthday, dear friend or relative, I hope you have a long healthy life, and when it's time to die, may you drop dead."

That was my final punch line.

The students were taken aback, including the teacher who asked, "What kind of good wish is that?"

"Given a choice," I said. "Do you want to drop dead at

the end of a long, healthy life, or do you want to die slowly and agonizingly while hooked up to wires and tubes?"

Everyone agreed it made sense, but it didn't sound good for a birthday wish. Nobody wanted to face their mortality. Perhaps they believed that if they didn't talk about it, it wouldn't happen. But if we liked it or not, death was part of Nature, like the seasons; we were born, we grew-up, we matured and then we moved on, much like spring, summer, autumn, and winter, each a graphic portrayal of our stages of life on earth.

When I came home, there was no one to exchange any further thoughts with. Al took everything I said as a joke.

I wrote to Michael about this and more, but the long letter was not as lighthearted as the last one. "The theatre is not the same without you. I miss our long talks while driving in the countryside. Thank God for college where I can spread my wings and express myself."

"Bathroom Humor," by Billy Van Zandt, was a crowd pleaser. But the props for it became one of my biggest challenges. I was about to give up when I found a store in Howell that sold bathroom fixtures. They were willing to work with me, in exchange for two tickets, two free dinners and a full-page advertisement in the playbill. I borrowed the three most imperative props: the tub, the toilet and a matching sink. They not only delivered them to the theatre, but also put everything on the stage for me. I was the luckiest theatre producer in the world.

For the second Public Speaking class I picked the subject of smoking. But I knew I had to come up with a serious visual presentation, since everybody already knew how bad smoking was for the health.

I kept it short and sweet, and saved the best for the end. "Do you want to see what happens to your organs inside your body, when you smoke?" I turned my back on the class and inserted into the right side of my mouth a brownish plastic roach and on the left side a black spider. They couldn't be more realistic, the reason I bought them.

Keeping my lips closed, I pulled a tight smile toward the class, lit a cigarette and with my tongue I slowly I pushed the black spider out of the opposite corner of my mouth. The look on their faces of repugnance and the sounds such as "Oooh," "Yuck," "Oh, no," and "Oh, my goodness," was like music to my ears. The teacher had his hand over his mouth and his eyes were a bit bugged out. I took that for a positive reaction and encouraged by the effect on the students and the teacher, I slowly moved the black roach out to the other corner of my lips and then spit it out toward the students. The ones on the front row backed away. It was unanimous; everyone was grossed out but they did clap including the teacher.

A young female student walked up to me. "Your talk was very illustrative. I'm going to skip my next smoke. Who knows, maybe I'll quit smoking." She shook my hand and added, "Thanks."

The teacher said I sure knew how to bring my point across, with my speeches. It helped being Portuguese; I had a natural streak for the dramatic just like my mother, who was Brazilian. Coming up with the ideas and presentations were a challenge but not as tough as the science courses.

My son Steve was very busy doing massages. He had never learned how, he had been born with a natural ability, and his clientele were mostly women. He got paid one hundred dollars an hour plus tips. When he massaged my back or my neck, I instantly felt better. Maybe that was what Dr. Holdman meant by using intention when treating a patient. When Steve gave a massage, his intent was to take away the muscle ache and it worked like magic.

I was nearly done with General Chemistry I. If all went

well, next quarter I would be toggling General Chemistry II and Physics I. All my life I had used the creative side of my brain, and it was a challenge to put my brain into science gear. The only thing motivating me not to quit was that Ralph assured me that if I passed pre-meds, chiropractic college would be a breeze. Physics scared me, so I told myself that I was going to have fun, fun, fun.

Mr. Johnson, our neighbor above our apartment, hurt his back at work and was talking about having back surgery. He was going through the same suffering I had experienced. I spent a lot of time with him and his wife, trying to convince him to go see Dr. Peruzzi, but he didn't believe in chiropractic and his doctor had recommended surgery. He acted as if chiropractic was some kind of religion. He didn't believe in it? What kind of dumb statement was that? In many ways I used to think like him, so I should be more understanding but the difference between him and I, was that at least I had the courage to try it.

For my third and last speech, it took me a week to come up with a topic, but inspired by the knowledge that Laurie, Rosanna's daughter-in-law was having her second insemination—by the same donor, because she wanted the two children to be related, I believed it would make a strong topic.
   After introducing Laurie's choice and reasoning to have the same donor, I added, "What happens if Laurie's neighbor happens to get the sperm donation from the same donor, doesn't it mean that her child is a sibling to the kid's neighbor?" I waited about two seconds for a response but no one raised their hand. "Of course, they are related," I walked to the front of the class. "They have the same father. Now, what if by any chance they were to grow up and fall in love and get married, then what?"

The teacher raised his hand. "That's a good question to ask the clinic involved."

"I did already. My friend Rosanna gave me the clinic's phone number, and they are located in Pennsylvania. I called them last Monday. 'No comment,' was the clinic's director response before she hung up." I was on the roll and kept going, "Rosanna showed her apprehension by observing that a semen donor might even marry his offspring without knowing it, since a lot of men nowadays marry girls that are young enough to be their daughters."

The insemination subject turned into a controversial debate, with the students getting upset that nobody was investigating such disturbing findings.

I was awarded an A with high honors in Public Speaking class. Gosh, how I missed my A's. All I was able to achieve in science courses were a B and sometimes a C.

Mama sent me a very disturbing letter. "All the money I saved for years and years in a locked box inside my bottom dresser drawer disappeared. I found the box empty except for ashes. Verónica, the money burned inside the box. Verónica, that money was to cover the funeral expenses for Papa, José and me, when the time came. I'm so heartbroken." The usual thin crispy onionskin paper she used for mailing long letters was tarnished at different spots as if she had cried over her writing.

I called Mama who upon hearing my voice began to cry unable to speak. "Mama, where did you keep the key to the box?" I asked.

"On a chain around my neck, and I never take it off."

"And who keeps the key every time you go to the hospital?"

"Alice, my employee. Why?"

"The robbery had to be from someone inside the house that knew where you kept the money. Mama, you need to be aware of Alice, the woman taking care of you. I bet she's the one that stole it.

"No, not her. She's like a loving daughter to me. I trust her with my own life."

"So, the money burned inside the box, like instant combustion, hum?" I waited for an answer but none arrived. "Is that what you been told? Mama, I don't trust the woman that works for you, you told me she's the one that gets your mail downstairs and the money I used to put inside your letters never got to you, don't you see that something is wrong?"

"Alice is a decent, kind woman. I trust her completely. She's the one that takes care of me when your father is not around. When I'm alone or not feeling well, she'll even cancel visiting her daughters just to keep me company."

In my heart I believed Alice was the culprit, even though I hadn't met the woman, it made the most sense. But Mama was completely sold on Alice's devotion and nothing I said made her change her mind.

Three days later Mama called again. Papa fell while putting on his trousers. He had lost his balance and hit his head against the corner of the bedroom armoire. He suffered a severe head concussion, and at the hospital, they had to make a hole in his skull to draw out the blood. Being that Papa was eighty-nine years old, the doctors said it was absolutely remarkable that he had survived the surgery. He would be coming home in a week.

I called Mama a week later and Papa was home and doing well. As luck would have it, she had been the one constantly in and out of the hospital, but once Papa came home, she got busy caring for him and would not allow herself to be sick. She also mentioned that she couldn't even imagine living without Papa and she prayed every day that she would die before him. She got up at least three times during the night to make sure he was breathing and sleeping comfortably.

My brother José was another story. While Papa was in the hospital, being treated for the head concussion, José had overdosed on drugs, and had been taken to the hospital. Mama and Alice were convinced that he had tried to kill himself.

Television viewers of soap operas believed the stories they watched were a dramatic concoction of fiction that couldn't possibly happen to anyone in real life. Well, they did, and my family was a good example of it.

~ *Chapter Five* ~

FREEDOM HAS BEEN GRANTED

1992

Spring of 1992

I awoke early this morning, looked at Al sleeping peacefully next to me and said to myself, *I must do something to save our marriage. Maybe it's not too late to go back to the way we were when we got married.* I awoke him, "Al, I have an idea," I curled up to him with one leg over his and my arm over his chest. "Let's re-do our marriage vows. Let's go to Portugal and re-do our vows. What do you say?"

"What for, we're already married."

"Because it's romantic," I gave him little kisses on the cheek and brushed his chest softly with my fingers. "Just imagine Al, a second honeymoon!"

"If it makes you happy, okay then." He went back to sleep.

I began planning the start of our life together, with a new beginning like newlyweds. The first four days in Lisbon would be dedicated to my parents, and when Al arrived at the airport, I would be there waiting for him, just like the first time we met. After doing our wedding vows at my parents' house with a little celebration, we had a rental car waiting for us at the airport and then travel for the next four days to the Serra da Estrela, which was very famous for its panoramic mountains.

I didn't tell Mama the real purpose of my visit to Portugal. She would flip out if I told her I was not happy. I simply wrote that thirty years of marriage deserved some kind of celebration. I planned on leaving while "Room Service" was on, which coincided with my spring break from college.

Al refused do any kind of handyman work on weekends and he stuck to his guns not to be a like a slave. I agreed with him. But one weekend he went beyond limits when it came to having an attitude problem. Arlene, the neighbor on the third floor of the building across from ours called us on the phone screaming, "Get Al here right away. There is a tire on the roof!" The heavy Swedish accent always made it difficult to understand her.

I covered the mouth piece on the phone handle with my hand. "Al, our neighbor Arlene says there's a tire on the roof, and she wants you to take a look right away."

"Yeah, yeah, just tell her that I'll take care of it on Monday."

I told Arlene what Al said and she yelled back, "You stupit! There a tire on the roof! How many times I tell to you?"

"Okay, compose yourself. I'll talk to Al and sooner or later he'll take care of it, don't worry."

She kept on screaming and calling me names so I hang up.

"Arlene is hysterical. Why don't you at least go talk to her?"

"You go talk to her. She's nothing but a pain in the neck." And he continued watching television.

I walked out and saw Arlene on the third floor of her

apartment standing on her balcony pointing to the apartment building across from her, "Look, look, the tire on the roof!"

The smoke from the fire was not only coming off the roof, but also the windows of the third floor. I ran inside our apartment to call the fire department and Al ran out to see what was going on. Thank God, the firemen got there in time to prevent the fire from spreading throughout the whole complex and were able to stop the flames from burning the building to the ground.

Nobody got hurt except Roy the tenant from the apartment where the fire had started. He couldn't cross the living room to reach the front door and had to jump from the small, narrow bathroom window, falling on the outside hard-concrete ground below. He was taken to the hospital for burns and both legs broken, but apparently, he was in fair condition. According to Mr. Stuart his friend and next-door neighbor, Roy had put a turkey cooking in the oven and then drank too many beers and fell in a deep stupor on the couch. He didn't wake up until the flames engulfed his apartment. All the apartments in that building section suffered serious damage either by fire or smoke.

Al and I got the okay from the insurance that did the appraisal of the burned building to start cleaning up the apartments of furniture debris, clothing and so on. We were promised a hefty bonus attached to our paycheck that month. There was a lot of smoke damage. Mostly putting things into large garbage bags and throwing it into the dumpster.

I was emptying the drawers from one of the burned rooms and throwing the contents into a trash bag when I found a brooch designed like a Picasso odd face. Instead of throwing away the singed trinket, I kept it to sew onto my jean jacket. I also found a hand-written diary that curiously enough had not burned completely in the fire. It was from a woman writing about her indiscretions with other men. She loved her husband but she needed more than one man in her life to be satisfied. I tossed it into the garbage can that Al was using to dispose of smaller items. After an hour of listening to Al complaining about everything under the sun, I excused myself with homework and left.

I was on a plane to Portugal the day after my last exam. I found Papa standing by the front door of his apartment waiting with arms open to give me a hug. His white hair had grown down to his shoulders, and the top of his head and sides stuck out as if he had put his head into an electric socket. He asked me if the hair made him look like Albert Einstein.

"Yes, but you're a lot more handsome." I knew the association would please him.

"Thank you for the compliment," he beamed. "I stopped going to the barber once I knew you were coming to visit us. I rather have my loving daughter cut my hair."

We walked arm in arm down the hallway toward their bedroom and before entering he said in a low tone of voice, "Your Mama is very weak lately. It's her heart as you know. She can't do much walking. It will do her good to see you again."

I found Mama sitting in her rocking chair and after we kissed and hugged several times I tried chatting with her but she said softly, "We have plenty of time to talk to each other later. Go ahead Verónica, your father really needs a haircut." I had never seen her so calm.

Papa sat in his old wingback chair with a scissor on one hand and a comb on the other, gazing at me with a beaming smile. When he was that happy his eyes always smiled along with his mouth making him look like a pampered happy child. I felt very special that in less than ten minutes after arriving at my parent's house, I was already giving Papa a haircut and using my tweezers to pull the little hairs off his ear lobes. He showed me, not one, but two holes on the right side of his skull, the result of the head surgery. He put one of my fingers into each indentation in his skull. He was like a soldier proudly showing his scars. My brother José walked in quietly and stood in the middle of the room, with the straight posture of a soldier. "Hello, Verónica, my sister, I'm glad you are here." He sounded like a robot. I walked speedily up to him and hugged him. "I'm also very happy to see you again, José." He hugged me back but unbendingly. I said playfully, "Am I shrinking or are you getting taller, since we last saw each other?"

He put out a forced smile, lowered his gaze and left the room.

I told my parents, "José looks drugged, what's going on?"

Mama said, "He needs the medicine he takes. It keeps him alive." I looked at Papa for a response. He shrugged his shoulders.

Later that day when Papa had left their room Mama confided, "Now that your father has his own bed, I'm sleeping so much better by myself," her face showed a glee of satisfaction. "Your father suffers from terrible nightmares about the Nazis coming after him and I used to get hit several times during the night by his flying arms and kicking legs as he ran away from them." Then she dropped her smile and shook her head. "But I have a problem with my twin-size bed it may be new but the mattress is hard as a rock, and in the morning, my whole-body hurts, I get very sore from lying on it."

I was glad to have the opportunity to observe Alice, my parent's employee. My mother used a small hand-held service bell made of brass that rang loud enough to be heard anywhere in the apartment. She called for Alice to come all the way from the kitchen for things like pouring a glass of water from the water jug in the room, or to bring a cup of tea, or snacks and also for when she needed help to stand and walk from her rocking chair to the bed or to the wooded commode across from her. Not once did I see Alice frown or show any signs of frustration, as she ran back and forth as if she couldn't wait to serve and always with a smile. Each time Alice was called in by Mama's hand bell, she would come running put her arms around her shoulders, and hug her, then take off to do the task as it had been requested. I had never seen such a loving display of servitude and even though I was thankful for Alice taking such good care of my mother, such excessive demonstrations of loving care seemed a bit exaggerated. Her overzealous attitude reminded me of a certain theater director I had worked with a few years back, who overacted to cover his dubious character.

That night after dinner I walked to the kitchen and found Alice washing the dishes. She caught sight of me, dried her hands hurriedly with a towel and closed the kitchen door. She stood against the counter next to the sink facing me and shook her head with the eyes closed as if tormented by what she had to tell me. "Miss Verónica, I'm so sorry to have to tell you this, but your parents are very, very sick. I closed the door because I don't want them to hear me tell you that I'm distraught and absolutely heartbroken about their health. They love me like a daughter and I feel the same way toward them." She sobbed copiously. "I never knew my parents." I gave her a hug and some tissues and thanked her for taking such good care of my parents. She was beyond kind; I could see why my mother felt so strongly about her. I put away all my suspicions and previous negative feelings toward her.

I went back to sit with my parents watching their black and white television.

Papa told me he felt humiliated having to sleep in a new bed, where the side rails were to be pulled up on both sides once he got in. Since his head concussion, the doctors insisted he needed protection from falling off the bed during the night. "They're treating me like a nincompoop and sleeping in a separate bed from your mother is very devastating to my ego. I may be eighty-nine years old, but I'm still a proud man and I like having my woman next to me, if you know what I mean," he smiled with a mischievous look in his eyes. I had to control myself from laughing but I did smile.

At 9:00pm Alice came into the room to get Mama washed and ready to bed. Papa was still weak but he did everything on his own He couldn't wait to have carte blanche from his doctor, to go out and do his daily errands as he was used to do.

I went to my room and stood by my window just like I used to do as a youngster when it was too early to go to sleep. I noticed a new apartment building at the end of our street where once a vacant lot had stood for over twenty years. Even thought it was the same street it had lost its familiarity. The cars drove by as if without engines, only the sound of the tires going over the cobblestones being heard, the street lamps were brighter than the old ones, people walked by but they were all in a hurry, no one stopped to talk. Alice knocked at my door. "Miss Verónica, I just want to make sure you're comfortable, do you need anything?" I told her I was fine and thanked her.

"Do you mind if I come in and join you at the window?" she walked in. "It is a beautiful night, isn't it?" she added.

I welcomed her company. I wanted to know more about her. She was three years younger than me and had been working most of her life as a maid. She was planning on being married in about a year. The love of her life had been in prison for two years for silly stuff he did, but he would be out in one year. She had two grown daughters who lived on their own in Lisbon. Every weekend she looked forward to visiting her fiancé in prison.

She asked a lot of questions about me and how much money Americans made a month, and how come they were so rich. "I would do anything to go to America with you Miss Verónica, I'm willing to cancel my wedding and become your employee instead."

I told her I was not rich, I worked for a living, and when it came to having an employee I couldn't afford it and didn't need one. She grew quiet, but after a minute or so she said, "Miss Verónica, it is in your best interest that you give me all the cash you brought with you, so that I can put it somewhere safe. There are a lot of robberies happening lately in our neighborhood, you know?"

It hit me as an odd request but I figured she was just being nice. "I only have five dollars on me, so I'm not worried about getting robbed. I use my charge card for everything I need." My instinct told me not to share with her, that I had three hundred dollars inside my money belt, along with my passport, driver's license and plane tickets and the only time I removed my money belt was while taking a shower, otherwise it remained around my waist even when I slept.

With my mind set on making Mama's bed more comfortable, the next morning I rode a bus to downtown Lisbon, to look for a store that would carry thick foam material to put over her mattress. It took me the whole morning, but I finally found a place specializing on foam of all sizes and thicknesses. I bought a four-inch-thick piece large enough to cover Mama's mattress.

Mama told me the next day that she had slept like a baby. And it was the first time she awoke in the morning without pain all over her body.

Later that morning, a young physical therapist came to their apartment to help Papa with therapy.

Papa winked an eye at her and then at me. "If I had known a physical therapist looked this pretty, I'd have requested one sooner."

She asked Papa to lie in his bed on his back, raise his feet and legs and move them as if he was biking. He definitely enjoyed the attention and decided to show off by doing the exercise as fast as he could. I could see in her face that she was not expecting to see an eighty-nine-year-old invalid in such good shape after a head injury.

Mama and I were laughing as Papa kept his hands behind his neck as he peddled hard and fast as if on a racetrack. It was quite impressive at his age.

"Mr. Wartenberg, you really are in very good shape!" The therapist gazed at him and nodded several times.

Without stopping or showing a hint of losing his breath Papa bragged, "This is child's play. I can do it all day and I can also do a dozen push-ups. Would you like to see?"

She took his pulse, blood pressure and left.

Papa couldn't help being a show-off but at the same time what he did was easy for him. Before he had fallen, he kept in shape by walking at a fast pace, up and down the hills in Lisbon and doing all kind of errands on a daily basis. He walked to the supermarket and carried the groceries home, five blocks away. When his errands took him further, to the pharmacy to pick up Mama's medicine or to the German Embassy to get his retirement check he used the subway, the trolley car or the bus. He liked visiting museums, principally the Guggenheim Museum on the other side of the city. I hoped to be just like him when I got to be his age.

I made several phone calls to pharmacies, hoping they sold or rented wheelchairs preferably a motorized one for Mama to use. I was thinking that if I could get her out of the apartment she could drive her wheelchair around the block and get some fresh air. To my shock, a handicapped person living in Lisbon was stuck at home. There were no wheelchairs of any kind available. I called two hospitals, but they needed them for their own patients.

On the third day, their forty-year-old refrigerator went kaput. My parents couldn't afford to buy another one and I told them I would take care of it.

The new refrigerator cost me $950 American dollars. It was the least expensive and made thin like a tin can, also the smallest they had in the store. I could have carried it home on my back! I was also disappointed that after paying for the refrigerator, which was overpriced to begin with, the storeowner, Mr. Silva, informed me that I needed to buy an electrical cord to plug into the wall. I had never heard of anything so crazy. Why did I buy the refrigerator from him? Because my parents knew Mr. Silva, and they felt he would give me a good deal since I was their daughter. If anything, I had been over charged for a fridge that didn't even have a plug. I had to take a trolley and then a local bus to reach the other side of the city to a specialty appliance store where they sold the cord with the ridiculous price tag of $75.

Before going to the appliance store, Mama had warned me about Mr. Silva.

"Swear on my head that you won't tell him your age. Mr. Silva is dying to know how old I am, and as long as he doesn't know how old you are, he won't be able to figure out my age. If he asks you, tell him that a man never asks a woman's age," a split-second brightened her eyes and then she added, "Because, it's sacrilegious!"

Mama had been right. After Mr. Silva asked me the usual polite question, "How are your parents doing?" he said, "And you, Miss Verónica tell me please, how old are you?"

"If I told you my age, I'd be betraying my mother and that would be... sacrilegious!"

Mama laughed with tears. "I'm proud of you. That bastard has been trying to find out my age for fifty years, but he'll never know."

Okay, nobody including myself knew Mama's age, but being in school had to make me a little smarter. I did the math, fifty years she knew Mr. Silva plus twenty-five to thirty years more—which was about the age she got married—Mama had to be around eighty years old!

While I was out buying the refrigerator, someone at home had gone through my luggage. I could tell because my things were not in the same manner I had left them, and my eye tweezers had been switched for a used one, with no grip. The swapping of my tweezers showed me that it had to be a woman who did it. May God forgive me, but it had to be my mother or Alice, since there were no other females in the apartment. I didn't mention anything to either, it was too petty, but I couldn't help feeling violated. I would gladly have given away my tweezers. All *she had to do was ask.*

I noticed that the water being served at meals was far from clean. I bought a large bottle of purified water at the grocery store, hoping to encourage my parents to drink that instead of the water from the faucet, but it didn't go well.

During lunch, Papa raised his glass of water and pointed at the dirt floating at the bottom, "Look at all the nutrients in the water, these particles at the bottom are very important minerals for keeping us healthy. I'm sorry Verónica, I know you mean well my daughter, but I don't like the idea of drinking purified water. We're doing fine with the water we have from our old but faithful pipes in our apartment."

I also tried to convince Papa not to use Saccharin in his morning coffee, because of its cancer association.

"I'm not going to worry about that at my age." He was 92 and set in his ways.

While Papa took his nap, Mama asked me to sit with her in the sunroom—as I used to call the pantry area when I was a kid. Mama wanted to have a woman-to-woman talk.

She asked me the dreadful question, "Verónica, are you happily married?"

"No. Al and I can't talk about anything without ending in an argument," I confessed.

Mama said she was glad I had confided in her, then she

took my hands and put them against her chest and pleaded, "For me, for your Mama, please try being submissive to your husband and don't argue back. Don't give your opinion on anything. Whatever he says, just respond with a yes and then later you can do whatever you want. If you say yes and agree with everything he says, you're going to notice your marriage will be a happier one. I do the same with your father. Don't you think he drives me crazy? He's hardheaded and has to have his own way all the time, so I make believe that I agree and go along with whatever he says, and that's why our marriage has lasted this long. He's a very difficult man to live with but our marriage is strong and we love each other." She then let out a deep sigh and added, "You're always such a good little girl when you were growing up."

I took her last remark as an encouragement to speak up. "Mama, if I was as good as you say, why did you use to beat me all the time?"

"What are you saying?" her eyes opened wide and her mouth dropped. "I never, ever hit you."

"Mama, I remember the beatings," I had waited all my life to confront her and I was not about to back off. "You used to hit me a lot. Those beatings have remained ingrained in my brain."

"That's not true," her voice trembled with indignation, "Verónica, how can you accuse me of something like that? Verónica, my dear, dear daughter, it's not true what you're saying." She stared at me in disbelief, tears fell.

There was no point arguing. She had forgotten the beatings that caused me to have so many bloody noses; not only from her, but also from Papa who was told as soon as he got home that I deserved a good spanking, for not behaving. Oh, well; I guess those were the blessings of old age; you only recalled the good old times. I hugged her and said I was just kidding.

I promised to follow her advice and be submissive,

when Al arrived the next morning.

While my parents were having their siesta, I took the opportunity to visit the Fonte Luminosa (Fountain of Lights) only a twenty-five-minute walk from our house. I carried my video camera over my shoulder and was looking forward to taking some good shots of the fountain. Four boys between the ages of eleven and thirteen years old were diving between the marble horses and naked statues when one of them saw me filming the fountain, and called my attention with gestures, then pulled his shorts down and exhibited his penis, shaking it back at me. I didn't even blink. In front of me was the opportunity to film a statement by a young punk and I even had the audacity to bring the lenses up closer.

When I got home I showed my film footage to Mama who got a real kick out of it and laughed with gusto. Papa, on the other hand, called it a representation of a doomed world of lost morals and values.

Mama winked at me. "Your father has a gloomy personality and you shouldn't pay attention to him." Then she reprimanded him, "Joachim, my love, it's just a young boy acting his age. Stop depressing us with your negativity."

Mama was a lot more free spirited and in control of her emotions than Papa who had become very philosophical and sensitive. He was far from the way he used to be when younger, where he barely spoke or showed little emotion. Now Papa got emotional and cried easily, like when they announced on the news one evening on television about a man that had suffered a stroke in bed but his dog saved his life by keeping him from getting dehydrated with a wet towel. The dog would dip a small towel into the toilet and then bring it to the old man's mouth so that he could suck on it. This went on for four days until a neighbor noticed the old man hadn't come out of the house for a while. She found him in bed, unable to stand but alive.

Papa wiped his tears with his handkerchief, "Imagine, a dog with a heart and soul, caring for his master and keeping him alive with toilet water. We may feel sorry for the poor man, but he was cared by the best friend anyone could ever wish for." He blew his nose. Mama looked at me and sighed. "Verónica, please give your father some water."

I couldn't sleep that night thinking about Al arriving the next morning. I got up before dawn and left my parents apartment to take the bus to the airport. I was so excited that I left without a jacket. The gusty chilly winds penetrated my bones. I ran the five blocks to the bus stop. Only one thing was going through my mind, keeping warm, Al and the restart of our lives together.

Our reunion wasn't exciting and romantic as I had imagined. He was tired and cranky from the long flight. When we got to my parents' house he crashed for the rest of the day.

The next morning, I showed Alice how to use the video camera which had been the reason I had brought it along, just for the occasion. Then I walked to the Praça do Chile where I knew a bakery sold real vanilla cakes decorated with delicious fluffy merengue and fresh fruit and bought one big enough for us to share after lunch.

I wore my favorite pink flower-print dress and put a piece of baby's breath in my hair for a touch of white. Mama and Papa held hands and looked joyously at Al and me while José, did a prayer at the table before we had lunch. Mama had Alice prepare my favorite food, green soup and codfish Gomes Sá style. We took our time eating and talking. Finally, it was siesta time, so Al and I said goodbye to my parents and we left to pick up the rental car at the airport. Al didn't like the idea of driving, so I gladly offered to do it since it would be a lot safer.

Before heading out to the famous Serra da Estrela, we stopped for a quick visit at Aunt Morena's apartment in

Oeiras, a suburb of Lisbon. She was my mother's sister and I had promised her that the next time I returned to Portugal I would bring her an American brand lipstick. I surprised with three lipsticks. She was thrilled and after trying one on, she kissed me on both cheeks and said, "That color looks great on you too, now all you have to do is spread it gently with your fingertips and it's the best rouge you can use. Here," she handed me the lipstick. "Put some on your lips to match."

Her husband had died two years ago, but she was still having difficulty living without him. After her husband's death, she had suffered a nervous breakdown and tried to kill herself by jumping out of their bedroom window, but she lost her balance and fell backwards into the room and broke her right ankle. I was moved by such beautiful love story.

Half-hour after being with Aunt Morena, her son Leão an ugly ghost from the past, showed up. I did not like him when I was a child and my feelings had not changed toward him, I hated the sight of him.

"Verónica," he said. "You haven't changed a bit since you got married and went to America. I thought by now you'd look older and as fat as your mother."

I couldn't help thinking, lousy pervert, it wasn't enough that you tried to molest me when I was a child, but you were successful with our little cousins Marcia and Lorraine, and as if that had not been enough, you also tried to take advantage of my brother José when he was nine years old. And there you are Leão, a bald-headed toothless old man with stinking tobacco-smell coming out of your pores. You deserve to rot in Hell.

I stood put on a smile for my Aunt Morena's sake and after giving her a heartfelt goodbye hug, I left without a word. Al was glad to leave too since he didn't understand Portuguese, but also because he knew all about Aunt Morena's depraved son, the child molester.

While driving to the Serra da Estrela, I felt I was going to go mad traveling with Al. He really loved me and would do anything under the sun to make me happy, but we had nothing in common. The trip was a reminder of why I had sold our motor-home after two or three trips together, it wasn't just because I was allergic to formaldehyde. I couldn't share my thoughts with him. Whenever I expressed an opinion it became a struggle between us, so I followed Mama's advice and become a yes wife to everything he said. Talking to each other became a one-way conversation. Either he slept, made remarks that he thought were hilarious, or complained about our surroundings. That night we stayed at a pousada, a bed and breakfast and while he slept I stared at the ceiling waiting for the sandman, while in the distance I could hear fireworks and the sound of singing and guitar music from a festive gathering in the nearest square.

For breakfast we had Papo Secos, small Portuguese bread rolls crusty on the outside and soft inside and baked in a brick oven. They were still warm when they reached our table. Al liked it with butter and jam and I had them with white cheese and jam. Neither drank coffee or tea but we had a glass of hot milk each. We were on the road after breakfast. Whenever I saw a castle or a panoramic view that I would like to have shared with him, like I had done with Ralph, I opted for not awaking him. I was by myself driving to a place he could care less. There was no enthusiasm, no passion, there was nothing left but sharing a honeymoon with a bored companion who would much rather be shopping at a mall or watching television. I stopped at a small village and called Mama to tell her the advice she had given me didn't work. José was in the hospital due to an overnight drug overdose. I had the perfect excuse to return to Lisbon. The way I saw it, if a marriage needed a second honeymoon in order to survive, then it was over. I had to accept the reality of our relationship and to stop fantasizing over something that didn't exist.

On the way back to Lisbon we stopped at a festive country fair. Al needed to go to the bathroom. I was waiting for him, on the side of the road when a young man slightly shorter than me with a pale face severely marked by pox scars sneaked up on me, and said with a terrible English accent, "Give me camera or I kill you!"

My memory became jolted by all the Portuguese curses I believed I had forgotten, and a spray of profanities came out of my mouth like bullets from a machine gun. I raised my arms and thrusted my hands out to grab him by his throat. He backed away startled and ran off. Eventually Al returned none the wiser.

The next day Al and I visited José at the hospital. Mama and Papa told us that every so many weeks José was taken to the emergency room due to a drug overdose. My parents were puzzled because José had no money to spend on such things; matter of fact, the only money he ever received daily were the equivalent of two quarters, just enough to buy a morning cup of coffee at a café. They believed he might be selling his books, to buy the drugs. But if that was true, his books would be gone by then, since drugs were expensive. It had to be something more profitable than books, but my parents were not missing anything from home. The only medicine José took was what Alice added to his food, as Mama had taught her, to make sure he didn't kill himself, and medical doctors were the ones prescribing them.

We found José seated in the hospital recreation room working on a puzzle. He stood when he saw us and hugged us wholeheartedly. He was in good spirits and talking quite coherently in comparison with when at home, where he seemed to be in a fog. I took advantage of his clear mind and asked, "José, tell me where do you get the drugs when you're living at home?"

"I'm sorry sister Verónica but I can't tell you. I promised not tell anyone." And he swayed his attention back to the puzzle.

I brought my chair close to his. "That's right I'm your sister, so you can trust me. Now tell me, go ahead." I put my arm over his shoulder.

He gazed around the room and then lowered his voice, "Verónica, my dear sister, if you promise to take me with you to America, I'll tell you where I get the drugs."

"Okay, it's a deal." I didn't translate to Al what José had asked. Al would not have agreed with our pact.

"Alice gives them to me," he smiled. "Now you take me to America with you?"

Wow, I really thought I had him, but he was a lot smarter than I gave him credit for. "That's the most ridiculous thing I've ever heard. Alice would have to be a criminal to give you drugs that can kill you. José, you are lying to me. If you don't tell me who is supplying with the drugs I can't take you to America with us."

José answered once again in the same, child-like tone of voice but this time he put his right hand over his chest trying to emphasize his words, "I swear to you that I'm telling you the truth, cross my heart and hope to die." And then added with an imploring look in his eyes, "Please, don't tell Alice I told you, she made me swear that I would not to tell anyone and if she finds out she won't be my friend anymore."

When Al and I got to my parents' apartment I told them José had incriminated Alice as the drug supplier. Like me they felt José had lied to protect the real drug dealer. Alice having heard the conversation from the kitchen, burst into my parent's bedroom, "What an awful thing for José to say about me. I love him like a brother. He's lying!" She dropped on her knees next to my mother and cried. "Your son is lying, he's a liar!" she sobbed. "I'd never do anything to hurt him. I'm so heartbroken, so heartbroken."

Mama felt so bad for Alice, that she offered some of her medicine drops to help her calm down.

That night I compared my brother's life with mine. He had been born unlucky. The same could have happened to me, but fortunately, I had been born with an angel on my shoulders. What else could explain our paths in life? I thanked God for having me grow up in Portugal with two very special mentors: Aunt Heydee and Encarnação.

Aunt Heydee, my mother's older sister had taught me to appreciate life's ups and downs and the ugly as well as the beautiful. She had died, but in my heart she lived permanently. Encarnação had been my loving childhood friend. She was now ninety-two years old.

Al and I walked to Encarnação's apartment on Rua Ponta Delgada #5 just down the street from where my parents lived. Encarnação still smiled a lot, and never complained, but I remembered when I was nine years old, she cried from deep within her heart when she showed me a picture of her first child, a little boy who had died when he was only two years old. Then Eduardo her older son, who used to let me play with his airplane toys, when I was a kid, died when he was twenty-seven years old, while flying a plane for the Portuguese Air Force. His plane crashed, killing him, and his co-pilot. I bet Encarnação cried a lot when she was by herself.

Mama always said, "May God never show us how much suffering we can carry." But Encarnação had so much love to give that not long after Eduardo died, God provided her with a baby to love. Maria, Encarnação's maid got pregnant and she offered Maria, and her husband João, room and board. Maria's baby was born with several birth defects of his hands and feet. That didn't stop Encarnação from loving the innocent child, and she offered to be his godmother, and that she was, to the full extent of the word. He received a proper education and lots of love, and he grew up to become a successful architect.

Maria and João still living with her and came into the parlor and hugged Al and me. They still remembered being at our wedding. They had aged, and I was sad, but also glad because they were still alive.

"Would you like me to bring your guests tea and cookies?" Maria asked Encarnação.

About twenty minutes later, she returned with a large silver tray with tea and home-made butter cookies. After the tea and reminiscing about the old times, Encarnação stood, "Come, let me show you around the apartment." She always did that every time I came to visit her. I followed her to her husband's study where as a child I had spent many hours seated cross-legged on the Persian carpet looking and reading his oversized books with black-and-white illustrations about Africa. They were still on the second shelving of the wall to wall bookcase.

She put her arm around my waist. "And now, I want to show you my godson's office," and she led me along the hallway to the last room in the apartment, next to the dining room. It was a typical architects' room with two large tables covered by papers with drawings, two large bookcases with books and lots of rolled up papers stacked on one corner. "I'm so proud of him and what he has accomplished in life," her voice was soft but raspy and tears welled up in her eyes. I was sorry to have missed him. Before we left Encarnação handed me a silvery mini box. "For you, to remember me by, I made it from aluminum foil. Isn't beautiful?"

"Yes, it is very beautiful, perfect as a jewelry box for my earrings. Thank you."

"Good. I knew you would come to visit me again and I made it just for you."

After visiting Encarnação, Al and I took the subway to downtown Lisbon to pick up cookies for Papa. Mama had asked me to buy them since she was running out of them. She felt that the dry cookies were perfect for making Papa thirsty, because he had been diagnosed with bad kidneys and he needed to drink a lot of water every day.

We were waiting on the platform for the subway train when Al took his wallet from his back pocket and said, "I wonder how much money I still have." He always did that at home when surrounded by people so everyone could see his shiny First Aid silver emblem, which looked a lot like a sheriff's badge. It had been years since he last volunteered for the First Aid Squad, but he still carried the badge attached to the inside of his wallet and whenever he opened it he made sure everyone caught a glimpse of it.

"Al, please don't count your money here," I begged him. "We're not in the US please put it away."

But he wouldn't listen. How much longer was he going to count his money? I guessed until everyone around us had seen his shiny badge. He was such a showoff.

"Great," I sighed and shook my head. "You have just put us into a dangerous situation when we get into the train."

"You're always imagining things. You're becoming psychotic in your old age." He laughed.

I heard the bird whistle sound. The gypsies always whistle like that to each other when they catch a "bird," otherwise known as sucker.

I immediately pulled my jacket pockets inside out and said as loud as I could, "Oh! No, I forgot to bring my money with me. See, my pockets are empty!"

"You're beyond weird. What the heck are you doing that for?"

"I'm just making sure they see that I don't have any money to steal."

Al hit his right backside pocket with his hand. "Oh yeah? Well, let them try and get it from me."

I couldn't believe it, now they knew exactly which pocket he kept his wallet. A rush of people pushed us along as we entered the train like sardines in a can. Al was being squeezed and pulled in different directions. A Portuguese man was aware of what was happening, and in his crude manner he stated, "Some idiot is getting robbed."

I looked away. Al was better off not knowing. Male gypsies doing that kind of work were known for carrying thin blades on the side of their boots, and had no problem using them if necessary.

When we got off the train I waited until we were above ground to ask, "Check your wallet."

"Stop bugging me; it's right here," he reached for his empty back pocket. The wallet was gone with the money, driver's license, charge cards, and his beloved silver badge.

During the last two days in Lisbon I went along with everything that Al said. There were no arguments, and he was happy. My purpose to go to Portugal to save my marriage had failed.

Mama kept reminding me, "Don't be a fool, Verónica. He adores you and takes good care of you. What more can you ask for? You must accept that you're married to Al for the rest of your life, for better or worse."

To make her happy I nodded while wishing I was already divorced.

Mama's advice to be more submissive meant living like a mute. It would be like going back to the way I used to be when I first got married, except I was no longer that person.

The day before we left I was walking in the hallway to see my parents when I noticed that José's bedroom door was open. He stood in front of his full-length mirror staring at himself as if in a trance. "Are you okay, José?" He didn't answer, so I walked up to him and stood next to him gazing at both our reflections. "Look, Verónica my sister," he said pointing to his image on the mirror. "That's not me. That's an ugly monster." Then he walked silently to his desk on the corner of his room and opening a geometry book got immersed into it. I did not know what to say. It had to be emotionally devastating for a young man his age to see himself as a monster, and I wanted to cry. He was right. He was obese, and his face was enlarged as if every cell in his body had duplicated and gone crazy. Mama told me one of the side effects from the medication she gave him made him gain weight. My brother had been a vivacious wild kid when he was younger, but he had a heart of gold. I remember when he took the chickens and turkeys from our backyard, and hid them in the neighbor's chicken coop, trying to save them from becoming our meal for the holidays. My brother deserved more in life than spending the days eating, sleeping, and working on his geometrical drawings.

I couldn't wait to return to the US and back to my studies, and the theatre. I was dying to see my friends, to laugh freely, and be in my own environment. I no longer belonged in Portugal. The city of Lisbon was a memory of times that no longer existed. I was a foreigner in my own country, and except for my parents and my brother José, there was no reason to be there except for a short visit.

Among all the mail waiting for me when we returned from Portugal was a letter from Michael's mom. She wanted to know how I was doing. I wondered if Michael had put her up to writing.

I answered her letter.

I couldn't be happier than when Ralph announced his final decision; he was ready to follow me to chiropractic college. Since he had most of his pre-requisites already completed, he was going to continue working until I was about done with mine and then he would take those he still needed. Meanwhile, we made plans to check out a chiropractic college in Pennsylvania, only an hour and a half from where we lived.

Ralph and I drove to the college in Pennsylvania this morning. Coming home every day would save us room and board, but we came to the conclusion that we would be gambling like fools if we attended a school still waiting for accreditation. What if they never became accredited?

Dr. Peruzzi recommended Life Chiropractic College in Marietta, Georgia. There was also New York Chiropractic College. Putting things into perspective, the cost of living in Georgia was a lot less than New York; the weather was a lot warmer even in the winter, and the tuition drastically less than the college in New York. Ralph and I voted on going to Georgia. Al said no way was he going to move to Georgia. He liked New Jersey. I didn't ask why.

When I heard Aunt Coty's voice on the phone, I pulled a chair to sit and held my breath. I knew she wouldn't call me from Portugal unless there was bad news. In the thirty years I had been in the US, she hadn't ever called me.

"Verónica," her voice was trembling as she repeated my name, "Verónica ."

"Go ahead, Aunt Coty, I'm listening." I closed my eyes and held the handset with both hands curling my shoulders around it and pressing it hard against my ear and my neck.

José had died in the hospital on June 9th. Five days after Al and I had left.

I called my parents immediately. Mama was not available. Papa told me that after we had left Dr. Silva called my parents and told them that this time he wasn't going to release José until he knew who was supplying him with the drugs. On June 9th Alice offered to visit José, and when she returned from the hospital she told my parents that José was doing great and had told her that he liked where he was staying. A couple of hours later after Alice's visit, Dr. Silva called Papa to tell him that José had lunch and about a half an hour later collapsed on the floor, dead. Dr. Silva felt that José had taken the drugs that killed him at lunch.

I prayed to God to put his arms around my younger brother José and hold him like the child he was, an innocent victim of drugs and the society we lived in.

Ralph offered a most remarkable suggestion on how I could financial aid to attend chiropractic college. Being divorced I would most likely be entitled to receive financial aid. I was all for it, but Al thought it was the most ridiculous idea Ralph had ever come up with. Ralph explained to him the financial benefits—and where the heck were we going to get the money to pay for my tuition—Al agreed to start proceedings immediately.

We did not need a lawyer; under Ralph's guidance, Al got the proper documents from the courthouse and we were filing them ourselves. We still had to go before a judge, but as I saw it that was just part of the process. My wish of getting divorced had finally come true, even if only on paper.

Summer of 1992

Two weeks had gone by since José had passed away but with each day I developed a growing anxiety concerning his real cause of death as well as my parents' safety. I called Papa. Mama was still unable to come to the phone; I imagined she was severely sedated.

"Papa, I need to share with you a gut-feeling I've been having. I know you and Mama love Alice but I think she had something to do with José's death." I expected him to call me crazy and start defending Alice.

"I've started to wonder that myself," he said. "I'm not stupid. Alice knew that the doctor at the hospital was keeping José under observation to find out who was supplying him with the drugs. Odd, very odd that the day José died was the morning after Alice visited him at the hospital."

"I know, it's too much of a coincidence. Please be careful, she could be dangerous. She even fooled me into believing her, instead of my own brother." My throat tightened as tears engulfed my vision. "Papa, please make sure she's not around when you talk to me on the phone, if she knows you suspect her she could be dangerous."

"I know, I know, she's in the kitchen now making dinner, so I'm safe talking to you, don't worry. I want José to have an autopsy, but your mother is adamant that she doesn't want José's body to be cut up. This is something that Alice has put into your mother's head, by constantly bringing it up. But an autopsy will let us identify what killed him." There was a moment of silence. "I'll have to wait until your mother recovers from the loss of our son."

Papa told me not to fear; he was going to wait until the right moment. I knew Papa would be very tactful and not do anything to jeopardize his life or Mama's.

"Let your enemy talk, and then you will know what he's up to." That was one of Papa's favorite quotes.

When I got home from classes that morning, I found a message from Michael on my answering machine. "I need to talk to you Ronnie but since you're not home I'll write to you, instead."

Thank God, I wasn't at home. What could I say, after all this time without seeing each other? We had written twice, but that barely counted as any kind of communication. The more I thought about it the more my chest hurt making it hard to breathe. I told myself, I didn't care if he loved me, he could suffer all he wanted. My life and my future didn't include him since nothing good could come of it.

Someone was finally buying Michael's house, but the future owners wanted certain work done before they signed the final papers. He finished the letter with; I love you and miss you so much. He included a cassette tape he had done while driving to work. I could hear in the background the familiar sound of his noisy pickup truck. He talked for a while about where he lived in South Carolina and how lonely it was out there in the boondocks, and then he sang along with the radio, "... I'll be your friend; I'll help you carry on. For it won't be long till I am going to need somebody to lean on."

I loved the sound of Michael's voice; he could have been a blues singer. I wrote back and told him about my trip to Portugal and my brother's death.

I spend the days in school, and the nights at the theatre, and in the morning, I looked forward to his mail.

I got to the lab at the college a bit too early one day and there weren't any students around so I figured that would be the perfect opportunity to try and make glass sculptures from the long glass test-tubes, not being used. I cautiously looked around to make sure no one was around. It would be my first time at glass blowing. How difficult could it be? I used the tiny flame-blower to heat a thin glass tube. *I'm going to create some quality glasswork,* I told myself. But it wasn't that simple to come up with anything recognizable. I played with a few more tubes, and after messing up more than a bunch, I gave up on the project and threw them into the trashcan.

I was still by myself and I would have to be a fool not to take advantage of such rare opportunity to mix all kinds of chemicals and see the reactions produced without anyone looking over my shoulder. A little bit of this and a little bit of that went into two glass containers. One of them created soft low flames. I picked it up, but my hand shook a little, I was nervous that I might get caught doing stuff that had nothing to do with my regular lab work and then my hand bumped the other glass over and the counter became covered by a flammable liquid that dripped to the floor. I immediately got rid of the glass in my hand by throwing it into the trashcan. Then like any fireman would do, I ran to the sink and filled a small plastic container with water and threw the water on top of the counter and into the trashcan. I could only guess that the water had turned into a fire conductor making the flames spread all over the counter and the glass contents inside the garbage container came out flying in all directions. Luckily, I didn't get pierced by the glass bits, and the fire extinguished by itself. I had a mess in my hands. I cleaned everything the best I could with paper towels and I did use water again but the chemicals had burned out and there was no further reaction. The place looked good when I left, except for a pungent odor and two brown stains on the off-white tiled floor.

Rosanna invited me for lunch at her favorite seafood restaurant in Belmar. I considered us like sisters, since we shared all our personal tribulations and I told her that I wanted to get a real divorce, not a temporary one just for financial reasons.

"Don't be silly, financial reasons or not, according to the law you're now officially divorced." Rosanna assured me.

But I knew that I was not divorced until Al agreed. In his mind we were still married even though he had chosen to remain in New Jersey while I lived in Georgia. I was not complaining, but four years away from each other, was no marriage of any kind. Movie stars were a good example of what happened when two people were away from each other for long periods of time while filming. I admired Paul Newman and his wife, they had the perfect formula for a happy marriage; they worked as a team, like true soulmates.

Michael called me at the Kobe. "It's been so long since we've seen each other," he said. "Ronnie, I've missed you so much."

"Me too, me too, when will I see you again?"

"I'm going to be in New Jersey to work on my house for a few days. Let me see if I can manage the trip, to make it happen." He gave me his phone number so I could call him on Wednesday from a payphone, for more details.

I called him Wednesday, during my lunch break at school. "Okay, I have great news." he said. "This Monday I'll be driving north on 95 and according to my map there's a park between Pattison Ave and S. Broad St. in Philadelphia, where we could meet and not worry about being seen together. I'm planning on starting very early from here and drive straight through. Depending on the traffic I should be there between 3 and 4 in the afternoon. And then we can follow each other back to New Jersey. How does that sound?"

"It sounds wonderful. I'll be there."

If he had suggested the moon, or another planet, I would have found a way to get there just to spend an hour in his arms like in the old days.

I saw him in the distance and when he caught sight of my van pulling into the parking lot, he dropped his cigarette on the ground and after stepping on it he ran toward me as I did the same. Our lips met so hard when we kissed that I thought my front teeth were going to shatter. We sat at a park bench with our legs intertwined, talking, kissing, enwrapped in each other's words. We had a lot to catch up on. He told me about his lonely, boring life in South Carolina and I told him about my exciting plans of going to chiropractic college, and my past work at Westwood Greens as their activity director. We talked about theatre, the plays and musicals I had produced lately and he mentioned that he had seen "Annie" ten times that year and if he had to hear the musical score one more time he would commit hara-kiri.

"I've never seen the show," I said. "But the thought of hearing the song "Tomorrow" more than twice would make me sick, unless of course my own child was involved in the production." I talked while in back of my mind the jealous green-eyed monster took over me. Ten times? But he didn't do theatre anymore. There had to be an actress in the cast that he was involved with, most likely a mother with a talented small child playing the part of Annie, not that it was any of my business. We kissed and exchanged words of love, but we were only friends no matter how I looked at it. I had no right to feel jealous. I quickly put those thoughts away in order to enjoy our get-together.

We had an hour and a half to drive back to New Jersey and I followed him. Somewhere in New Jersey he pulled his pickup into a small park by a river and I did the same. We stood by the water holding hands silently. The sun was setting, and the shadows of the evening slowly began to cover the water and the surrounding trees with a thin gray blanket. A chilly breeze brought his arms around me, and I was comfortably warm. We stood like that together for another half-hour. It was dark now. He said he was going to spend the night at a motel. He had been driving since 5:30 that morning. I told him I would follow him since it was on our way home and then go on my way.

He pulled over into a motel in Cherry Hill, but instead of saying goodbye I followed him silently as he opened the door to his room.

He sat at the foot of the bed and lit a cigarette. I sat next to him. He stood and walked to the window. "It's better if we don't sit together on the bed," he said.

"I trust you." Was I out of my mind?

"But I don't trust myself," his face was flushed and visibly nervous as he added, "It's really hot in here."

I told him if he was that hot he should take his shirt off.

He did.

We sat on the carpeted floor by the end of bed making small talk. And then he said, "If you're not comfortable spending the night with me and want to leave, I won't hold it against you."

I immediately sat on his lap, since I knew that was his

favorite way of holding me closer, and I was very sure of myself when I responded, "I would like to spend the night with you. That is, if you want me to."

"I was hoping you would say that."

We kissed each other as if it was the last day of our lives. We couldn't take our clothes off fast enough as we rolled on the bed and fell on the floor, laughing. I pushed him gently on his back and kissed him all over. Being that I'd never been with anyone else but Al, I assumed that was the way all men liked being loved. I wanted to please him more than anything else. But then, to my surprise, he got on top of me and began penetrating me. He moved very slowly with each movement, as if calculated to purposely bring me pleasure, and I was carried along with a multitude of fireworks exploding, followed by the delicious feeling of a calm ocean. We didn't pull away from each other; we stayed joined, like glue, for a long time. I was dumbfounded; I had been able to express my satisfaction without being ridiculed.

Being married to Al for close to thirty years, he had me convinced that intercourse was only good for one purpose, making babies. After Steve was born and a few years into our marriage I remember Al laugh as he said, "You're such a faker," he said. "You can't possibly be enjoying it. It's a known fact that women only get pleasure from oral sex. So, stop acting!"

Al's remark, hit me more like a slap in the face than anything else. I felt humiliated and at that very moment my worth as a woman vanished into thin air. I immediately closed myself from showing any further emotion as I held back my tears. I knew Al enough to know that it was a waste of time to defend myself or to even bother to argue the point. From that day on, when we had sex I began to fantasize that he was a woman and I was a lesbian.

I didn't share these thoughts with Michael, but I thanked God for giving me the opportunity to learn that there was nothing wrong with me physically.

It was 10:30 in the evening and we were hungry. On the way to the restaurant I ignored the voices in my head warning me of the consequences of cheating on my husband. I was legally divorced but not morally.

I called the house. I left a message in the answering machine, "Al, I won't be home until tomorrow morning. Sorry, but it's late so I'm spending the night with a friend."

After dinner at a diner across the highway we went back to our room. We lay naked in each other's arms. We were the only two that existed as we whispered the universal words of intimacy, where there was no yesterday or tomorrow. When he fell asleep I could hear his heart beating close to mine, and I tried to stay awake for as long as possible as I wanted that moment in time to last forever. It was seven in the morning when we awoke and made love and talked and made love again. We showered together, got dressed and went out for breakfast. He would be working on his house for the next three days before heading back to South Carolina and at night staying with his friend Morph. He promised to call and let me know when he would be back to New Jersey.

I got into my car and drove off. And that was the last thing I remembered doing when I found myself of all places in Atlantic City. I had no recollection of driving. I pulled into a gas station and remained in the car trying to focus my mental abilities into driving north to Lakewood. When I got home an hour later I went to bed and didn't wake up until the next morning.

Two weeks later Michael called. He had more projects to do at his house and planed on coming a day earlier so that we could spend it together. He said he was due for a visit to a barber for a haircut when he got here and I told him not to bother, I would be happy to do it. We met at Morph's house that Thursday and spent the day in a motel room.

I never thought there was anything sexy about cutting someone's hair until I cut his hair. Michael made me feel like a woman. While he was seated in a chair, I maneuvered my body around him like a professional barber, except that it was accented by the mutual pleasure of being so close. I purposely took my time cutting each strand as he wrapped his arms around my waist every time I stood facing him.

"The Owl and the Pussycat" was a hit. Robert Kras directed and played the main character. It was very good, but to me it was missing the charm that Barbara Schiavonne had put into the same production, six years prior.

Meanwhile I had started offering the latest type of entertainment, I called it "Murder for Lunch" and in the evening "Murder for Dinner." The audiences loved being part of the plot and at the end, guess who the criminal was.

Last Saturday I was accused of being the killer because my pink silk outfit, had ruffles around the hips making it perfect to conceal a handgun. That would have made sense but I spent most of the evening behind the bar, running the stage lights and sound effects. Some people shouldn't even try being detectives.

The main chef at the Kobe Restaurant quit. It was a disastrous situation for all of us who loved his salad dressing. The other cooks tried and tried again to formulate the same salad dressing but it didn't even get close. Ralph was very disappointed when he asked me to buy a bottle of Kobe salad dressing. When the chef quit, he took his secret recipe with him.

On weekends I still worked most mornings at the Kobe answering phones and taking reservations while closed. Mr. and Mrs. Ounuma used the time off to recover from the long grueling week at the restaurant and to catch up on their sleep. The quiet soothing atmosphere of the restaurant was great for studying.

On Saturday morning, I did my usual before sitting behind the front counter to study and answer phone calls. I went into the kitchen for a cup of pistachio ice cream. I didn't even bother to turn the light on; a stream of natural light coming from the main dining room was enough to light my way to the ice cream box. I felt being watched but I attributed it to a figment of my imagination.

I sat on the bar stool at the counter, opened my notebook and laid my pencil next to it. I had just put a spoonful of pistachio ice cream in my mouth when I looked up. Kuno the guard dog stood at the top of the steps by the front door and had his eyes on me. Kuno hated Americans. He had attacked Tracey when she was innocently walking in the back of the restaurant's parking lot. She had to defend herself with the roll of posters she was carrying under her arm. They were chewed up to pieces when he attempted to go for her throat.

On the first day I worked at Kobe's answering the phones, I had written Mr. Ounuma's home phone number on a tiny piece of scrap paper and tucked it away under a bunch of papers on one of the shelves behind the counter, figuring that I would never have the need to call him. I began to doubt I would find the damn piece of paper. My hands shook as I rummaged through a bunch of bills, letters and junk mail. I had heard that animals could tell when you were scared. I hid my shaking hands behind my back and tried to smile confidently. The closest to a sharp object to use to defend myself with, was a pencil. I looked up; Kuno had not moved an inch and his eyes were transfixed on me. I guess I had more brain memory cells than I gave myself credit for, when to my utter amazement I was able to recall Mr. Ounuma's phone number.

I whispered, "Mr. Ounuma, please hurry and come to the restaurant. Kuno is not tied up; he's going to attack me anytime."

He laughed. "Kuno likes you."

"Mr. Ounuma, he only likes me when I'm wearing my kimono, and right now I look like an American." I started to cry hoping he would feel sorry for me. "I swear to you that he's looking straight at me in a very strange way, and he's showing his teeth, and believe me when I say that he's not smiling."

"Okay, Okay," responded Mr. Ounuma in a condescending voice, "I'll be right over, just try to remain calm."

I stayed calm all right, more like frozen in time, until Mr. Ounuma showed up. "Kuno is a big dog it's true, but he's a nice doggie, he would not hurt you," he said before taking Kuno with him.

Yeah, I thought, *doggie my foot. He loves Japanese, not Americans, and Portuguese people are most likely on his hate list too.*

"The Murder Room," from September 11 through October 17 was to be my last theatrical production at the Kobe Japanese Restaurant. Mr. Ounuma had given up trying to make me stay; he knew I had my mind made up to be a chiropractor and theatre was no longer the most important part of my life.

Once it became official that I was selling The Simy Dinner Theatre, I was getting several calls daily. But I had to consider Mr. Ounuma's feelings in the matter, it was important that he liked the people I sold the theatre to.

Autumn of 1992

The chemistry teacher made an announcement on our first day of class. "More than half the students in this class will drop out before the end of the quarter, and of those remaining only very few," he put out his hand and brought his thumb and index close to each other and focused his sight on his two fingers. "Maybe two percent of you will pass the course and those are the ones that already took my class before." His laughter echoed in the quietness of the room and in my skull.

As soon as I got home I called Ralph. He said the teacher sounded like a total jerk and he encouraged me to get a chemistry tutor right away.

Michael called Sunday. He was coming over Tuesday, but his mom and two other friends would be accompanying him. They were all staying until they finished repairing their house. The closing was at the end of the month and it was dependent on all the repairs being performed. He had to fix the roof, put on a new garage door, lay down some concrete, and re-do the wooden steps going into the house. The list was absolutely unreasonable. It would be easier to just level the house and build a new one.

I drove to his house prepared to give up everything in my life. All he had to do was ask me to move to South Carolina with him and I would quit school and go live with him. On the way to his house, I couldn't help thinking about our age difference, when I was sixty, he would be turning forty and most likely he would no longer think of me as young looking for my age, he would see me instead as an old lady. I pushed away the negative thoughts, by telling myself, *the present is all that matters.*

Michael saw me driving up his driveway and dropped his tools on the ground. I jumped out of my van and ran towards him. He held me tight and would not let go, swaying me from one side to the other. His mom stood waiting patiently for Michael and me to come apart so we could also hug. I missed her too; it had been a long time. He announced to his helpers that he was taking a break and then, putting his arm over my shoulders, he led me to the side of the house.

We sat on the grass and then he said the most horrible thing I could have heard him say, "I want you to continue going to college. Ronnie, we must not see each other again until you finish what you have been working so hard for."

"You don't mind waiting five years without seeing each other?" I bit my bottom lip. He was saying goodbye. I felt exposed and even ridiculous for having thought that when it came to love our feelings for each other could withstand any adversity.

"Ronnie, I love you too much to destroy your future. It's the right thing that we both go our way and meet again, if it's meant to be, when you're done with school."

I put on my happy face mask. "You're right. I don't know what's got into me," I stood. "I've got to go now, it's getting late for my next class. Goodbye, Michael, I'll see you when I graduate." I walked away at a fast pace, climbed into my van, and drove off as fast as I could. I didn't look back.

I had been a fool to believe in love, that amazingly supreme passionate love that writers wrote so much about only existed in romance novels. I opened my window, picked up from the passenger seat the little brown teddy bear he had given me six years earlier for my birthday and without a second thought I threw it out. I really had no choice, if I was going to survive without him I needed to break all my ties and leave no memories to haunt me.

When I got to school I removed the silver necklace he had given me when we spent the day at the Renaissance Fair, but instead of throwing it away, which had been my first impulse, I laid it carefully on top of the school's bathroom counter and left it there.

While walking to my classroom I came upon a jewelry fair in the cafeteria. I bought a necklace made of tiny black stones shaped in the form of hearts. The stones felt like tiny bits of ice around my neck and it brought me comfort. I would wear it every time I needed to remind myself that I could be as cold as those stones, and still be happy without him.

I found an Asian student that taught chemistry for only twenty-five dollars an hour, but I had trouble understanding his quick mumbled answers. He became very impatient when I asked him several times to repeat what he said. After two unproductive lessons and wasting precious time driving back and forth to his apartment in Red Bank when I could be studying on my own and possibly get a lot more done I came to the obvious conclusion that I was better off on my own. The problem was to figure out how to tell him I was quitting, without hurting his feelings.

Talk about male chauvinism. The chemistry teacher told Nancy, a girl in our class, that she was too pretty to waste her life in college and that she should be thinking instead about getting married and being a wife and mother. She ran out of the class sobbing.

We were in lab this morning when he started nagging Nancy again. "Leave me alone," she cried and covered her ears with the palm of her hands.

"It just shows how sensitive you are that you can't even hear the truth," he said mercilessly. "For your own good I'll say it again, college is a waste of time for someone as beautiful as you. A good man will take care of all your needs."

That was the last time I saw Nancy in school.

She was a weakling. If I was her I would not allow the chemistry teacher or anyone else to bully me on account of being a woman, and if anything, I would work harder to prove myself.

I called my chemistry tutor, he wasn't home. I left a message in his answering machine that he was great at teaching but I no longer needed his help.

I was not as smart as Ralph but I did have a brain. I would do my best with what God had given me. At present, Ralph was taking biology at Ocean County College as the only one of the pre-requisites left that he needed to enter chiropractic college the following summer, with me. If I got stuck with a chemistry problem all I had to do was call him.

After lunch on Saturday, Al went to do his rounds around our building complex, and I began cleaning the kitchen and putting the dishes into the dishwasher when I noticed a tiny piece of the lasagna crust still attached to the side of the baking dish. It was crustier than I thought and got stuck in the back of my throat. It wouldn't go down or up and worst of all I could barely breathe. I picked up the phone to dial 911 but realized I better come up with another idea since I couldn't talk. I couldn't stand the idea that I was going to choke to death on a piece of food like Mama Cass, the singer in The Mamas and the Papas band. I had no choice but to perform a self-imposed Heimlich maneuver. I positioned my fists between my breasts and dropped as hard as I could several times against the kitchen sink. I was ready to say goodbye to life, when the piece of crust popped out from the back of my throat. I shook so hard that I let myself slide down to the kitchen floor where I felt as if I was going to pass out from shock and I was better off being already on the floor. It had been my first experience face to face with death. I sat in the couch thanking God for helping me out and realized how one day we were here laughing or crying whichever the case and then the next day—or even a few minutes later—one could suddenly be gone for no darn good reason.

I was having fun with the psychology class until the teacher told us to team up with another student and go into the library for ten minutes where we were to sit across from each other and one of us was to make something out of a piece of soft clay. While the sculptor worked on his masterpiece he was to encourage his or her partner to guess what was being created, while using the same encouraging words over and over again. It sounded easy. Marc my partner would be the sculptor. It turned into the longest minutes of my life. Marc started by slowly rolling the soft piece of clay on the table.

I said right away, "It's a hotdog!" Talk about an easy assignment.

"You can do it, keep trying." He was not allowed to say anything else.

"It's not?" I was shocked. Okay, it's a small candlestick."

"You can do it, keep trying." He continued to smile at me, and as he held it in his hands.

"It's a pickle."

"You can do it, keep trying." His tiny crooked yellow teeth showed when he smiled. It was very distracting.

"It's a small cucumber."

"You can do it, keep trying."

"It's a small carrot."

"You can do it, keep trying."

"It's a tiny zucchini."

"It's not a vegetable, keep trying."

Since he had broken the rules of encouragement I dared to ask, "Is it a body part?"

"Yes, and that's all I can say."

I no longer could look into his perverted eyes. *Shit!* I thought, *he made a penis, and there's no way I'm going to say that word.* I crossed my hands in frustration and sat back into my chair. "I give up."

"Do you want to know what it is?" He asked obviously enjoying the psychological torture he was putting me through.

"Sure, go ahead, tell me," I dared him.

"It's a finger." And he laughed like the little rat he was. Knowing how much trouble I had with numbers of any kind, Ralph lent me his Casio scientific calculator, which was also equipped with a keyboard to enter data that could be viewed on a tiny but elongated screen. I couldn't believe that we were allowed to use the calculator in class during algebra, calculus or physics' tests, but who was I to question the college's guidelines? As I was playing with it one evening I noticed I could type not only equations but also words, complete sentences. I spent a week entering everything I found of any importance from my chemistry notes in class and the chemistry book. I was amazed at how much information it retained. I was going to pass my chemistry test even if I got caught cheating and thrown out of college. I didn't share my plans with Ralph but I did complain, "What am I going to do with chemistry, as a chiropractor? This is such an ill-use of my time and energy."

"There is a reason for it," Ralph possessed an old soul. "They make you take all those unnecessary and difficult courses to see if you've got what it takes to being a doctor. It's their way of weeding out the weak that don't have what it takes to make it through a four-year degree. Mom, if you pass your pre-meds, you've got it made after that."

I could only hope he was right. I used to brag of never suffering from headaches, but now the pounding kind visited me daily to the point I had to lie down and shut my eyes.

I sold the dinner theatre to Kyle and Gregg. Over the last seven years, they had worked for me as directors and actors. Kyle taught theatre at the Ocean County College and Gregg was an English teacher at the same college. They had been involved in theatre for twenty years and worked well as a team. Of all the people inquiring the purchase of my theatre, I felt they were the best-qualified.

They wanted to keep the theatre name, and that meant The Simy Dinner Theatre would continue to live on. They offered me $5,000 and I signed the theatre over to them. Mr. Ounuma liked them and approved of my choice.

When Mr. Armstrong passed the final chemistry exam papers around the classroom I courageously took my sophisticated hand-held calculator from my backpack and rested it innocently on the side of my table, close to my reach. First question on the test I didn't even know what it was about. Second question, I didn't know it either. Everything became foggy and a migraine took over my brain.

The teacher had his back to me and seemed busy sorting a stack of papers on his desk. Shaking from head to toes and barely able to breath I used the opportunity to reach for the calculator. I had entered my notes in alphabetical order, but nothing was even remotely associated with the first two questions on the test.

I turned it off, closed my eyes and started praying, "Dear God, please help me. As you know I studied very hard but I need a little help to pass this test. As you can see this teacher is an egomaniac and he made the test impossible to pass on purpose. He wants us all to repeat the course so that he'll never be out of a job."

I opened my eyes when I heard next to me Mr. Armstrong sarcastic words, "Nifty little thing you have here," he held my calculator in his hands. "I bet it can store a lot of information, hum?" he emphasized each syllable on the word information.

I looked up and dared him, "Yes it does, but there's nothing in there that even comes close to the questions in this test."

He kept his obnoxious smile as he turned to the class and spoke loud enough for everyone to hear him, "Like I said; nobody is going to pass my class unless they repeat it."

Bastard, I'm going to show you, I told myself. God knows how hard I studied; I am going to do great. And then I answered the questions the best I could.

Psychology was a very interesting subject. By learning about Ivan Pavlov and his dog's behavior associated with the sound of a bell with food, I learned something about myself. The reason I loved chocolate was because, just like Pavlov's dog, I could recall vividly, at least in my case, the satisfaction of the taste, smell, and feel of chocolate melting in my mouth. My mother's chocolate pudding, was a very rare and special treat, as she would say; "You have been a very good little girl, so I made you chocolate pudding, just for you."

I did not salivate at the thought of chocolate, but mentally I was induced to longing for it. According to Pavlov's discovery on the science of behavior, my addiction for chocolate was called a conditional reflex, caused by knowing that chocolate would give me emotional comfort. When I ate chocolate, I was emotionally satisfied.

As tradition went, for closing night Mr. Ounuma offered the cast and crew a free dinner at the hibachi table. It was also my last night at The Simy Dinner Theatre and I sat quietly eating while watching the cast and crew, who no longer were part of my life. One of the male actors sitting next to me was being rambunctious toward the young waiter, "Honey, bring me another glass of water, will you?" And he would try to touch the waiter's hand while the cast and crew laughed at his friskiness. He was rude and so were the cast. Being gay or not, one should always show respect for another human being.

That night was the closing chapter of my life at the Kobe and my beloved dinner theatre.

Rosanna had a good friend that worked for the Holiday Inn, and she gave me ten coupons that would allow me to stay free at any of their associated motels as I traveled back and forth between Georgia and New Jersey. The coupons were good for one year, and all I had to do if anyone asked was to say that I worked as a housekeeper for the Holiday Inn in Lakewood. Talk about lucky!

I did it! Yahoo, hooray! I passed all my classes including the abominable chemistry! But since my brain cells had to change gears from the arts to science courses, I had gone from being an A student with high honors, to a plain B. But after thinking it over I was proud of my achievement, B stood for Best, Bingo, and Bravo! And the few C's I got, oh well, that stood for congratulations.

Passing all the exams at Ocean County College gave me a lot of self-confidence. It proved that I could memorize anything if I studied hard enough—or in the case of being chewed up by Kuno the dog—panic could also work to my advantage. I was also proud to say that I memorized my social security number from repeating it over and over again at the college library. All my life I had been aware of my deficiency at memorizing a simple poem or the words to a song but I had just proven myself wrong, I did have a reasonable amount of memory, and should be able to handle all further studies.

I no longer feared science courses. Besides, Ralph had sworn that once I was done with pre-meds the worst was over. Ralph never lied not even to make me feel better.

I called Life Chiropractic College to confirm that in January, I would be taking the last two pre-requisites needed, Organic Chemistry II and Physics II at their college. If I signed up for those courses in New Jersey I couldn't start chiropractic college until the fall of the following year. That was too long to wait. I wanted to get on with my life. I chose to sign up for the ten-week course instead of rushing through the shorter option of five weeks. The lady I spoke to from the registrar's office told me not to worry about a place to stay, there were plenty of students renting rooms around the campus and she would let me know of one close by.

I liked the idea of finishing my last two pre-requisites at the college I would be attending for the next four years. It would give me a chance to get acquainted with the school. Once I finished those two subjects I would return to New Jersey and take a short break until Ralph and I moved to Georgia for the more serious studies ahead.

Ralph encouraged me to keep my eyes open for scholarship offers while at Life Chiropractic College.

I had absolutely no luck with used cars, so I asked Ralph his opinion on new ones. The old jalopies I had been driving were not to be trusted even if free. I needed a reliable car to drive to Georgia. Ralph found in Consumer's Report that the Saturn brand had gotten rave reviews. I'd never been to Georgia, but I knew it wouldn't be a skip and a jump and making the trip alone I needed dependable transportation.

I took the $5,000 I made on the sale of the theatre, added the difference from what I had saved, and bought a brand new red Saturn. I left the rest of the money in the bank.

Winter of 1993

Steve's new girlfriend, Diane, was pregnant and it looked like they were not only staying together but possibly getting married. I crossed my fingers. My grandson was due around July and I couldn't wait.

Papa called this morning. He had not given up on the idea of having my brother's body autopsied. "Don't worry," he lowered his voice. "I'm being very careful not to let Alice know that I suspect her. You're the only one that knows my plan. I won't even share my suspicions with your mother. Alice is her confidant and she tells her everything."

Papa was a very cautious person and I felt better after talking to him. But now I carried an unforgivable burden to haunt me for the rest of my life, my brother had told me the truth and I had not believed him. Alice had us all baffled and in many ways, I had also fallen prey of her charismatic personality.

Over the weekend I said goodbye to my chiropractic friends and mentors. Dr. Peruzzi made me swear that I'd write to him. Dr. Holdman's came to the front door as I was running down the steps and yelled at the top of his lungs, "Remember what I said, if you use the intention of healing on your patients, you will be a great doctor!"

I waited until the day before leaving New Jersey to say goodbye to Mr. and Mrs. Ounuma, Jerry the bartender, and the waitresses. Mrs. Ounuma handed me a large basket with all kinds of Japanese dried goods to take with me to school. I cried, and Mr. and Mrs. Ounuma hugged me instead of just bowing.

January 3rd, at 6:30 in the morning, my car was packed with a pillow, a blanket, a set of bed sheets, my classical guitar, Mrs. Ounuma's gift basket, a suitcase with clothes, the two wooden barrels used as props for "The Playboy of the Western World," the dissection picture book, and a map with directions on how to get to Life Chiropractic College in Smyrna, Georgia. I hugged Al, Ralph, and Steve, adjusted my car seat and buckled up. I took a lungful of its intoxicating new car smell and waved back as I drove away.

On the highway I felt light as a feather, empowered by the classical radio station playing a Bach piece, it befitted my newfound independence. I let myself be emotionally transported as if in a trance to the beat of what sounded like a prolonged drum roll that kept on beating. I drove straight into the welcoming horizon ahead.

Once the sun went down, I began looking for a Holiday Inn. I found one in Fayetteville, North Carolina.

Once in the room, I set my suitcase on the extra bed, took my shoes off, pulled off the starched flowery bed cover and threw it over a seat. Then I laid on my back on top of the thin brown blanket. Kind of silly, but it was the second time that an eye specialist in Freehold came to my mind. He entered the exam room with a partially stained white shirt not quite tucked into his pants. He was out of shape and his disheveled unkempt look took away my confidence of him as a doctor. Earlier on, while taking my pre-meds; his image had also been on my mind. He was there to re-assure me that I could do just as good if not better. Characters like him had become my biggest source of self-confidence. Anything they had achieved I could do it too. I went to turn the shower on in the bathroom. Then I returned to my room to get my pajamas from my suitcase.

When I returned to the bathroom the smell of the hot water running made me gasp for air. I immediately turned the water off and closed the bathroom door so the polluted fumes would remain away from the bedroom. I went downstairs to complain to the front desk girl that their water smelled like some kind of nasty chemical. She told me that was normal in North Carolina and she was used to it.

I didn't feel like having who-knew-what kind of chemicals were in the water penetrate through my skin pores. I skipped the shower.

I awoke exactly one minute before my alarm clock went off the next morning and I lay there appreciating the self-discovery that over the years I had developed a special talent, a dependable internal clock. Such aptitude had grown most likely from teaching guitar for thirteen years.

After a while I just knew when a half-hour private lesson or a one-hour group class was over without even checking my wristwatch. But for occasions like these where waking up on time was a vital necessity I still used my faithful alarm clock.

Once back on the highway I got myself comfortably situated behind a truck. If the truck driver speeded I knew it was safe to speed too. Being up high in their cabin, they had a great advantage point, they could see the highway police cars way ahead of them. In many ways, I missed my old music van where I sat a lot higher than in my Saturn. The other thing I noticed about my car was that it possessed no pick-up power but being brand new made me very happy.

Marietta, Georgia

I imagined that driving through the southern states I would encounter narrow dusty road, lots of polluted lakes and at least one old farmer seated on a rock holding a fishing pole, and folks like Elly May and Granny from the show *The Beverly Hillbillies* would be standing by an old rundown wooden shack and wave at me as I drove by. Instead, I found the southern roads to be super modern highways no different from the northern states, except for the weird large vegetation along the road. They owned odd-shaped heads and long stretched-out arms that could be taken for green monsters out of a science fiction movie. If I were a child growing up in the south I wouldn't be caught dead looking outside my window at night. Those tall, weeping cypress trees—as I learned their names later on—were a bizarre sight.

I had driven through some major traffic jams in my life, New York City, the suicidal city traffic of Lisbon, and crossed many long bridges, and tunnels but was taken by surprise when I reached Atlanta and found myself in a super highway of five lanes that ended in a roundabout circle. I drove around and around looking for a sign that read north or an arrow pointing to Marietta or Smyrna. Finally, I got my courage up and began cutting into one lane at a time until I was able to exit. The price of gasoline was one third of the gas in New Jersey. I filled my tank like a gas glutton and got directions to Cobb Parkway and the apartment where I'd be living for the next ten weeks. The college's admission office had arranged for my stay with two other chiropractic students.

   It was late when I arrived at the address, an impressively large apartment complex. A tall girl half asleep in pajamas opened the door and when I said my name, she led me to my room and then pointed to the bathroom across the hallway and disappeared on me. To my astonishment, the room being rented had no furnishings. It was late, I was tired and for one night only I figured I could sleep on the floor. I got my suitcase, bed sheets, blanket, and pillow from my car and after brushing my teeth I was ready to go to sleep. There was no heat in the room. I remained dressed, wrapped the blanket around my shoulders and lay on the carpet with the pillow under my head. But in order to sleep on a hard surface, fat was needed to compensate for a missing mattress. And that was the night I wished I had a weight problem. The carpet had no rubber padding. It had been laid directly on the cement floor. After rolling from side to side for maybe a half an hour, I doubled the thin cotton blanket in half and lay on top hoping it would provide a cushion to my hips and shoulders. But it was hard to relax the muscles while shivering, and when the calves' muscles went into spasms, I stood swiftly and began doing jumping jacks. It helped to raise my body heat and get rid of the charley horse but I knew better than to lie on the floor again. *I need to get myself tired enough to fall asleep sitting down,* I told myself. I started dancing like I had seen the Native American Indians doing during a Powwow a while back. Keeping the blanket over my shoulders and holding it tight around my chest I jumped and jumped and jumped, and when I was out of breath I sat on my pillow against the corner wall waiting for the morning to come.

I awoke with the sun on my eyes. My roommates were gone. After a super long well-deserved hot shower, I looked up on the yellow pages of the phone book in the kitchen, for the address of a military surplus store, close by. Michael had told me several times how much he loved sleeping on an army cot when he was living in the attic at the Arnold Theatre. I figured it would be cheaper than buying a mattress to use for only ten weeks.

After purchasing the cot, I headed to the chiropractic college. It was only a ten-minute drive from the apartment. The campus was not much different from the community colleges I had attended, and I felt comfortable. The staff was very welcoming, and their southerners' accents, made them even more charming. The only thing that shocked me into complete disbelief considering it was 1993, were the Ku Klux Klan members going about their business of hate. Seeing them on television and in the movies, was not the same as when they stood a few feet from me, like poison snakes ready to bite. Five of them, dressed in their customary white gowns and hoods, were standing by the traffic light handing out their propaganda pamphlets. One of them began walking towards my car. I rolled my window up. The light turned green and I pressed my foot hard on the gas pedal.

Oh, my goodness, what a horrible night, the cold creeped up from the cement floor up the cot's thin canvas material, and because of the position I was being held in, I couldn't find a comfortable position. As if I didn't have enough to contend with, Melinda the roommate next to my room liked to sleep to the loud sound of rap music.

Still, I wasn't going to give up that easily, and made up

my mind to try one more night sleeping on the cot; maybe I could get used to it and to the rap music.

Exhausted from two nights of barely any sleep I slept straight through. But in the morning my legs and back didn't respond to my brain's order to get up. I told myself not to panic and instead to analyze the situation like a mature adult. Slowly I turned on my belly and used my legs and feet like a small child would do to reach the floor. Once I was off the cot, I curled up on the floor, in a fetal position, then extra carefully I stretched my back on the ground and kept repeating those two movements over and over again until I felt comfortable enough to stand. To my surprise I was able to walk. I carried the cot to the car and drove to the military surplus store hoping they would take it back.

The owner and his wife were very kind and exchanged it for a four-inch foam pad. From there I paid a visit to the Salvation Army and bought two thick sleeping bags, one to cover the foam, the other to be used as a blanket.

I couldn't believe it, the foam pad turned out to be more comfortable than any mattress I had slept on. Monday would be my first day at the chiropractic college and I was more than ready to start.

My two roommates, Sally and Melinda were as different as night and day. Sally was a tall, shy twenty-four years old. When she spoke the soft tone of her voice reminded me of an eight-year-old. She had an angelic face and wore a constant smile that came across as forced. I had never met anyone so sensitive but it fitted with her romantic ideals. All she talked about was how much she loved the boy at school, two quarters ahead of her. They had sex twice in his car, and then she made the mistake of confessing her crime to a church member. She had to go before a board and was almost thrown out of the church. Her religion required her to wear a chemise while showering to protect her from sinful thoughts while bathing. And she had to read the bible every night before going to bed.

Melinda made it clear as soon as we met, that she was the boss in the apartment. She had long straight red hair, the color my father referred to as tomato soup. He hated tomato soup. Melinda was obese and just over four and a half feet tall. Her head seemed too small for her body but being twenty-two years old she got away with it. Like Aunt Heydee used to say, "There's no such thing as an ugly young girl."

Melinda was also a control-freak, and Sally and I were reprimanded daily if things were not run her way. Neither Sally nor I were allowed to touch the thermostat even though it was winter and some mornings the temperature read 55 degrees. Melinda warned us, "This is my place and you're renting it from me. I don't like heat in my apartment. If you don't like it, you can move." Maybe because she was so plump, she had extra sweat glands.

The roads in Georgia amazed me. They had been built to go through Marietta, Smyrna and other towns, with a middle lane that very few drivers used unless they were making a turn into a parking lot on the other side of the road. Even during traffic jams nobody used that lane. What a waste of road space. I concluded that it was a southern thing. But I was from the north so I drove on it. Drivers would give me the finger and others just stared at me as if I was committing a crime. I just waved back at the fools and went on my merry way. It was their choice if they wanted to remain stuck in traffic.

Physics II and Organic Chemistry II was going well. I liked the teachers, they didn't mind answering questions or overseeing the lab experiments. But I was a nervous wreck during chemistry class, from witnessing some of my classmates act like spoiled children. These were the future doctors of chiropractic and their malice was the worst I had ever seen towards a teacher.

Poor Dr. Gounder, he used to teach at a medical school and was probably used to being respected by his students. The wise-guys in class made him repeat the stuff over and over again, laughing at his Indian accent and then complained straight to his face that he should quit teaching and go back to India. He definitely had the patience of a saint to put up with so much verbal abuse. Luckily, I was able to follow what he wrote on the board, because he explained each problem, over and over again, for their benefit.

I finally got my courage up last night, and at one in the morning I knocked at Melinda's bedroom door. She yelled, "What is it?"

"It's me. Do you think you can lower the music just a little, so I can sleep?"

"I like my music loud. Just keep your door closed." She yelled back from her bedroom.

I did keep my door closed, but her bedroom was next to mine and the sound came straight through the walls. She was such a spoiled brat!

Ralph called and reminded me to take a look at the scholarship opportunities. I found them posted on the wall of the financial aid department. The one that made the most sense to apply for was the Harvey Lillard Scholarship, which offered full year tuition. They required three letters of recommendation, my own letter telling them why I deserved to get the scholarship, and also proof of what I had done for the betterment of a minority community.

I had all the requirements they asked for. One free year of school would mean less money I had to pay for my government loan when I graduated from chiropractic college.

A very flamboyant student walked into the chemistry class wearing a red wide-brim hat, a long dark blue coat, a red scarf, and carrying more than she could handle, like one overflowing backpack on each shoulder and two handbags full of books and papers. She always arrived late and it was almost guaranteed that she would inadvertently drop something before reaching her seat in the front row. But I noticed that she was not nasty like the others, she made her questions politely and always said thank you. One day, she sat next to me in class and said, "Hi, my name is Leila and I've noticed that you're always taking notes. Do you mind if I borrow them? I'm so lost in this class."

I wondered if I had a sign over my head, come get your chemistry notes here. Of course, I took notes, and at home I reviewed them, and cautiously compiled them into an understanding reading format. From those notes I created a log of questions and answers. I told Leila she could borrow everything I had, but she was only interested in the logs. She was five years younger, a little overweight and a tad shorter than me. We became friends.

The refrigerator in our apartment was always crammed with Melinda's food, leaving Sally and I barely any space available to store our food. Sally used a spot on the upper shelf of the refrigerator door where her weekly ration of seven small veggie burritos were perfectly squeezed in as if saying, sorry for taking so much space.

I liked having fresh vegetables and fruit on hand, but because the refrigerator was always packed tight with Melinda's food, I kept my fruit in a bowl on top of the dining room table and I only bought veggies to last two or three days.

I divided the meals I cooked into three tiny plastic containers, but I still had a hard time placing them into the freezer box. If I was not careful opening the freezer door, I was guaranteed to have a package of Melinda's frozen burgers or a frozen chicken fall out. Last night I injured my right toe when one of her frozen packages of ground meat fell out of the crammed freezer.

I did not mind helping Leila with her studies, by coaching her it reinforced my own knowledge. She had been professionally diagnosed with dyslexia and as such she was provided with special arrangements for testing, like longer time to finish a written test and our college even provided her with a private tutor. I told her not to feel bad, I also had multiple learning disabilities, and even though I hadn't been tested, I was most likely also dyslexic because I was very slow at comprehending physics and chemistry and often I even caught myself writing in reverse. I also had a weak system; I was highly allergic to formaldehyde, a serious problem in hand if I was going to handle the fumes in dissection lab in the near future. I was also partially deaf, the reason I always sat in the front row. And the English language was hard for me even after so many years in the US. Oh yeah, and I had to use glasses, otherwise I couldn't see the blackboard from far away. She agreed with me, we were special and our weaknesses made us sisters under the skin.

Leila took me under her wing. She invited me to go with her to the free chiropractic adjusting clubs at the college.

The clubs were open classes being held by students about to graduate in a year that were eager to practice their technique by offering adjustments to other students. I attended three adjusting clubs: Gonstead, Activator, and SOT which was short for Sacral Occipital Technique. I was a bit scared, to be in the hands of students but I did volunteer to be adjusted at each meeting so that I could experience at firsthand how each technique felt and worked.

All the techniques followed a very strict list of rules in order to find the subluxation, the vertebra that needed to be adjusted. For the Activator Technique the students used a hand-held instrument to deliver a gentle impulse force to the spine and address the subluxation. SOT was practiced by using blocks under the hips. Both techniques were very gentle but used numerous and detailed steps to get to the subluxation in need of correction.

On the other side of the spectrum, The Gonstead Technique was done manually and very harshly. The method had been created by a man, named Gonstead, supposedly a former farmer and a butcher, prior to becoming a chiropractor. The problem was that he not only had arthritic hands, but he was also a tough heavyset guy, and when you added force with big fat crooked fingers the technique was close to a lethal weapon in my humble opinion. The students at the Gonstead club, mostly guys, were fanatical about the method, and twisted their fingers and made a fist to apply the adjustment and they were like Gonstead clones. I went to that club once with Leila and swore never to let them touch me again. One of the students moved my neck and my lower back in both directions like a nutcracker, and I was so sore afterward that I couldn't walk straight for the rest of the evening.

What I really wanted to learn was the Toggle Technique, which was what Dr. Peruzzi had used on me. But that technique didn't have a club, and I was stuck with having to wait until I started my regular chiropractic curriculum.

The students walked around the campus roaring about their elected method being better than all the rest. I became overwhelmed and confused with so many choices. I thought there was only one-way of adjusting the spine but it looked like there was more to adjusting than I had imagined possible. I told Leila not to count on me to attend anymore clubs with her, they took away the time I needed for studying.

Sally invited me Friday night to go with her to a party at the clubhouse on campus. It consisted of a large room packed with young people standing and talking to each other and drinking.

Sally wouldn't let go of my arm as we walked into the crowded room and kept right on walking until we exited through the other door. "I can't stand places like these," she cried. "It's like a meat market, for men to pick up women."

I didn't see anything bad about it except for being noisy and filled to capacity, but just to make her happy I rolled my eyes to show I was in complete agreement with her and drove her home.

Sally wanted to go to the party because she was hoping to see Larry the love of her life. She cried all the way home.

Leila told me that Dr. Williams, the president of Life Chiropractic College, believed that it was not important how well we did scholastically, what was most important was how good we were at adjusting the spine and getting people well again. That sounded a lot like Dr. Peruzzi. She encouraged me to take advantage of the free Wednesday morning lectures to learn more about chiropractic philosophy.

Dr. Williams had been responsible for starting Life Chiropractic College and supposedly he was a great speaker. Leila took pride in teaching me the ropes around the college. I planned on attending the philosophy seminar with her.

Since arriving to Life Chiropractic College, I had to let go of my nickname, Ronnie and use my given name on all paperwork including written exams. The name Ronnie now belonged in New Jersey. I thanked God, for giving me the opportunity to be me.

Just about every night Sally came to my room to talk about Larry. I felt more like a mother than a roommate. She just wanted someone to listen and I didn't have the heart to tell her to get on with life. "I never meant to sin," she said last night. Her eyes were red shot. "I just wanted to please him so that he would love me," she sobbed. "We met at the cafeteria this morning and he said he loved me, but if I'm not available to be his, he'll have to date someone else. What am I going to do?" She made a question but didn't give me time to respond. "I wish he would ask me to marry him." Her eyes were fixated into space. She was expressing her romantic thoughts out loud, and I understood her completely. "But we can't be married. He'll never be accepted by my church. My only hope is to find a boy in church who will fall in love with me and ask me to marry him and then," she stopped as if experiencing a lovely vision. "Then, I don't have to continue chiropractic college." Her eyes lit up and her voice became joyful. "I want to get married and have at least five children. I'm not asking for too much am I?"

Her brother was gay and her mother had a girlfriend. As far as the church she belonged to, her mother and her brother were not welcome due to their so-called aberrant lifestyles. Sally cried a lot. I could hear her reading the bible at night in the bedroom next to mine. Between the pounding music on one side and the priestly words of the bible on the other, I came to appreciate my one side deafness by sleeping on my good ear.

When I think back to those days I wonder if Sally's wishes to become a mother came true. I hope she did and she's happily married.

Wednesday morning, I followed Leila to a huge gym-like auditorium on campus, to hear a guest speaker on chiropractic philosophy. It was like a scene from the movie

Logan's Run, where all the young people under thirty, hurried in eagerly to find the best seats in the house. Dr. Strudel entered center-stage and put his hands up as the crowd clapped cheerfully. He then went on to talk about the healing power of chiropractic, and how pathetic it was to spend so much time and money on education when all we needed was to learn to adjust the spine.

"Why are you here?" he asked.

Someone yelled from the crowd, "To be chiropractors."

Dr. Strudel pulled a twenty-dollar bill from his pocket and waved it in the air so that no one could miss seeing it, and yelled out, "No. The truth is that you're here for the money."

He kept the twenty-dollar bill up in the air, chanting on, "Money, money, money, money! Everybody sing with me. Money, money, money, money!"

I noticed several students shaking their heads, while others were laughing. But many were having a jolly time chanting along with Dr. Strudel.

I was so disillusioned with what I had witnessed that I called Ralph to let him know that I was experiencing second thoughts about becoming a chiropractor. Yes, I had a school loan to pay back, and wanted to make a decent living, but money was not my only goal. My priority was to be a healer like Dr. Peruzzi and Dr. Holdman.

Ralph told me what I already knew, but I needed the reinforcement of his words. "Mom, remember the crooked dentist in Freehold? In every profession there's always a bad seed spoiling it for everybody else. There are good and bad presidents, just like priests, lawyers, and of course chiropractors are no different, they're just people."

I did express my disappointment to Leila, but she loved and admired Dr. Strudel as much as Dr. Williams. "Veronica, trust me when I say that Dr. Williams is a great man and he has accomplished many good things for the future of chiropractic. If it weren't for him, this college would not exist. He made our college a reality and we must be more forgiving when a guest speaker is acting silly." I agreed with her only to make her happy.

I was doing okay with physics and chemistry, not great, just okay. I had come to terms with the fact that no matter how much I studied and knew my subject, I was not a good test taker; I passed them but not with flying colors. I blamed that on my language barrier. But I did feel confident that I had done reasonably well when I finished taking the first chemistry test. I came out of the classroom and noticed that about half a dozen of the students taking the test with me were already hanging out in the hallway.
"Not too bad, huh?" I said joining the group outside.
Gary an older student looked at me with fuming eyes. "Why do you say that?"
"You finished before I did, you must have done well," and not knowing when to shut up I added, "Everything the teacher taught us in class was on the test."
He made a closed fist in my direction. "Oh, I see, Miss Smarty Pants. You think you know everything, don't you? How would you like me to punch you in the mouth?"
I backed away as I was sure he was going to hit me.
Probably the only reason he didn't was because there were other students around. I walked away shaking from the experience, swearing to myself that from then on, except for Leila, I wouldn't talk or mingle with any students in my classes.

Sally must have knocked on my bedroom door, while I slept on my good ear; I awoke with the startling feeling of someone close to my face. "I think Melinda is a lesbian," she whispered.
"What?" I said half dazed. I got up and turned the light on. It was 10pm. I sat back next to her.
"Melinda uses all kinds of excuses to touch me; like

when we pass each other in the hallway," her eyes were wet and red and she took one of my Scotch tissues to blow her nose. "Melinda bumps her body into mine when we go by in the hallway as if it's an accident, and when she talks to me sometimes she touches my shoulders."

My goodness, she was homophobic. Poor thing, if Sally was a glass vase, she would have shattered a long time ago. It was beyond me how she was going to survive with the ups and downs of normal life once she finished college.

Friday night, I placed my acoustic guitar in the trunk of my car and drove up to the clubhouse at the college hoping to find some students to play guitar with. It was later than I thought, the crowd was dissipating. I was leaving the building and going through the foyer by the bathrooms when I saw two guitarists jamming-up on their acoustics. I stood watching them while thinking about my old days of teaching guitar. When they stopped playing, I asked the one smiling at me if he would let me play a tune on his guitar just for fun. He handed me his Yamaha classical guitar and I sat down and played "Romance Antigua." I had hit gold! They wanted me to play it over and over again. One of them told me he was disappointed that I didn't have my own guitar since he would like me to join them. I told him I had a guitar in my car and would be right back. I tuned my guitar to one of theirs and I started playing "Romance Antigua" once again. Chris and Justin, the two guitarists, were addicted to the tune, and a couple of people stood listening as one of them played bass and the other strummed along.

"Do you mind if the three of us go play inside the men's bathroom? I bet the acoustics in there will make this song beyond real!" Chris suggested.

Who was I to question something out of the norm? We took our guitars and the metal chairs with us and settled down to play close to the sinks. The bathroom was better than a music studio in the sense that the acoustics made our ensemble a phenomenal theatrical sound experience. Each time a guy would come in and remark what the heck was a woman doing in there, never mind that we were playing guitar in the bathroom, we would just keep playing as Justin would yell out, "Don't worry, she's cool." A musical bond had been created.

College students all over the world were naturally that way, they were the first to fight for liberty and freedom of expression, it was part of being young and I was definitely stagnant in the young mental mode. I loved school; and the simple atmosphere of pure ideals where one could learn the secrets of the wise. While I played with the two students I forgot all about Michael.

Melinda enjoyed strutting out of her bedroom butt-naked, while patting her wet red hair with a towel. Her breasts were humongous and since she was so short they drooped down to her waist. Poor Sally every time she caught sight of Melinda in all her naked glory walking around the apartment; she ran into her room and slammed the door behind her. I just remained seated at the dining room table and looked down at my books wondering if I should encourage her to have breast reduction. She sure enjoyed creating turmoil. When she saw me staring at her the first time she put on an exhibition, she shook her flabby butt at me and with a contempt look said, "This is the way I was born, and I've nothing to hide."

"I agree with being proud of whom we are, but do you see Sally or me flaunting our naked bodies around the apartment?"

"Sap, yeah, yeah, scrap, snap, strap, yeah, yeah," she called each word swiftly to a pulsating rhythm as her butt swung from one side to the other, on the way to her bedroom. She banged her door closed and within two minutes I heard the blasting thumping sound of her stereo.

Rosanna, my friend back home had become my pen pal and in her last letter she encouraged me to stick my foot out when Melinda walked by to make her fall on her face. If Rosanna was a cop she would probably shoot anyone that got in her way.

I spend the weekends studying, and whenever possible I rewarded myself by playing my acoustic guitar in my room. I sat cross legged on my foam pad and played sad love songs and classical tunes. Every day I thought about Michael, I couldn't help it. Often after playing a love song I stopped to wonder how he was doing.

I saved the more popular tunes for showing off my musical talents when Melinda or Sally was home. They were a lot younger than me and I assumed classical music was not their scene.

I made an appointment to see a gynecologist and have my breasts examined. I had a tiny blister on my right nipple, that wasn't going away. A gynecologist in Lakewood had told me it was nothing and that it would go away on its own, but three years had gone by and it was still there. It was the size of a pinhead but it leaked what looked like milk, and at times it bled for no reason. I just wanted to make sure I didn't have breast cancer. I asked Leila if she knew a woman doctor. She recommended Dr. Lawoski.

Dr. Lawoski confirmed that my nipple was fine and it was the result of one milk duct leaking. But, I had trichomoniasis, a common sexually transmitted disease. I knew Al could not have been the carrier since I couldn't even remember the last time we had been romantic. I told Dr. Lawoski about Michael and she recommended I let him know so that he could take care of it. Usually men didn't have symptoms either, but they kept spreading the infection to their partners. She gave me enough metronidazole samples to cover for the full treatment and told me I'd be fine in two weeks.

Michael wrote back apologizing, and also thanking me for letting him know. He had gone to see a doctor who told him he would be fine after taking the medication. He also wrote that if I wanted to finish our relationship he understood how I felt.

My first impulse was to write back and ask, "What relationship?" Instead I wrote, "I love you too much to make such a decision." But during the night I couldn't sleep so I tore up my note and wrote, "Since you're so understanding, I accept the responsibility of terminating our relationship forever."

"P.S. If I don't get a response from you, it means you accepted my resolution. In that case this is the final chapter of our love for each other and we'll never meet again."

I found an underarm hair on my roll-on deodorant, this morning. Were my roommates using my toothbrush too? The thought of someone using my personal toiletries got me upset enough to give me the courage to question them. I waited for the right time to approach them preferably at the same time. That evening in the kitchen, Sally stood by the microwave waiting for her burrito to get heated and Melinda was busy chopping carrots on the counter, for her chicken soup. I held the deodorant at eye level. "Which of you is using my deodorant?" I did my best not to project any agitation in my voice.

"I don't use deodorant," Sally said. She took her burrito from the microwave and went to her bedroom to eat her dinner.

"I used it," said Melinda keeping her back to me. "I ran out of mine and haven't had time to buy another. You don't mind, do you?"

I laid the deodorant on the kitchen counter next to her peeled carrots. "It's yours now." And like Sally I walked away and closed my bedroom door.

The next day I bought a deodorant and a small straw basket just big enough to carry all my toiletries along with my hairbrush and soap to and from the bathroom and then storage it on the shelve under two bath towels, in my bedroom closet.

One morning, I was getting into my car in the school's parking lot, when I noticed an old pick-up truck with a South Carolina's license plate. The first thought to enter my mind was that Michael had come to my college to look for me. With my heart fluttering and visions of us hugging each other again, I remained seated in my car waiting. Half-hour later, two students climbed into the truck and drove off.

Children had more brains than me. I knew it was a pathetic self-created illusion and didn't know when to let go. Michael smoked and drank too much, he had a depressive nature, and I had seen him lose his temper with other people. With time, it would be only natural that we would lose our patience with each other.

Melinda and Sally couldn't remember the last time snow had fallen in Georgia and said I had brought the snowstorm, from the north.

They tried to dissuade me from going out since everything was closed and the roads would be like ice. I looked forward to the excitement of having my car skid just a little and told them, "In New Jersey five inches of snow is like drizzle for us Northerners."

I didn't know that in Georgia if it snowed they were not prepared to make the roads safe like in New Jersey. There were cars stranded all over the roads, and it felt great to be driving without any tribulations. A large lit up billboard at the Convention Center proclaimed that they were open and were holding a gun show event. It would be a unique experience to check it out. Besides, everything else was closed. When I drove into the Convention Center's parking lot there were maybe two dozen cars parked. The lot glittered with a thin sheet of slippery ice. But I refused to acknowledge that I had made a mistake driving there. Stubborn like a bull, like my mother used to call me when I was growing up, I got out of my car and taking baby steps while extending my arms out in case I fell, I made it across the lot and into the Convention Center.

I was done looking at guns within twenty minutes. I didn't like guns and would never own one. That day I must have had an ice skating angel on my shoulder, because I also made it safely back into my car.

Feeling lucky that I had not slipped on the parking lot and broken my back I drove home at five miles an hour.

While waiting to be called in to take the Physics exam, I sat cross-legged against the wall on the hallway, and concentrated on breathing and relaxing with my eyes closed. Smiling would help a lot before a test, but I didn't want anyone to think I was weird. I figured if I could relax by letting go of all thoughts, I could reach complete mental relaxation and do a lot better during the exam. The teacher called everyone in. I sat to take the exam but I didn't feel like rushing. Instead I looked around the room watching the other students taking the quiz and then I stared into the air, singing no particular tune in my head and in good spirits.

The teacher stopped by my desk. "I've been watching you. Aren't you taking the exam? You've only got twenty minutes left to answer all the questions."

"Oh, okay. Thank you for telling me." Like big deal! What was the urgency anyway?

I finished the test along with the other students. It wasn't until I left the room that it hit me. What had I done? Hypnotized myself into a state of careless stupid abandonment? What if I answered the questions wrong? If I had to stay in Georgia and live with Melinda for another ten weeks I would kill myself.

Whenever Whitney Houston came on the radio singing "I will love you forever," Michael came into my mind. I needed to be in love. I liked the feeling of being in love, even if nothing derived from it. Being in love meant that I was alive, even though I had lost all hope of ever seeing him again. He had not answered my letter.

Waiting with a bunch of other students to enter the next classroom, I found a corner spot and got busy writing a letter to my friend Rosanna, when a young man—blonde, blue eyes, and a smile that could sell any brand of toothpaste on television—sat next to me and introduced himself. Rick's interest in me took me by surprise. I didn't inform him of my marital or divorce status. I answered his first question with a lie. With the second question the lies flowed more easily. I became aware that I was purposely doing my best to attract him by giving him the answers he most likely wanted to hear from a sexy older woman. Greek Gods were not supposed to bother with mere mortals like me, and he was the personification of Adonis. His undivided attention made me feel as if I was the only real woman in the hallway. Obviously, he was fascinated by my mature looks and I felt the physical attraction between us growing with each second that ticked away. Reality only hit me when my class was called into the room. Rick was twenty-seven years old and would be graduating the following quarter. I was glad to say goodbye and leave things as they were, two ships passing in the hallway.

I received a letter from Rosanna. "Before you come back to New Jersey you must take your revenge on Melinda. Steal something of value, something that she finds dear to her heart. Later, if she refuses to give your rent deposit back you can use the stolen item to blackmail her." Rosanna didn't stop there, she called to reinforce her instructions and that I was a coward and had no pride and lacked any backbone if I didn't follow her advice. I said, "Okay, I'll do it."

Even though the idea of revenge sounded great, the thought of purposely stealing something from Melinda made me feel sick to my stomach.

Dr. Gounder didn't show up at the testing center. He had suffered a stroke and was in the hospital. Gary and other students were going around laughing as they announced aloud that it was the best thing that could happen, and they hoped he never come back. They were hoping for the chemistry exam to be cancelled on account of the teacher dying! I was horrified; it was at times like those that I felt ashamed of being part of the human race. But the test went on. God bless Dr. Gounder's soul, he had prepared the written test the day before he was taken to the hospital. I had no doubt in my mind that those immature malicious students had induced the professor's stroke from so much aggravation.

After the test I wrote Dr. Gounder an anonymous letter, "Dear doctor and teacher, I wish from the bottom of my heart that you recover soon and I want you to know that I admire you for putting up with so many ignorant people in chemistry class. In my opinion you are the best chemistry teacher I have ever had, and it is an honor to be in your class." I signed the bottom of the letter, "Please get well soon, from an anonymous student that cares."

I slipped the letter into his mailbox slot on his office door.

Melinda heard me playing guitar in my bedroom and knocked on my door. "I'm on my way to school but I wanted to tell you that you play very well." I opened my door to say thanks and she said, "I want you to know that I also appreciate good music and I love to sing too. I would love to sing in public someday. Okay, Gotta go to classes, goodbye."

Her birthday was in two weeks and it would be nice to make her dream come true. I made a note to find a place with karaoke and take her there for her birthday.

I was studying at the library in school when I heard my name. I looked up and it was good that I was seating. Rick stood in front of my table. Talk about charisma coming out of his pores. He was beyond handsome, everything about him was to be admired, his smile, his eyes, his blonde hair, his tall physique, his hands, his voice. I uttered one word, "Hi," and grasped my book closer to my chest like a life preserver.

"Do you want to go out with me Friday night?" and he pulled himself a chair. "I know a cozy Italian restaurant in downtown Atlanta." I wanted to say yes, and why wait, let's go right now, but instead my common sense took over. "Finals will be here soon," I could feel my face turning red. "And I'm very busy studying for them." It was the only believable answer I could come up with. A man had asked me out, a very attractive man, and that scared me. If alone with him I knew I'd be like a tiny insect caught in a spider's web.

"Okay then. How about going to the movies Saturday night? You need to have a break away from your studies." His voice was like music to my ears, but the wrong tune.

"Maybe another time." I opened my note book indiscriminately to a page. "And now if you'll excuse me, I need to get back to my studies." I looked down at the page in front of me.

He scribbled his phone number on a piece of paper and left. I threw the paper in the trash can. He was too young and too beautiful.

The following Monday Dr. Gounder showed up for class, much to the disappointment of several students. He entered the room without greeting us. He put his papers on his desk and stood for about a minute facing us, with his hands behind his back as if in deep thought. Everyone remained silent and all eyes were on him when he spoke. "I want to say thank you for the anonymous letter sent to me while I was in the hospital. It gave me the strength to get better faster." He pointed to the row where two students were seated way in the back of the room and putting his hands together as if praying he gracefully bowed toward them. "I know it was you who sent me that letter, thank you," his voice quivered with emotion.

The two students had a dumbfound look on their faces. I was the only one who knew. I thanked God for giving me the insight to write to him.

Melinda glowed with happiness when I told her I was taking her out for her birthday. When we entered the Karaoke bar she realized why. I ordered her favorite drink, a martini and to make her comfortable I asked her to join me singing one of my favorite songs, *Sweet Home Alabama*. Afterward she took over singing other tunes on her own. She did have a good voice.

On the way home, she demonstrated that she had some human qualities. "I appreciate what you did for my birthday," she said. "Thank you for taking me out to sing, on my birthday. That was very special, I didn't expect it."

The next day she was still in a pleasant mood, and she made dinner for Sally and me and the three of us had a good time talking about the man of our dreams. Melinda was not a lesbian like Sally told me. She just liked attention.

After taking Melinda out for her birthday, she became more amicable, so much so that she invited me to go dancing with her the following Friday to her favorite bar. She wanted me to meet Tom, whom she had met a week ago. She wanted to know what I thought of him. Sally couldn't go dancing with us, her church would not approve.

The bar scene was not for me. The music was too loud and it made it difficult for me to hear her. Neither Melinda nor Sally knew that I was partially deaf. I heard fine on a one to-one basis, it only became difficult when there was a lot of noise around me; then I was completely at a loss. I walked straight to the dance floor with the intention of spending the night dancing, that way I would not have to talk to anyone. I shouted to Melinda, "I'm going to stay here, dancing!"

"Why are you yelling?" she shouted back. "I'm not deaf, I can hear you."

I danced to two tunes when Melinda waved at me from the bar to come and join her, but I made believe that I didn't see her and kept dancing. She came to the dance floor, seized my hand, and without letting go she led me to the bar to meet Tom. He was an average-looking guy, and I wondered what he liked about Melinda. She was wearing her lowest cut blouse, so I figured that he liked short, red-haired girls with huge breasts. I also noticed that Melinda was flirting more with him than he did with her. When Melinda excused herself to go to the bathroom he must have felt that I was in line for his affection. I could tell he had asked me a question by the way he slightly tilted his head and then smiled, but I was no good at reading lips. I nodded a lot, hoping the answer to his questions was a yes. Finally, I began relying on the usual, "What?"

I felt his beer breath on my face. "I really like you," he said. "Do you like big-band music?"

I nodded even though I preferred rock and roll music.

I stood getting ready to go back to the dance floor. He stood too, and put his arm around my waist, just as Melinda approached us.

"Can't wait for me to leave so that you can make out after my girlfriend, huh?" She pushed him briskly away from me.

"I was just going to ask Veronica to dance," he said, sheep-like.

"Well, we're leaving," she said. I followed her. Surprisingly, she was not angry with me; instead she thanked me for going with her, it had helped her make up her mind about Tom. "Now I know he's the wrong guy for me, "she said. "My best bet is someone I met on the internet two weeks ago. I have this thing for tall, heavyset men, and a jelly-belly really turns me on," she laughed. "He's six foot tall, and according to his description, some extra weight around his middle. He likes the idea that I'm short and also a little on the heavy side." If Melinda was happy, that was all that mattered when living with her.

Sunday morning, I was studying at the dining room table when Sally came in and without a word sat by the window in the living room twirling her chair slowly around and around. Just as I was going to ask what bothered her, someone knocked at the front door. Two young men about Sally's age, dressed in black suits, white shirts, and black ties asked for her. One of them carried a black attaché case. I thought they were insurance people, but Sally had been waiting for them and welcomed them to come in and sit on the couch across from her chair.

"Do you want me to leave the room?" I stood.

"No, I'd rather you stay." She wriggled her hands on her lap and sat with perfect posture in her chair.

"So, tell me Sister Sally, have you had any sinful thoughts lately?" asked the one with severe acne.

I couldn't believe what I heard; those two guys were as old as her if not younger. I admit it; I was paying more attention to their conversation than my studies.

"Yes," she murmured. And said something else

afterward but I couldn't hear.

"You'll need to repent to clean yourself from damnation," said the other guy.

I had enough. I went into my room and played my guitar softly, just for me. A while later I heard a soft tap on my door. "They left. You can come out if you want."

"Thanks, but I'm going to take a nap." I heard her cry. I figured the two young men had made her feel like dirt and given her some sort of penance for having the normal feelings of a human being.

I was finally done with the finals in chemistry and physics and Thursday night I shared my dinner with Melinda and Sally and said our goodbyes since I was leaving early the next morning. I asked Melinda for my security deposit but she said, "Don't worry, I have your address in New Jersey, I'll mail you the check." That night Rosanna called me and I told her what Melinda said. She reminded me to steal something from Melinda or I would be sorry later.

My car was packed and ready to start my trip home within an hour after I got up. I left the foam pad in the room. Then, I opened Melinda's bedroom door. I stood in the doorway. I could hear Rosanna's voice in back of my mind, "Go ahead Ronnie, you know she's never gonna give you your security deposit. Take Melinda's favorite jewelry, make her suffer." *I don't want to make her suffer.* "Go ahead, take her favorite teddy bear; break her heart." *No! I'm not going to do such cruel thing.* I turned around and closed the door behind me, I *am who I am, and I choose not to do har*m. I walked out of the apartment feeling like I had accomplished a lot more than finishing chemistry and physics, I had finally grown up to stand on my own. If Rosanna asked me what I had taken from Melinda, I would tell her the truth, nothing. Like Papa used to say with pride before he retired, "I won't take a stamp from my office unless I pay for it. At night I sleep with a clean conscience."

But I was not as honest as my father and while at college I had become aware of my large collection of pens and pencils taken from banks, stores, or any place where I was handed one to sign something or another. I also collected at least one towel from each hotel or motel where I stayed overnight. But that was a tradition, a practice that started when I first came to the US in 1962. I didn't want to blame anyone but the truth was that Nelly, my mother-in-law and Al, were the ones that told me hotels expected their guests to leave with at least one or two towels and as such they were already included in the price of the room.

~ *Chapter Six* ~

COLLEGE, DATING, AND SEX

1993

Lakewood, New Jersey

Spring of 1993

Having to stay with Al until June, turned out to be unbearable. I was irritable, and far from being a pleasant person to live with. I even felt sorry for him. I began to look for a job that could keep me occupied until I left for Georgia with Ralph. I thought it would be a good idea to look for a position in a chiropractic office, so I could get an idea of what to expect when I opened my own practice.

    I stopped at a chiropractic clinic in Lakewood and was hired as a physical therapist. When I showed concern for not having any experience, Dr. Smith the chiropractor, told me not to worry; they were going to train me on the job, starting the following Monday.

I always thought Ralph would be the first one to get married, but I was wrong. Diane and Steve married over the weekend and my grandson was due at the end of July.

    The wedding was an intimate affair mostly family and

close friends of the bride and groom. I didn't have time to look for something to wear but Diane's older sister lent me a beautiful glittery bluish green long skirt and a silk white shirt.

Diane's mom prepared all the food for the wedding reception, including the wedding cake and several delicious homemade chocolate cakes. I liked Diane's family; her parents and her sisters were very kind and straightforward people. They were German and I associated their forthright ways with Papa. I prayed to God to bless my son Steve, his sweet wife Diane.

After a week of working at Dr. Smith's chiropractic office I found it dreadful going to work even though it was only temporary. Dr. Smith was a dishonest person and Laura and Suzanne the front desk girls, were part of the fraudulent click. Dr. Smith wanted me to enter patient visits on the charts as if they had been in for treatment. He also had an arrogant attitude problem which was complimented by the front desk girls, and Roger, his parrot. Dr. Smith had taught Roger more than a few words. His parrot repertoire was a mimic of Dr. Smith's sentiments and Roger's high-pitch voice made it most annoying as he repeated over and over again, like a broken record lines such as, "Get me the hell out of here!" and "You f…… idiot, stop staring at me," and "I hate working here."

Dr. Smith used to have Roger in the waiting room but the patients complained about the language and he was forced to move Roger into his private office at the end of the hallway.

One morning I witnessed a male patient asking Suzanne, with an angry tone in his voice, "I received these papers from the insurance company and noticed that you're charging them for treatments on dates when I didn't come in." He positioned the papers on the counter facing her.

"And on these days," he pointed at the bill and then taped on it vigorously. "I did come in but you charged them for a bunch of services that were never provided. I demand to know what's going on!"

Suzanne answered unsympathetically, "Do you want to collect a good compensation for what you suffered in the car accident?"

"Yes, but."

She cut him off, "There is no but here." She stood from her seated position behind the front desk and moved her upper body forward. I thought she was going to punch him. Maintaining her contemptuous look, she said, "The more money we show in care provided to you, the more money you get. But if you don't like that, I'll be happy to take those charges off." She sat back in her chair.

"Oh no, if I'm gonna get more money, you go right ahead and charge them whatever you want."

I was very disappointed with the patient's greed. I did not look forward to going to work anymore if anything I felt that by working for them, I was a member of their gang.

I applied for a government loan to pay my tuition at the college, but thanks to Ralph's encouragement I also collected three letters of recommendation from friends, and several copies of newspaper clippings, awards, and letters showing my past community involvement with minority groups. Like Ralph said, I had nothing to lose by applying for the Harvey Lillard Scholarship. He really believed I deserved to get the award. I wrote my introduction letter, as they requested and then I asked Ralph to proofread it, and he helped me to cut it down to two pages.

I drove over to visit Dr. Holdman, but to my great disappointed he had sold his practice and moved to Florida, a month prior.

Dr. Peruzzi invited me to a chiropractic social meeting. They met in the evening once a month, to talk about chiropractic philosophy. I did not share with him my tribulations with Dr. Smith; I was too embarrassed to tell him. I knew he would tell me to quit or worst like going to Dr. Smith's office and telling him he was a disgrace to our profession.

At the chiropractic gathering he made his opinion heard, "It's demeaning to our profession the way modern chiropractors dress in jeans and a short sleeve tee-shirt when treating their patients."

The other chiropractors said they were going to dress the way they wanted. Dr. Peruzzi stood and yelled, "You're all pathetic!" I followed him out the door.

He could be a bit of a dictator, but at the same time I could see his point. He did look a lot more refined than the other doctors attending the meeting.

He was too old fashioned and adamant about his ways. When I drove him back to his house, he turned his negative attitude on me for wearing jeans. "A woman should always look like a lady and wear a dress or a skirt, particularly when she's going to be a doctor."

Feeling like a reprimanded youngster I decided to stop visiting him for a while.

I also had a horrible experience that night, actually two bad experiences. The first one happened at the chiropractic meeting when a plate of fresh strawberries came my way and instead of taking a small ladylike bite, I opened my mouth wide to insert a whole strawberry but it was larger than I thought and far from ripe. My jaw popped on the right side, followed by sharp jotting pain. I had just developed what everybody called, TMJ. When I was a kid I used to love listening to Aunt Heydee's clicking jaw as she ate next to me. I guess I liked it so much that God decided to provide me with the same affliction.

The second tragedy that same night happened while

driving home. By the time I dropped Dr. Peruzzi off at his house and stayed listening to him complaining about everyone he knew, it was one in the morning when I left him. Anxious to get home I took a short cut on an isolated road. Thank goodness, I was going slowly when I hit a pothole on the road. The car dropped right afterward on its back-right tire followed by the front left tire blowing out. The car went off the road and into a small ditch where it laid on its side like a wounded animal. I gave thanks for not being hurt and then took an assessment of my surroundings. It was pitch dark except for the silvery half-moon shining her guiding light on the country road pavement. I began walking at a fast pace toward a single light coming from a building in the distance. It was a gas station, and to my delight still open but the night attendant had no sympathy for my predicament and would not let me use the phone. Thank God, there was a payphone outside. I dialed the number for the Saturn road-help and speedier than lightning they sent a tow truck to fix the tires and I was back on the road in no time. Hurray for my Saturn!

Monday morning while going from one room to another, checking on patients at the chiropractic clinic I heard, "Help! Help! Get me the hell out of here!" I went to the front desk where Laura and Suzanne sat chatting and said, "Roger is being a pain again. Can one of you, please stop him before he starts shouting his usual profane list of not so decent words?"

"Stop bothering us. We're busy," said Suzanne. "You go take care of it."

I knew better than to bother Dr. Smith. He had taught Roger to speak and got his jollies from listening to him. As I walked by the last two treatment rooms, I became aware of the yelling coming from the treatment room on my right, not Dr. Smith's back office where he kept the parrot. I opened the door to find the patient's table no longer flat, instead it had gone up with the patient on it, and two of the electrodes on his lower back had gone flying into the air while the other two, still stuck to his mid-back were stinging him with higher electric impulses. "Get me the hell out of here!" He shouted at me.

I always forewarn the patients not to play with any of the buttons on the sides of the adjusting tables, when they were bored or curious. But sometimes they didn't listen.

I received a short letter from Melinda. "Dear Veronica, I hope this letter finds you well. I have great news to share with you. Remember Jason the guy from the Internet I told you about? We met, and it was love at first sight. He's wonderful and on our second date he surprised me with a pair of soft slippers because he knew how sensitive my tiny feet are. We are getting married next year." She had enclosed my deposit check.

It was a week for great news in the mail. Ralph and I received two letters from Life Chiropractic College in Georgia. I had passed my two final pre-requisites. The other letter stated we had been accepted to the college. Ralph and I began making plans to start school the following month. We also received a letter from Judge Buczynski, my divorce had become final.

Francis and Rosanna were happy for me. But Tracey got angry, "How dare you divorce Al after all he did for you? You're wrong to leave such a good man and go away to school for four years; how can you do that to Al?" Some years later, when her husband died she called to ask if it was alright with me if she asked Al out on a date. I gave her my blessings.

Dr. Smith told all his patients that he was against drugs, but he was a hypocrite. He had me go to his red sports car parked in back of his building to get his prescription drugs, as he sometimes would forget to bring them in with him.

But being that he was such a hyper-neurotic individual I could see why he needed to take so many tranquilizers.

Twice a week he sent me out on a specific errand. He would take from the safe in his office three to four thousand dollars in cash, and I was to go to the post office or the bank and change it into cashier's checks. He bragged about soon having enough money to open a restaurant. He also said he wished he had become a surgeon, instead of a chiropractor, because then he would be making a lot more money. He was a disgrace to the human race.

One morning he entered the front office and unexpectedly threw his car keys at me, and when I didn't catch them, he laughed and said, "Look at those slow reflexes," he turned to the two office girls that were just as amused as him and added, "She's definitely retarded. How are you ever going to make it in chiropractic college, is beyond me."

I felt emotionally abused. Even if I was retarded, he had no right to make fun of my inadequacies.

His abusive nature didn't stop there, the next day Dr. Smith yelled at me for not entering in the charts that all the patients had come in.

"You want me to lie?" I said flushed with frustration.

"You work for me, and you do what I tell you, if you want to keep your job. Do you understand English?"

I didn't like being yelled at, and out of desperation I wrote on the charts that the patients had been there every single day of that week including Saturday when the office was closed. I expected him to fire me when I handed him the charts. "Is this what you want me to do?" I asked.

He looked briefly at one of them, "Exactly. Now you're doing your job!" Then he took hold of my arm and hauled me to what looked like an x-ray room. I had never been in there before. "It's about time that you earn your money, you need to learn how to take x-rays," he said.

A female patient was waiting in the room against a wall

plate, probably brought in by one of the girls in the office. He told me to get behind a metal partition. "Stay, and watch what I'm doing," he said. He pressed a couple of numbers into a keyboard that looked a lot like a mini computer connected to an old metal box as tall as me. "Go ahead press that button, and then this one," he ordered me.

"Shouldn't I first learn what the buttons are for?"

"You ask too many questions. Just do what I'm telling you."

I was not ready to give in so easily. X-rays were too medical and invasive in my opinion. Besides all that, I didn't feel safe being in his x-ray room. What if his old equipment was leaking radioactive material? "Am I not supposed to have a license to do this type of work?" I asked.

He pushed me with his body against the machine, his belly against my back like a large rubber tire. He pressed the buttons and then released me. "Get out of here."

I was more than glad to be out of there.

Every morning Dr. Smith held a staff meeting, and it was all about reinforcing his crooked business. All his clientele come directly from referrals by a specific lawyer in Freehold. If anyone came to his clinic and asked to be treated by Dr. Smith we were to say, he didn't work there, unless they had a referral from a certain lawyer in Freehold. The building he owned had already been put under his mother's name so it couldn't be taken away from him. I told Al about all this, but he said, "Don't worry, you only work there, it's none of your business if your boss is a crook." But my mind was made up, I wanted my paycheck, and quit.

Rosanna asked me to wait until the end of the week. She wanted to do a little investigating of her own. She was going to visit the lawyer that Dr. Smith worked with, and act as if she had been in a car accident. Rosanna called to tell me about her experience with the lawyer. "I liked him. He was not pushy if anything he was very nice, even offered me a cup of tea and really listened to what I had to say, as I acted like I had been in a major car collision. Before leaving his law office, he handed me Dr. Smith's card and said, "'I heard this chiropractor is very good with cases like yours, if I was you I'd make an appointment to see him. Just tell him you spoke to me, give him my card and he'll take good care of you.'" Ronnie, if I had been the victim of a car accident most likely I would be seeing Dr. Smith."

"Two slithering snakes," I said. "Okay, I'm going to write my letter of resignation tonight."

"Let me write your letters."

"I feel like I should be the one writing, since I work there," I said meekly.

"You need two letters. One should be addressed to Dr. Smith and the other to his staff," she said, "I'm a professional writer and I'll do a better job than you. Besides, it will give me a lot of pleasure to do that."

Her insistence in writing the letters made me feel like inadequate, but I didn't have the courage to speak up since she was my friend.

Rosanna stopped over at our apartment the next day. She had written not two, but three letters. One was addressed to Dr. Smith, his dishonest conduct and his obnoxious parrot. The other two letters were very specifically addressed to each girl. Rosanna had a lot of anger inside her and didn't even get along with her family. Writing gave her the opportunity to air out her personnel frustrations. Still, I took the three letters to the chiropractor's office and put them in his mailbox outside, along with a side note stating that I'd be back after their lunchtime to pick up my paycheck as I had no intentions of returning to work. I was at their front door at two exactly, and Suzanne came out and handed me my paycheck without a word.

When I got home, there was a message on our answering machine.

"This is Dr. Smith and I just called you Ronnie to wish you a happy, but short, life."

Such nasty message prompted me to call several insurance companies and the New Jersey Board of Chiropractors. I shared with them my experiences as an employee of Dr. Smith.

Having suffered several mishaps with medical doctors I did not look forward to using them, but I thought it would be a good idea to see a gynecologist and get a clean bill of health.

"It looks good. You're in good shape, nice and clean," said Dr. Madison, putting his tools of the trade on the metal tray next to him.

The next morning, I awoke with a serious white vaginal discharge. I called Dr. Madison's office. His nurse told me to go to the hospital immediately. I walked into the emergency room like a cowboy, with my knees wide apart.

"I've never seen a yeast infection this bad!" said the emergency room doctor. "How long have you been this way?"

"I woke up this morning with it. I was fine yesterday when I saw my gynecologist. He even remarked how good everything looked."

"Are you married?"

"If you're thinking that I got it from my husband, I can tell you that would be impossible. We have no sex. Maybe the doctor forgot to clean the instruments he used on the patient before me? Is that possible?"

"You didn't hear it from me, but that's most likely what happened."

He swore that if I used the vaginal cream he prescribed, in a week it would all be gone.

I called Dr. Madison before I left the hospital. He was

not available. I gave his nurse the whole story and that I was putting the responsibility for paying my hospital bill and the medicine I needed in Dr. Madison's hands. She put me on hold for about five minutes and then said that their office would take care of the hospital bill, and I'd be receiving a check in the mail to cover the medicine including a refund for my visit to their office. She apologized for the inconvenience.

The next morning, I awoke with an important realization, why did I need a pap smear every year? The test was done to rule out cancer of the cervix, but I didn't have a cervix or a uterus. Either they didn't read the charts with my medical history where I had entered that I had a partial hysterectomy—due to some medical error years earlier—or they were doing the procedure blindly without any idea of what they were looking for. Maybe Al was right, that they were a bunch of crooks. They read my chart but figured they would charge for the Pap smear anyway, even when they knew well in advance that there was nothing to "smear" about. Dr. Smith was not the only doctor with lack of ethics.

Barbara stopped doing theatre after falling at her son's wedding. I was devastated to find her bed ridden at home. She was scheduled to have back surgery the end of the month. I tried to convince her to go see Dr. Peruzzi, but she didn't believe in chiropractic.

Summer of 1993

I bought an extra thick mattress from Crazy Joe's Furniture store to take with me to college. After so many years of borrowing his furniture for the productions at the Simy Dinner Theatre at no cost to us, it was only fair that any furnishings I needed I should buy them from him. Ralph and I were planning to leave the following week, on June

25.

Al insisted on coming to Georgia and staying with us until July 2nd, and then he would take the train back to New Jersey. Rosanna's hotel coupons were going to be handy, since we needed a place to stay while looking for an apartment to rent.

The day before leaving for Georgia, the delivery truck company picked up all our belongings, Ralph's television and computer, the new microwave, our mattresses and bed frames, the dining room table and chairs, kitchen stuff, clothing, and so on that we knew we would need for the next four years while attending school. The dispatcher for the trucking company guaranteed that everything would be delivered to our door as early as June 29th. All we had to do was to call them with our apartment address once we got settled.
    That evening I drove to the Kobe Japanese Restaurant to say goodbye to everyone, but I didn't go upstairs to the theatre. I didn't want to feel sad. I also didn't go to Westwood Greens. I didn't want to say goodbye.
    Ralph and I took turns driving and we did a lot of talking about our future as students, and then as chiropractors once we graduated. Al slept most of the time. We drove straight to Georgia. When we got to Smyrna we were not only tired, but also hungry. We couldn't help notice a large sign on a building that read, "Go-Go Buffet Special."
    It wasn't a family restaurant. The dancers were young girls dancing around metal poles, naked except for a string like bikini. Interesting though what hunger did to people. All we wanted was food!
    While we ate I couldn't help notice one girl dancing while seated on a guy's lap and I thought she might be his girlfriend—but he was more interested in the other girls dancing on the platform. I felt sorry for her.

Ralph said we must have looked like a typical family, because none of the dancers approached our table.

Marietta, Georgia

We spent the next day looking for an apartment. Al was bored and told us he was ready to take a train back to New Jersey the next morning.

As soon as Al left, Ralph and I headed to the college admissions office to make sure everything was going well with our student loans. To my utmost surprise, I had been granted the Harvey Lillard full-year scholarship. I remained seated and reacted very properly with a straight face and said to the friendly lady behind the desk, "That's nice. Thank you." I glanced at Ralph who gave me a puzzled look.

When we left the building, I started jumping up and down. "Oh, my God!" I yelled out. "Oh, my, God! I can't believe it!"

"I was starting to worry when you acted so calmly," Ralph laughed.

"I was too dumfounded for any form of reaction." And I began jumping and twirling around and screaming.

"That's more like you, mom." He laughed.

We celebrated by going to a restaurant called Pig-N-Chik BBQ, where we experienced our first delicious southern meal of pulled pork. Afterward I felt sick of my stomach, but it was worth it.

The first time I was sprayed with pesticides had been while walking in a bird sanctuary in New Jersey. I heard the sound of a helicopter in the distance and as it got closer I could see a cloud of bright yellow powder being dropped over the park. I didn't run fast enough into my car and no matter how much I held my breath I could still feel the taste in my mouth and the foul acid like dust, up my nostrils.

Why they did that when there were people below I did not know, but it was to my benefit, from that day forward I become an expert at identifying the smell of insecticide spray in corn as well as in fruit and vegetables. I always took a whiff first, before I bought anything from the fresh produce department in the food stores.

My developed extra sense of smell came to our rescue when Ralph and I were checking an apartment in Smyrna, near the college.

He was ready to take the apartment, but I told him, no way. It was below the ground floor, and the sunlight barely made it through the narrow windows. Along with the cold dampness inside the apartment, I could smell the familiar smell of insecticide.

"Mom what does it matter what the apartment smells like, we'll be spending the days in school anyway."

I opened one of the kitchen drawers, and found a mummified cockroach covered in white paint. I said firmly, "Let's just check one more apartment."

The next apartment was like a dream come true. It had a swimming pool, hot tub, laundry room and beautiful garden surroundings. It was less than one mile away from the college. We could walk to school if our cars broke down, and the apartment was like new, fresh and clean. It was on the ground floor, and I knew that Ralph would rather be on the second or third level for safety, but it had sliding glass doors from the living room to a private patio, and I loved the idea of sunshine at my doorstep. The kitchen had an open modern look, with a counter peninsula big enough that we could use it to eat on. There was also a nice size living room and dining room and two spacious bedrooms. Ralph immediately took possession of the larger bedroom with a private bathroom. The other bedroom was about the same size, but the bathroom was across the hallway. There were windows everywhere and plenty of sunshine; I also liked the modern white window shades, for privacy. The rent was $400 a month, $200 each and included all utilities.

Ralph called the moving company to give them our address, and their secretary said they would deliver our belongings the following Monday morning.

We went to the Salvation Army and bought two high stools so we could sit by the kitchen island not only to use it as a table to eat on but also to study. While there we also shopped for summer clothes and luckily, we found two thick foam pieces, for two bucks each. They were perfect to sleep on until our furnishings and mattresses arrived in a week. Thank God, we had the insight to bring with us a couple of bath towels, two blankets, and our pillows.

Monday came and our stuff had not been delivered as it had been promised. Ralph called them on Tuesday and they apologized and promised the following week everything would be delivered to our apartment. We had no dishes, or pots to cook with, but it was sinful to buy anything when we knew in another week we would have all our kitchenware back. We bought a large, deep frying pan that we used for cooking just about everything.

Ralph bought a car, a brand new red Plymouth Duster, not my favorite look for a car, but he liked the way it drove and also how much power it had on taking off. My Saturn was very nice, but when it came to taking off it was like a stick-in-the-mud.

When I first arrived to Georgia I couldn't find direction for driving north. Ralph encountered the same issue. We concluded that the word north didn't exist in the south. I also found out that the middle lane I had been driving on was called suicide lane, and it was illegal to use it unless I needed to make a turn. Whoops!

Classes started. Our first quarter curriculum consisted of Embryology, Osteology, Histology, Anatomy &

Physiology and Lab., Public Health, Clinical Experience, Health Care Terminology, Introduction to Chiropractic Philosophy, and Introduction to Business Principles I. Ralph and I attended the same classes and studied together every evening and also on weekends. Whenever I had a question, he was ready to help. He was even smarter than I thought, he could read something and not only did he understand it but he had it committed to memory. Having Ralph as my roommate and friend was a blessing.

Besides being study buddies, Ralph and I held lots of good heart-to-heart talks and he was well aware of my difficulties being married to his father.

"I want my divorce to be real but I'm scared that he'll come down to Georgia and kill me," I said.

"Mom, you're so dramatic. When I go to New Jersey on the next school break I'll explain to him, how you feel and he'll understand that this is your decision."

"Tell your father that he can have the condo and all its contents."

"Stop worrying about it. I'll tell him you want the divorce to be final and that's all. Everything is going to be all right."

I was very lucky that Ralph and Steve were aware of the situation between Al and me and understood how I felt. But to be sure, I called Steve. He promised to be with Ralph when conveying my request to Al.

Hopefully Ralph was right that Al would not come down to Georgia and shoot me in the head. The idea of gaining my freedom and then die soon after was too much for me to handle.

Ralph and I were seated at the kitchen island studying when he made an announcement which took me for a loop. He said point blank, "If I keep tutoring you, you'll never become independent. Mom, you need to study on your own from now on."

An overflowing feeling of being abandoned and casted aside took over me, but I also understood. Most likely I had been dragging him down.

The following Saturday, I bought a long folding table to use as my desk and a used office chair at Goodwill and set them in the corner of the empty living room. Ralph bought a smaller folding table and a chair and took them into his room.

The days were spent in school and the evenings at home studying. If I had a question regarding something that I didn't understand, Ralph was willing to explain it to me, but he no longer held my hand while I studied, he wanted me to figure things out for myself.

We were still sleeping on the foam pieces and waiting patiently for our belongings to be delivered.

Mitchell, one of the students at school, dropped dead while walking to one of his classes. He was only fifty-nine years old. A student that knew him stated that Mitchell was always too stressed out and that was probably the reason his heart had given up. Sarah, one of my classmates, who was sixty-two years old, told me, "I don't care if the same happens to me; at least I'm living my dream of being a chiropractor." And she was quick to add with a smile in her eyes, "And if that happens, I won't have to pay my student loan!"

With English being my second language and unquestionably being right-brained I blamed my lack of aptitude towards logic such as in science on my defective left-brain. That plus my loss of hearing being a learning disability in a crowded classroom and sometimes having to guess what the mumbling was about, it made me a most dedicated student. At home I studied into the wee hours of the night and was up early the next day. I relished sleeping 9 hours but since school had started I was down to five.

On weekends, I studied all day Saturday and got up

early Sunday morning to continue my revisions. It was Sunday noon when I felt a strange fluttering of my heart. I checked my pulse and asked Ralph to check it too.

He said it was wiser if he drove me to the emergency room. An exam was performed which included an EKG and then I was asked to remain in the hospital bed and wait for the results. While waiting I began looking over the Embryology notes, which I had taken along. When I heard a cough, I looked up, a doctor had been standing on the doorway for who knows how long, trying to get my attention. He walked in and moving my papers to one side, sat on the edge of my bed. "What are you doing?" he pointed at my notes and the book on my lap.

"Studying," then reading his reprimanding frown I added, "I can't waste any time, I have a test next week."

"How long have you been in school?" He gently took the book from my hand, and looked at the cover.

"A month. I'm taking a test next week…"

"I have good news, and bad news." He handed me the book back. "First let me tell you the good news. There's nothing wrong with your heart. Now for the bad news, you're suffering from stress, and you're not going to make it at the speed you're running your life."

Then he gave me the best advice any doctor could give a patient. "If you don't take care of yourself and take one day a week off to rest, you will soon return to this hospital, and I can't promise in what state of health you will be. Take a walk in the park on Saturday or Sunday. Go out for dinner or to a movie. Get a life; you'll do a lot better when you take a test."

I thought about what happened to Mitchell and decided to follow his advice.

Every weekend I took either Saturday or Sunday off from studying. I started taking walks in the park next to a river not even twenty minutes from where we lived. It was a great place to hike or walk a pet, and it was fun to watch the dogs swimming after the sticks their owners threw in the water. There were lots of kids playing and joggers all around including a guy who proudly walked his pet pig on a leash.

Thursday night, Ralph and I treated ourselves to a Middle Eastern restaurant in downtown Atlanta. The restaurant was ironically called the Casbah and quite pricey but we were taking advantage of the coupon offer, received in the mail; buy one dinner and receive the second meal free. It was a great deal and we couldn't pass it.

   The restaurant was decorated close to what one would imagine a sultan's palace. It was far from the no-frills, washed off grey painted four walls restaurant Ralph and I had eaten while in Tangier, Morocco. Here, all the waiters wore a silk greenish turban matching in color to an embroidered ankle-length garment with long sleeves, similar to a robe. In Tangier the men wore simple cotton garments mostly white and they didn't use turbans with feathers. We figured the restaurant owner had the staff dressed that way to provide a more touristic atmosphere. The waiter showed us to a corner of the large room where beautiful red and gold curtains hang from the ceiling behind us. We sat cross-legged on pillows by a low round table and we were served an array of exquisite food in small dishes for us to eat using our fingers. That was the best part of it, eating without the conservative rules of table manners dictated by society. We laughed while using our fingers to pick each delicious morsel, even the wet dripping ones. Putting our cares aside of how messy it could get, we made use of the white towel on our shoulders, provided by our attentive waiter who encouraged us to use it to dry our hands, after he brought us a bowl and poured rose water over our greasy hands. I had never seen belly-dancers performing, but it didn't start until eleven at night, and sadly enough, we couldn't stay any longer since we had early morning classes. Being out with Ralph was always an adventure. I counted my blessings, being his mother.

Ralph and I took turns at calling the moving company every week, without any results. Rita, one of the secretaries promised me to call back as soon as possible and let me know what the delay was about.

She called an hour later and just like the other people in the company had done in the past, she assured me, that the following week, most likely on Monday morning, our stuff would be delivered. They were going to call Sunday evening to confirm.

I confided in Leila how much Ralph and I were frustrated with the teaching staff at our college. Half the time they came in late and when they did show up they talked about their hobbies, or the news. Russell, one of our classmates, who used to be an engineer, was just as disappointed as Ralph. I always found them talking about how—if they had a chance—they would choose another college. But Russell was married and had a child. It would be very difficult for him to just pack and go. And besides, he had a house and a mortgage; his roots were definitely in Georgia with his family.

I couldn't bear the idea that Ralph might quit school.

Friday night, Ralph invited me to a local pub to play pool with him. The place was packed with young people, mostly students from the college. I partnered with Ralph in a game of pool against two other students. After the second game where Ralph lost once again because of my inadequacy at shooting pool, he went to talk to a girl at the bar. There was music in the background but no dancing-floor, so I couldn't hide. I walked around and around the room several times with a smile as if I was having a great time. I was bored out of my mind but I just couldn't go up to Ralph and ask him to take me home. He was busy talking to the same girl. The feeling of being alone in a crowd became more painful when one drunken student decided that we should hug since we were attending the same college. When we left I told Ralph how I felt and that I had no intentions of frequenting any more bars or clubs.

"Mom, you're single now. When you see somebody you like, you need to be more proactive. Just go up to that person and start a conversation."

"Ralph, I've never dated and I'm not good at starting conversations with strangers."

"You need to lose your fears. When we go out; start practicing."

Sure, that was easy for him to say. I could just see myself going up to a guy at a bar and saying, "Hi, my name is Veronica. So, do you come here often? Oh yeah, and I should also tell you that it's too noisy here, so don't even bother to talk to me because I won't be able to hear a word you say."

The following Friday night I stayed home. I told Ralph I'd find other ways to meet a guy. And besides, I didn't drink.

Leila still struggled with the curriculum. It was rare when a week went by without calling to let me know she was on her way to my apartment to talk. Ralph got upset, saying that she was interrupting my studies, and I needed to put a stop to her visits. But I lacked the courage to tell her not to bother me when I was studying. Friends were supposed to help each other. Knowing her kind nature, I knew she would do the same for me.

Ralph didn't have to spend as much time as I did studying. He used his free time talking on the phone to friends, went out at night, slept during the boring classes in school, and then at twelve midnight he would make an announcement, "Mom, I need to study for the exam tomorrow, and I'm not to be bothered." Then he closed his bedroom door and studied all night. In the morning we went into the testing center, and he whizzed through the exams. I, on the other hand, had to study daily like my life depended on it and if lucky get a B or a C on the tests. The only class that I was truly a wiz was Healthcare Terminology. Those three years of high school in Portugal learning Latin had finally paid off.

We finished our first quarter. I should say we survived our first quarter of neglectful teaching. We were basically on our own during those three months, since everything we learned had been self-taught from the books we bought. Several of the teachers were right-out wackos on chiropractic philosophy and Ralph had a lot of trouble coping with such morons most likely because of his higher IQ and engineering mind. But once we got to the party at Sylvia's house, one of the students at the college—it was time to celebrate with glee, the end of the first quarter and the potential of a second quarter with better teachers.

Everybody at the party was having fun talking, laughing drinking and eating. It was a vegetarian potluck party. I had never been to a potluck before, and I liked the idea of enjoying the best of homemade cooking. I also noticed that everyone left their shoes outside before entering Sylvia's house. It made a lot of sense not to track the dirt from outside onto the carpets. Ralph and I agreed to start doing the same. Keeping our carpet clean meant less to worry when we moved out and getting our deposit back.

Bernice, one of the students was going around announcing, "Tomorrow morning, I'm driving east to one of the beaches along the coast, and read as many novels as I can."

"Three months of studying has been enough for me," I said.

"Nothing with letters is going to even come close to my

eyes." Bernice laughed and shook her head. The girl next to her did the same. I felt obliged to explain further, "I'm going to clean my apartment, instead."

"Are you crazy?" Bernice shook her head. "Why would you spend your free time cleaning your apartment?"

I wasn't going to tell them I had nothing else to do. "It's just the way I am, I guess," I said acting modest. They turned their back and disappeared into the young crowd. The loud music and gabbing inside the house made it hard for me to hear, not that anyone bothered talking to me, anyway. I filled my plate with a little of everything from the kitchen counter and walked out to the back porch to sit on a bench. It was a typical southern summer night, muggy and hot. I blamed the light from the stars for the overall heat. I had just put a fork full of chopped kale covered in a vinaigrette dressing into my mouth when a tall older student, stood next to me and bending forward asked, "Do you mind if I sit next to you?"

I raised my thumb up. That was not the first time I had been approached when my mouth was full. It happened at restaurants all the time. "How is everything? Enjoying your meal? Is there anything else I can bring you?" the waitress expected an answer. There was also the occasional person I had not seen for a while, "Wow, is that you Ronnie? How are you? Tell me, what have you been up to?"

My most embarrassing moment happened when I was still teaching guitar. I had bought a burger and fries at McDonald's in Freehold, and just as I placed a handful of fries into my mouth, one of my guitar students—an adult student no less—spotted me among the crowd and began hugging me joyfully. He told me he was leaving to Hawaii the next day and then he began, "Do you remember the song I composed a year ago when you used to teach me guitar?" I nodded.

He went on, "You have been so detrimental in my life and I can only thank you for inspiring me to write my own music. Ronnie, how can I ever thank you?"

I kept my lips tightly pressed, shrugged my shoulders and nodded my head. Then I waved goodbye and made a quick exit through the crowd.

The chiropractic student's name was Dexter. Luckily, he liked talking and I had enough time to clear my mouth of kale. It was very exciting to have someone of the opposite sex interested in a hearty intellectual conversation and when we finished eating we sat on the cool grass talking about religion in contrast with spirituality.

What helped me to feel relaxed while talking to Dexter was that even though he was tall, with a lean body, and closer to my age, his face reminded me of a very pale eel with yellowed teeth. He was very excited about starting first quarter, and I told him as long as he studied on his own he was going to be fine. Ralph interrupted our conversation, "C'mon mom, it's getting late. We need to go home. I want to get started early tomorrow morning if I'm going to make it to New Jersey in the same day." Dexter said it would be great if we could exchange phone numbers. I wrote my name and phone number on a paper napkin and he did the same. I slipped his napkin into my coat pocket. The college was so big that I doubted we would ever run into each other again.

That night I gave Ralph a letter I wrote to Al asking for a real divorce. I had spent two days on my typewriter refining the words over and over again until it was clear that I blamed myself and no one else for our marriage not working out. "Don't worry mom, Dad will understand how you feel and everything is going to be fine," Ralph reassured me once again.

When I got up the next morning, Ralph had already left. I paid a visit to our apartment's main office and asked them for a small can of white paint so that I could touch up the walls in the apartment. They never had a renter offer to do such a thing, and they were delighted to supply the paint and brush. After painting over a few fingerprints here and there mostly along the hallway, I cleaned the top of the stove, washed the kitchen floors with a mix of water and vinegar, and then borrowed a vacuum cleaner from my neighbor. Two hours later the still empty apartment of furnishings was sparkly clean with not much of anything else to do. Everybody from school was gone; even my friends Leila and Sarah had left. I lay down on my foam pad staring at the white walls; *I'm only halfway down to Florida. I'd be a fool not to take advantage of this opportunity and enjoy my school break.*

I called Steve and told him I was heading to Florida the next morning.

"Mom, please you can't go by yourself. Carjacking is rampant down south. It's all over the news!"

I told him not to worry, my buddy Joe was traveling with me.

Joe was a stuffed male doll, I had ordered from one of those crime safety magazines and it had arrived at our apartment a day before like an omen telling me to go wherever I wished. I had bought him to use as a patient when practicing my adjusting technique, but there was no law against taking him along on a trip.

Joe had a rough young-looking face, good strong neck, shoulders and torso like a body builder, but his stuffed cloth legs and arms, hang limp. It didn't matter, in the passenger's seat he looked quite real with sunglasses, a blue cap hat, and a sailor's shirt I picked up that morning at Goodwill. Everything fitted him like a glove. I had paid $99.95 for Joe, but he was worth his weight in gold as my valuable bodyguard on the road to Florida.

Eight hours later I checked into an Orlando hotel. The only nasty thing I encountered on the road to Florida was hundreds of ugly black insects called love bugs. They splashed against the front of my car, causing a sticky clogging mess. After apologizing to Joe for what I was about to do, I placed him head first inside my car trunk. He would become my road guardian once again when we drove back to Georgia.

I spent the next day at Universal Studios and shamelessly rode the ET ride, three times. Between Disney World and Epcot, my favorite was Epcot, where I bought a very eye-catching metal bluish ring for five dollars at the Asian Pavilion. I took my time walking through Epcot's World Showcase and then settled down for dinner in the Norway Pavilion where their buffet included my very favorites, herring in vinaigrette and herring with raw sliced onions and cream sauce. For dessert I gorged myself on a large piece of dark chocolate cake because I had not eaten chocolate for a long time. I reasoned with myself that maybe, just maybe, I was no longer allergic to chocolate. Afterward, I returned to the hotel to grab a jacket since I wanted to spend the night at Pleasure Island.

I was in the hotel lobby waiting for the elevator, when a man looking a lot like a young Robert Redford stood next to me. He wore a dark blue suit and tie; most likely he was there for some kind of business meeting. He said hello. I said hello back. When we entered the elevator, he asked me where I was from, and like everyone else did; he mentioned how much he liked my accent. Robert was very charming, and in view of the fact that he showed an interest in me, and I was getting out at the next floor, I felt safe being a little flirtatious.

On the way to Pleasure Island I couldn't help thinking about the man in the elevator. It would be fun to hang out with him for a little while, that would prove to me that Michael was out of my life forever. It was no fun walking around Pleasure Island by myself. I sat at one of their bars acting like a woman-of-the-world and ordered a light beer and a corn on the cob. I knew that I was a fool to order a beer, when I couldn't handle alcohol of any kind, but I was alone and slightly gloomy. Even the bartender asked if I was okay. I ate the corn and drank half the beer. It surprised me that I found my way back to the hotel.

Then, a sort of a wish phenomenon happened. The elevator door opened and there was Robert, a very coincidental first name, I should say. He had changed into jeans and a white polo shirt and on his way downstairs to get a soda. He was easy to talk to but when he said, something like it was one thirty in the morning so why stand in the lobby when we could go to his room and talk there, I wanted to say I may be a bit naïve, but I'm not that dumb. Instead I said, "It's getting late, and I have to go." I waved goodbye and started walking away. But I didn't really want to say adieu so I turned around and said something foolish like, "On second thought, I'm going to get my bathing suit and take a swim in the pool, if it's still open. Would you like to join me?"

He proposed we meet by the pool within the next fifteen minutes.

When I got downstairs Robert was already in the lobby, wearing just a white towel wrapped around his waist. I couldn't help noticing his well-sculptured body, with a small waist and wide shoulders. He winked at me, "The pool was closed but I was able to convince the night manager to allow us to use it."

The pool was outside, but the water was warm from the pounding heat of the sun all day. I was in a water paradise as I let myself submerge as far as the back of my head. I didn't like chlorine in my eyes and I was also a scary cat when it came to putting my head under water. He dove into the pool and swam across twice. When he started coming into my direction I got this weird feeling of Robert turning into a shark. He put his hands on my shoulders and began massaging my back. I had told him that I was a chiropractic student, so he used that information to ask me if I was also learning massage at school. I immediately defended my future profession by stating that chiropractic was a technique of adjusting the spine and not soothing the muscles by massaging them. Then I swam away.

Once again, he swam toward me, but I didn't put up a fight when he held me in his arms. All I had to do was close my eyes and I was with Michael. We kissed.

"Let's take our bathing suits off," he said.

"I don't see any reason to take my bathing suit off." I moved away from him.

"Okay, okay then, just let me hold you a little longer." He started kissing the base of my neck and then my lips as his arms were holding my body tight against his. I closed my eyes, hoping it would last forever. He slowly pulled my bathing suit straps off my shoulders. I didn't mind. I had my eyes closed.

"You have the most beautiful breasts I've ever seen," he said.

Of course, I did. Any woman in a pool without a bra, would have beautiful breasts, they float upwards. Like hello, where have you been? I couldn't help but laugh at his innocence. I opened my eyes, but it wasn't Michael; it was a stranger, a man I had met in the elevator. The water had become as cold as ice. I ran out of the pool, wrapped myself with a towel, and ran into the elevator. He caught up with me by putting his foot in between the closing doors and then stepped in. I backed into the corner. He stayed on the opposite side. He smiled at me and then displayed himself like a little boy showing his trophy. There was no way I could ignore it, but I managed to focus my confounded gaze on the elevator door. He must have read my mind, he immediately covered himself. As the elevator door opened on my floor I ran out as fast as I could and holding the key to my room I opened my door and quickly locked it. I waited a bit and when I didn't hear a knock except for my heart beating, I assumed that I had lost Robert for good. Then I heard two light knocks. I looked through the peephole. It was Robert. What have I done, I asked myself as I trembled from head to toes. He knocked twice again, but I could tell by the way he gazed from one side to the other that he was not sure if he had the right room. No way in heaven was I going to open my door. Finally, he walked away.

The phone rang; stupid me, I picked up the receiver. Robert must have gotten my room number from the manager downstairs, and he wanted me to come to his room. I told him that I was sorry but it had been an error on my part to go swimming with him, and I didn't want to go any further. He wouldn't take no for an answer, so I came up with what I thought was an ingenious excuse, "Look, my husband is sleeping in the room, and I can't keep talking."

He cut me off, "Are you pulling my leg?"

"No, I'm not." I lowered my voice even lower. "He's sleeping, but believe me, he's very mean when he's jealous. I better go before he wakes up. I advise you not to call me again." I hanged up.

On the way to Georgia I thought about what happened in Florida, but I was not sorry. If anything, I understood now what loneliness could do. And I considered myself lucky that I had not fallen in the hands of a crazy woman-hater. He could have squeezed my neck until I drowned. I could have joined the other poor lonely women of the world that died; victims of the same circumstances. Just another newspaper headline, "Chiropractic student's body found floating in swimming pool in Florida." Or worse, "Mass pool-murderer kills his seventh victim."

I found a message on my answering machine. "This is Dexter; I guess you're still in Florida. I'll call you tomorrow." I crossed my fingers that he would, because the white paper napkin with his phone number was nowhere to be found, and I really needed a friend.

The three days I had before classes started, were spent with Dexter. On our first get-together he invited me to his apartment. He made pasta with chicken and veggies swimming in butter, heavy whipped cream and cream cheese. It was delicious, but I refrained from eating more than a small portion as I knew my stomach didn't do well with creamy rich food. Dexter preferred foreign movies, and we went to see "Mediterraneo," an Italian movie.

From the way he talked about himself not being like other guys, I assumed he was gay, but that was fine with me. I enjoyed the friendship a lot better without strings attached.

I paid dearly for the chocolate cake I ate in Florida and the two chocolate bars I munched on while driving back. I was a chocoholic. I was aware of the consequences and yet I always found an excuse like, *a little brownie won't hurt me and it didn't, but the next thing I knew, I was having more than one.*

As always, the pain hit me two or three days later after my chocolate binge. It was unbearable; like sharp knives stabbing at my legs and hips. But I purposely didn't take anything for it, in the hope that the memory of my agony would remain ingrained deep into my brain so the next time I found anything that even resembled chocolate, I would refrain from touching it.

Autumn of 1993

The first thing that Ralph said to me when he got back from New Jersey was that everything had been taken care of. He and his brother had taken Al out for lunch and told him that I wanted a bona fide divorce. He also gave Al my letter explaining how I felt. Al was upset and hurt, but Ralph explained that when he and I had got married I was very young and still inside a shell, but over the years I had grown out of it. I was no longer the same person he had married. Ralph couldn't have explained it better.

Ralph also brought the official letter from Life Chiropractic College concerning my scholarship. It was dated June 22nd. The mail must have arrived right after we left for Georgia on June 25th.

Dear Ms. Esagui:

The Scholarship Committee met today and reviewed your application for the Harvey Lillard Scholarship. You have met all the criteria, and the Committee has voted to award you the Harvey Lillard Scholarship, which is for tuition for four quarters (D.C. PROGRAM).
The Accounting Department will be notified to credit your account accordingly, and awards will be given out at an upcoming assembly.
Congratulations! Keep up the good work.

Sincerely, Morris W. Lutes
Chairman, Scholarship Committee

I attended one of their meetings at the campus. I was the only white woman sitting in the back of the room. I shared my dilemma with Leila and Sarah and they were concerned that since Mr. Harvey Lillard was black, and the committee members were black they were going to withdraw my scholarship. Leila and Sarah came over to my apartment to assure me that with the appropriate attire I could conceal my skin by using dark stockings, gloves, a long dress with long sleeves, and creamy dark make-up to cover my face. I didn't want to discourage them for their effort but it didn't sound realistic to me.

I told Ralph about their plans and he said, "Mom, that's the most ridiculous thing I ever heard, the award was given to you because you deserve it. You did a lot for minority groups when you were living in New Jersey. And besides, the tuition for the year has already been paid by the scholarship committee; you have their letter confirming the award."

Thank God, Ralph had a lot of common sense when it came to resolving any serious issues.

Our second quarter promised to be a lot more challenging than the first. Our new classes were, Spinal Anatomy, Musculoskeletal Gross Anatomy, Motion Palpation & Static Palpation, Instrumentation, Spinal Biomechanics, Clinical Experience II, Chiropractic Assembly, History of Chiropractic, Cell & Neuromuscular Physiology, and Introduction to Business Principles II.

Ralph and I were stoked with our new curriculum. Perhaps first quarter had been a fluke.

I asked Ralph as my friend to explain how a man could have sex with a stranger and not be bothered by it.

"The difference between a man and a woman is that a man only needs a place and a woman needs a reason."

So that's what had happened in Florida. What an eye opener for me.

My parents were not doing well. Papa answered the phone, Mama was back in the hospital, and he was not quite sure why. "I feel very weak and tired lately," his voice was barely audible. "I think I have a virus or something like that. I'll call you when I'm back to normal."

I called him the next day. Alice answered the phone. I asked her what was going on with my parents. "Your parents are old, that's why they're always sick. It's expected."

"Put my father on the phone. I want to talk to him."

"He's sleeping and shouldn't be disturbed." Her tone of voice showed irritation.

"Then, wake him up," I was surprised at my

assertiveness.

"No," she said firmly. "I already told you that he's sleeping."

Worried that she was going to hang up I challenged her, "Oh yeah? Well, I'm going to get on a plane right now, and you're going to answer to me unless I talk to my father immediately."

"Give me a minute, I'll get him."

He came to the phone, but his words were hard to understand as he mumbled, "I don't know what's wrong, all I do is sleep. I can't even move my lips to speak, I feel as if in a stupor. I have to go lay down."

I didn't have my brother Max-Leão's phone number and didn't know where he lived in Portugal. I called Aunt Coty, the widow of Uncle Augusto, my mother's brother, and asked her to please check on my parents and find out what was going on. She was about to leave to Spain to visit her daughter and would try to stop by their apartment on the way to the airport. She would call me when she got back to Lisbon in two weeks.

After two weeks I called Aunt Coty. I got her answering machine. Three days later Papa called. He was in high spirits and seemed to have regained his health. He had a lot to tell me.

He felt that if it weren't for Luisa, a part-time employee my parents had luckily hired two months ago to take care of them when Alice was not available, they would have been dead by now. Luisa confided in Papa that she had witnessed Alice putting drugs in their food. Alice had been drugging my parents just like she had done to my brother José. Luisa took Papa to the German Embassy, and that was how he learned that Alice had been going to the German Embassy and telling them that Papa had given her authorization to pick up his monthly checks because he was too ill to get them himself. She was also falsifying his signature and cashing the checks along with the checks in the mail sent by my cousins from England, and now it was clear as a bell that she had been the one that had stolen the cash I had sent to my parents' months ago. Alice kept them doped up and unaware of what was going on. Alice's intention after getting rid of my parents was to keep their apartment for herself, her daughters, and her boyfriend who was coming out of prison in another month.

Luisa and Papa had put their heads together and devised a plan on how to get rid of Alice. He told Alice that she was to have a week off with vacation paid, because she deserved it after working so hard. Luisa would work that week and cover for Alice's absence. When Alice left, he immediately made arrangements with someone he knew and sold everything he and Mama owned inside the apartment, and then he called the landlord and told him that he would leave the apartment for a certain amount of cash. Everything got done in less than a week, and Papa got all the money he made from selling everything, including his apartment, gave some to Luisa and then put the rest in the bank. He was living with Luisa and her family, at present.

Mama was still in the hospital and had not been told what happened. According to him, Luisa was the salt of the earth and he was sure that Mama was going to be fine with his decision. Luisa out of the kindness of her heart had offered a room in her apartment—for a monthly fee, of course. She had three children. Her husband was a chauffeur and didn't make much money so they could use Papa's financial help.

"Verónica, my daughter, Alice, killed my son and was poisoning your mother and me. We owe our lives to Luisa."

"Papa, why didn't you call the police and turn her in, instead of selling everything and losing your home?" I doubted he had gotten paid fairly, since he was in such a hurry.

"I did. They're presently looking for Alice, to put her behind bars. But Luisa and I were afraid that Alice's boyfriend once out of prison would come over and get revenge on us for turning Alice into the cops. Verónica, my daughter, this is better, no one will know where your mother and I will be living, and they can't get to us."

I dropped the subject. I hoped Papa knew what he was doing and that moving in with Luisa was the best for them. He sounded very content with the way things had turned out. I could only hope that Mama would feel the same way. I couldn't even imagine the emotional pain she was going to feel when told she could never go home. The home where she had lived for the last fifty years with her family, were gone along with her personal memories and belongings, and she would have to adapt to living in a single room of her new employee's apartment.

I knew that a lot of old people sometimes were killed for their money or property, but I never thought it could happen to my parents. A few years back, in Toms River, right in New Jersey of all places, a woman had been caught and put in prison for keeping an old couple imprisoned in her cellar while she collected their social security. A neighbor turned her in and the police found the couple shackled, beaten and starving. I prayed with all my heart that Alice would pay for her crime. If there was justice in the world I wanted it to happen when she got old, I prayed that she would become a victim of a greedy bastard just like her. She had killed my brother and had tried to do the same to my parents. I was sure that this time even Papa was not ready to forgive her.

Aunt Coty called later that day and confirmed what Papa told me. She also told me that the first time she met Alice, she warned Mama that she didn't trust Alice and had a bad feeling about her, but Mama would not listen.

We finally gave up on calling the trucking company. Ralph called the FBI.

He was told to wait a couple of days; they were already

investigating the situation because there had been a lot of people calling them about the same issue.

The federales, as Ralph referred to the FBI agents, called back. Our belongings were being delivered in a week's time, and if anything was missing we were to call them back. The moving company was liable for everything, we had given them. Supposedly the moving company was not making any deliveries; and was keeping everything in a warehouse. Amazing how the FBI found the warehouse. According to them it was a very successful bust.

Dr. Shtick the Spinal Biomechanics teacher was proud to have been born in Georgia and raised in Georgia; even his farmhouse was in Georgia. Besides his devotion for Georgia he lived for racing, all he talked about was his car and car racing as if we gave a damn about it, and then on the way out of the class he would say, "Ba da way, naxt week there is an eyezam."

When he explained biomechanics, which was rarely and briefly, neither Ralph nor I understood his southern jargon.

We began to look for a private tutor to help us with the subject. Everyone in our class was in the same sinking ship.

Wednesday night, Ralph and I were sleeping when we heard loud knocking at our front door. It was two in the morning. Our belongings were finally being delivered. I was so excited that I ran out in my pajamas and no shoes.

A humongous super-duper truck was parked on the other side of our apartment complex. The driver and the other guy had already unloaded our belongings on the sidewalk next to their truck, making it a long stretch for us to carry our stuff through the front door. We opened the sliding glass doors to our living room and used that as the entrance. When we asked for a helping hand to carry the heavier items, the two men told us they were only deliverymen, not movers. They were ready to take off, but Ralph and I insisted on climbing inside the truck to make sure nothing had been left behind. The truck was crammed with stuff yet to be delivered to other customers, all over the US and as far west as California. I was delighted to see the antique umbrella that Katherine, the costume designer for "The Playboy of the Western World," had given me a few years back. It stood quite properly between someone else's couch and a plastic palm tree.

    Thank God that prior to having our stuff picked up in New Jersey I had marked all the boxes with numbers and kept a list and a basic statement of the contents. Most boxes were either smashed in or had been opened and the movers had neglected to close them. My mattress was seriously damaged, with an indent large enough for an elephant to sleep in, but the metal bed frames were intact. Ralph's computer and stereo were still inside the dented boxes, so we wouldn't know their condition until we opened the boxes in the morning. Finally, all that was left outside was my dresser. But there wasn't much left except for the drawers, which we carried two at a time. We were crossing the lawn with them when I stepped with my right foot over what felt at first like a fluffy mound of dirt. Ants, angry ants with needles for teeth, were biting my right foot and running up my ankle to sting me further. I jumped up and down screaming while slapping frantically at my legs and feet. Ralph led me to the bathroom, turned the cold water on in the tub and told me to get in. "Looks like you stepped on a fire ant mound, supposedly prominent in Georgia," he said in his usual informative calm voice.

    There were only three bites, but it had felt more like one hundred. I liked ants, I admired their work ethics and how social they were with each other. Poor things, they must have been pretty angry when I stepped on them.

Over the weekend Ralph put the bed frames together, but my new mattress was damaged beyond repair. Whatever had been stored on top of it all those months had created a crater in the center. Ralph's computer didn't look any better, as if it had been hit by a baseball bat on the side and the screen was shattered, the microwave was missing the door. I threw away what was left of the dresser and stacked the six drawers on top of each other to use them as a bookcase next to my study table. The dining room table was missing one leg.

What really broke my heart, was to find my beloved wine wooden barrels used on stage for the Irish play, "The Playboy of the Western World," barely holding up. The rusty metal rings that had held in place the wooden staves, fell off when we moved the barrels to the other side of the room and the barrels collapsed like dominoes. Ralph caught the dismayed look on my face and promised that when he had some free time he would help me put them together with glue. I loved those barrels, they remind me of the old, Portuguese wine barrels, and that made them very dear to me. I could not possibly throw them out. The boxes with clothing and kitchen and bathroom stuff were left unopen and we put them against the wall in the dining room space, next to the pile of wood staves.

It took me a while but I finally found the same white plastic panel I used at the Howell Music Center for writing down the teachers' schedules. I bought a full 4'x8' and with Ralph's help I nailed the board sideways to the living room wall. It worked like a blackboard without the dust and mess of using chalk. I like the idea of using colorful dry markers and writing everything big enough to read from the kitchen while I cooked. As I turned around I could quiz myself that way. The whole board was dedicated to Spinal Biomechanics.

Papa called just as I was leaving for school the next morning, "Your mother is making it very difficult for us to live with Luisa and we may have to move. After everything that Luisa did for us, your mother wrote a terrible letter to you about Luisa and it was a good thing that she got hold of the letter before it went out." I wondered what right Luisa had to open my mother's letter, but Papa was so upset that I didn't have the courage to say anything. Supposedly Mama had written that Luisa had the temper of an atomic bomb, and was a flirting slut, taking him for all the money she could get off him. Meanwhile, Luisa was so angry after reading the letter that she told them that if Mama was not happy they should go live in an old-folks home instead because no matter how much money Papa gave her, it wasn't enough to pay her for the aggravation she was being put through.

I told Papa I was on my way to classes but would call when I got back.

When I called they had made peace with each other and couldn't be happier living with Luisa and her family.

Sometimes a student would say something really dumb to Ralph and I like, "You're a lucky son of a gun that your mother is your roommate. I bet she's a great cook."

We lived together, but we didn't cook for each other. We felt it was only fair that neither one was burdened by the other. As students and adults, we were on equal terms. Once in a blue moon Ralph and I dabbled on a cooking experience, but it was rare. He usually added piquant things like chili peppers and peppery sauces to food and I didn't. One thing was for sure, it was nice to have all our cooking pots back, even though we had become masters at preparing just about anything in the large frying pan we had shared through the months we didn't have kitchenware.

Ralph helped me to throw my mattress into the dumpster and I went back to sleeping on my foam piece. I believed the reason my mattress was a lot worse than Ralph's was because while in storage they must have put a refrigerator on top of it. That was the only reasonable explanation to cause such a serious cavity on a brand-new mattress.

Ralph and I gathered all the bills showing the cost to replace everything that arrived damaged, and we sent it to the moving company just like the FBI advised us to do. We also enclosed the cost of getting a new dining room set, since the table was missing one of the legs.

Dexter came over one evening and as usual we sat in the living room floor talking. I noticed him glancing at the kitchen on and off with what seemed an anxious look. "Are you hungry?" I asked.

"No, but do you mind if I look into your kitchen cabinets and the refrigerator?" he stood while retaining his gaze toward the kitchen.

I shrugged my shoulders and said. "Sure, go ahead." My goodness, talk about being nosey.

He opened the lower cabinets, looked in, closed them and then reached for the top ones. "Wow, you really don't have a single can of food or sugary cereal stuff." He opened another cabinet and looked inside like a kid looking for hidden candy and followed up with opening the refrigerator. "Incredible, you really follow what you preach, I'm amazed.

All your food is fresh!"

Such excitement over my eating habits was a bit overwhelming. But we were friends and as such I needed to accept that he was eccentric maximum.

He sat at the kitchen island and I brought out the salad I had prepared. Dexter was a good cook and I took it as a compliment that he loved my cooking. He took a bite for the first time of my very favorite grapefruit salad, that evening.

"My God," he made a face as if he had swollen a whole lemon, "I've never tasted anything so sour in my whole life." The contorted look on his face grew acutely comical as he added, "Please, don't take this personally but...I can't eat it."

I burst out laughing as I watched him swallow ever so slow the piece of grapefruit already in his mouth and then, I raised my three middle fingers like I had seen my two sons do when saying the boy scouts' oath. "On my honor, I'll never again make grapefruit salad for you."

Grapefruit or orange salad was prepared with fresh pieces of fruit, minced garlic, olive oil, and just a touch of rice vinegar and salt. Aunt Heydee always made orange salad as a refreshing side-salad in the summertime. The grapefruit usage was my own invention; I figured if oranges were good, grapefruit would also be delicious. In Portugal there were no grapefruits available, I bet Aunt Heydee would have loved my salad.

The next day, Dexter treated me to lunch at the school cafeteria. He introduced me to the latest in health food, a veggie burger. I found it kind of dry on its own so I covered it with ketchup, mustard, lettuce, onions, pickles and sliced tomatoes, and it was quite tasty.

Ralph and I were absolutely stoked when we discovered a supermarket not far from our apartment that welcomed shoppers to sample their food. Twice a week we were there for lunch. But soon we felt obliged to buy groceries, as it was only fair that we support their business after their tremendous efforts at being super amicable and interested in making our shopping journey a pleasant one.

One day I happened to catch the butcher filleting a nice size fish for a customer and then threw the skin, fins, bones, and the head into the trash can. I waited patiently until he was done to talk to him. Raul was from Peru, and since I could speak Spanish he liked me enough to tell me to return in an hour and he would give me a bag of fish heads and bones at no charge. Lucky for me, Americans did not eat fish heads and wanted their fish spineless.

With the fish heads and bones, I made the most nutritious broth soup imaginable, and tasty too according to Dexter who believed to be a veggie soup of some kind. Ralph was the only one that knew the broth source. Another day, Ralph found in the deli freezer way deep in the back, cold cuts odds and ends at one quarter of the cost. He seriously stocked up. I didn't mind corned beef and roast beef once in a while but I much preferred egg or tuna sandwich.

When I cooked, I had one goal in mind, how many meals to make from the vegetable stew, the lasagna, or the large pot of vegetable soup. I bought a bunch of plastic containers, the perfect size for a single serving. Ralph thought it was a great idea and began doing the same. The freezer was well stocked. Except for having to buy fresh vegetables and fruit, I could go weeks with no need to cook. I always accompanied my dinner small bowl of fresh green salad.

It wasn't my intention to become a vegetarian; I simply let my inner intelligence dictate what was good for me. I ate fish or meat once or twice a month.

Mama woke me up this morning. "Verónica, my daughter, I don't know what to do, Luisa confiscates all my mail to you and if the letters don't meet her approval, she throws them out. Verónica, your father is infatuated with Luisa and in his eyes, she can do no wrong. Oops," she added hastily, "I hear her at the front door." She hung up.

Neither one of my parents were happy. Fifty years of marriage down the drain, that was how I looked at it. I thanked God for allowing me to get out of my marriage before it was too late. I began thinking about visiting my parents during Christmas break even though I had no idea what I could do to help them.

Dexter and I continued to see each other every weekend, and during the week we talked on the phone. One Friday night he came over and as usual we sat on the living room floor talking. It was ten in the evening when he said, "I hope you don't mind if I stay a little longer. I'm not looking forward to going to my apartment."

"I don't mind. But what's going on?"

"My roommate is having a bunch of her girlfriends over at nine for a meeting, and I already know that she'll try to connect me with one of her friends."

It was two in the morning when he left.

I never thought it could be possible to spend so many hours with someone and never run out of dialogue. Dexter already had warned me that he was not like other men and I could understand why he didn't want a bunch of women all over him. But I didn't care if he was gay or weird, I enjoyed his company. He listened and I felt very relaxed with him since I could express my philosophical thoughts without holding back, like I had done with Al and sometimes even with Michael.

Ralph asked me one morning when we were on our way to school, "Mom, how can you be attracted to Dexter? His face looks like a turtle."

I laughed. Yes, it was true about his face, but I only noticed it the first time we met. Since we had become friends, his features were not that important to me, I simply enjoyed listening to him, and I appreciated the opportunity he gave me to speak freely.

I was not attracted to Dexter the way Ralph thought. He would probably laugh, so I didn't tell him that I was seriously spellbound with Dexter's intellect.

Dexter spoke fluent Spanish, French, Italian, Dutch and Brazilian which was Portuguese with an added flare. He had traveled to exotic-far-away places all over the world and had lots of interesting stories. But what I liked mostly was his mysticism, which was ingrained in everything he said. Once in a while he went a bit too far with it, but I kept an open mind because he also respected my point of view even when I felt that some of the things I stood for were pretty much off the wall. When I was with Dexter I felt emotionally fulfilled.

Dexter told me that of all the countries he had travelled when he used to work for an airline, his favorite was Brazil. He had been pickpocketed while taking a nap on the sandy beach of Rio de Janeiro, but he loved the people, the language and the food and was seriously considering practicing in Rio. I told him about my cousins who lived in São Paulo and Rio and thirty years ago they had warned my mother that those cities were infested with criminals. I could only imagine how bad it was now. Dexter said he didn't care. I would. I wanted to walk the streets where I lived without having to look over my shoulder wondering if I was going to be robbed or kidnapped. I wanted adventure, but not at gunpoint, unless I was with the man I loved and he could keep me safe even when we were in a dangerous environment.

Sylvia, the girl that invited Ralph and me to her end-of-the-first-quarter party, saw me in school and yelled out from the end of the hallway, "How dare you steal Dexter from me." She freed herself from two other students, who held her arms trying to hold her back.

    I stood frozen from shock. "Dexter and I are just friends," and then I walked toward her.

    She let herself loose and walked rapidly toward me, as her two friends ran after her. We stood face to face. She yelled as if I was still at the end of the hallway, "Dexter and I were dating each other until you showed up."

    "You're making a big mistake. Sylvia, there's nothing, absolutely nothing between us."

"I called him yesterday and he told me that he was seeing you." Her face was red with anger. The two girls gave me the evil eyes. "You should be going out with old men, your own age. You have already been married and I want to be married too, you know." Tears poured out of her eyes.

"My goodness, go ahead and marry Dexter. You have my blessings. I swear to you that Dexter and I are only friends." Her two girlfriends lead her away from me as she cried.

I shook from head to toes and had to stand against the wall to take hold of myself. I had never been in a situation where I was the *other* woman. I hated when people accused me of things that weren't true. My goodness, no wonder sometimes innocent people went to jail and were electrocuted, all because of false accusations.

I called Leila as soon as I got home. "Oh, Veronica, don't you know that Sylvia is a jerk?" she said. "I don't talk to her and never go to any of her parties. If you had told me, I would have warned you. She's a crazy woman."

I didn't tell Dexter what happened between Sylvia and me. The whole thing was too dumb to even bring it up.

Al called every week to see how I was doing. On his last call he had the best news ever. He was taking special classes to become a detective, as this had always been his dream. Finally, he was doing something for himself, I couldn't be happier. He had also bought a pair of modern eyeglasses and a whole new wardrobe. This meant there was still hope and maybe he would start having a normal life.

I called Steve and asked if he would mind introducing his father to other women. It just happened that Steve knew a really nice lady a bit young, but since she was looking for a serious relationship it might work. According to Steve, Laurie was a real knockout. She was a part-time school teacher and he had known her for many years. He made plans to invite Al and Laurie to his house for dinner that weekend.

We received a package in the mail, from the delivery trucking company. It was the missing wood leg to our dining room table.

They had also enclosed a check covering all the items damaged. I made plans to go shopping for a new mattress that Saturday.

Ralph fixed one of my barrels, and Dexter helped me with the other. Like the barrels, my life was finally coming together.

Friday night Dexter invited me for a walk at the park by the college. We sat on the rocks by the pond and talked. The topic was religion and what we believed in. I didn't like to talk about religion with other people, but with Dexter it was different. He didn't try to convince me of this or that, or to push his beliefs on me. If anything, he told me I should be sharing my philosophy with other people.

I told him I was Jewish.

"So, what?" he said. "I love the way you speak, I get inspired by your positive insight. I took the liberty of telling some members of my church, about you and they want me to invite you to come over as a guest speaker."

I felt very flattered, but I refused to talk to a group of people much less to a religious group staring at me in profound silence waiting for my profound words. "I can only express my thoughts and feelings on a one-to-one basis," I said firmly. "More than two people around me are a crowd."

I knew my limits enough not to be easily persuaded.

In the spine analysis class called instrumentation, a

handheld instrument connected to a small metal box, was supplied to every student as a prerequisite tool. We rolled it up and down each other's spine, supposedly measuring the heat from one side to the other via a unique, non-contact infrared sensor, thus giving us a reading of where the subluxations existed. Subluxation was a chiropractic word used to describe a misalignment of the spine. The subluxations' findings were then picked up by a small metal box which printed the results for us to study. The teacher said we had to buy the hand-held instrument for the class, and it was automatically added into our tuition. Whether we like it or not, we were charged $350, even though after we graduated we had no use for it, unless we purchased the metal box that printed out the reading, for a couple of thousand dollars. Ralph and I were very upset, and believed the whole thing was just an excuse to make more money off the students.

I was studying for an exam when Leila called, "Veronica, I need you my friend. Can I come over? I'm at the end of my rope." She suffered from those bouts of depression at the oddest times, and I always felt obliged to stop everything and pay attention to her.

"I'm in the middle of studying for exams tomorrow morning," I felt a bit frustrated. "How about you call me later tomorrow?"

"Oh, Okay. I'll call you tomorrow." And she hung up. "What the heck did I just do, Ralph," I called his name louder. He came out of his room wondering why I was shouting. "I just hung up on Leila after she said that she was feeling down. I told her I was too busy studying to see her. What if she kills herself?"

Ralph shrugged his shoulders as he walked back to his room. "Don't worry. Trust me when I say, you'll see her in school tomorrow."

"What if she does kill herself, then what?" I asked.

"If she's that nuts, then you couldn't save her anyway," and he closed his bedroom door to go back to studying.

The next day I was walking in the hallway between classes and saw Leila. She waved at me with both hands, and called out, "Wait!" She approached me along with another student and said, "Veronica, I want you to meet my friend Howard. He's also a student here, and…" she stopped momentarily and then raised the tone of her voice to a higher pitch of excitement, "Howard is known for being the best hugger at our college."

"Would you like a hug?" he asked politely.

His big eyeglasses were thicker than the ones worn by the albino student in one of my classes. But Howard did have a nice friendly smile, and I figured a friend of Leila was a friend of mine. "Sure," I answered.

He wrapped his arms around my whole back as if they were two large wings, then, slowly but firmly, he shelled his body around mine like a plastic molding. He was the reincarnation of what a mother's hug must feel to a soldier that just returned from the war after being tortured in prison. When he let go, he smiled at me. He knew he was good.

Dexter called that night. He couldn't go to school the next day, a two-day low-grade fever had knocked all his strength and couldn't speak without breaking into a coughing spell. I told him I'd stop by his apartment the next day during my lunch break.

On the way to his apartment I picked up a small container of Vicks VapoRub at the pharmacy. I had been to his place twice but only to his kitchen where he had made me dinner. This time he was in his room but he wore a robe over his pajamas and his bed was still in disarray. I had him sit on the only chair available in his bedroom and gently massaged his head and neck, then worked on some trigger points to release the sinus pressure as I had learned in school from another student.

After doing set designing for so many years I could not help myself from automatically surveying his bedroom. A person's possessions, and even how clean they were, gave me a profound image of who lived there; it was a visual fingerprint of their personality. A full-size wall-to-wall bookcase displayed books about self-improvement, finding yourself, reaching within, and the joy of being better than you already were. I had just discovered Dexter's secret, he was trying to find himself.

I said nothing, but I had to admire him for not giving up even at his age. I applied a bit of Vicks on his chest and back and after washing my hands, left after telling him to get some sleep, and get better soon.

What a freak-out bug experience I had while seated on the toilet in my bathroom. As I pulled the toilet paper from the roll, a humungous black cockroach fell on the floor, from inside the toilet paper roll. I ran out of the bathroom screaming. Ralph didn't believe me when I told him how large the roach was and made fun of me.

I could understand a roach showing up in the kitchen to look for food to munch on but hanging inside a toilet paper roll was just too much for me to accept. While in school I couldn't help thinking that maybe Georgia's roaches also liked to live between bed sheets, and with that in mind, during my lunch break, I drove to the mall and bought a white set.

That night I threw away my flowery pattern sheets. They offered too much camouflage.

Last weekend, Ralph and I attended a birthday party for Russell's little girl. He lived far away, forty-five minutes from school to be exact. I felt spoiled living just ten minutes away from our campus; I could go home for lunch, I could even have a nap. Lucy, one of the girls in second quarter, was also at Russell's party and shared nonchalantly that she was a witch. I always thought that witches were characters in children's books, made up to scare kids into behaving, and my witty reply was, "Me too."

When we left the party, Ralph and I talked about it and came to the conclusion that except for Russell and his wife Margie there weren't many so called normal students in our school.

Ralph never made accusations unless he had proof. But after he caught Dr. Nicholls giving us false information several times he believed our teacher was not a medical doctor as he had introduced himself to our class. The truth came out, when Ralph asked Dr. Nicholls what the differences between a female and male pelvis were to make it easy for us to identify them apart. Dr. Nicholls's answer was, "There's no difference between them."

How could a doctor not know basic anatomy? But he was hired by the college so we had no one to complain to.

Ralph and I named Harold a student in motion palpation class, as Harold the Hateful, because of his hateful attitude accentuated by hard like metal hands, an example of his lack of lovability. My luck, the teacher teamed us during spinal palpation class. I told Harold not to touch me so harshly, but he took offense. During class break I ran to the bathroom, due to nausea and the discomfort inflicted on my back. Ralph had the same experience as I did, the prior week and agreed that Harold was going to hurt a lot of people as a chiropractor.

I complained to the teacher and asked him not to team me up with Harold.

"I'm sorry honey," the teacher was far from understanding "But you have to learn to work with whoever your partner is each week."

And then what did he do? He had a talk with Harold.

"How dare you whine to the instructor about me?" Harold put his hands on my upper back.

I pulled his hands away. "Several times I told you to be gentler when you palpate my spine but you got upset. So that you know, I'm not made of wood." And I walked out of the classroom.

Ralph talked to our teacher about Harold. I don't know what he said, but the teacher teamed Harold with a male student until the end of the quarter.

Except for a few much needed kitchen items and clothes, neither Ralph nor I had opened the rest of the boxes after they were delivered.

Being in school all day and then going home to study, decorating our apartment was not on our list of priorities. It amazed me how little we needed, when it came to stuff.

Saturday night Dexter picked me up and took me to meet his friends from school Donna and Cody. They were having a meditation gathering at their apartment.

I was very excited about learning to do the real thing. Donna was the facilitator. We were to sit cross-legged in a circle on the floor, put the palms of our hands up so the energy flowed through them, and with a slow rhythmic breathing and eyes closed, we were to get into a mental calmness and introspection and find peace within. I couldn't relax; sitting on the hardwood floor was painful to my tailbone. Twice I opened my eyes slightly, to see what everyone else was doing, and I couldn't help admiring how they seemed to be in their own mental space. As a kid I used to sit for hours on the soft sand above a small cliff staring at the ocean in front of me, blending myself into the Universe, listening to the waves hitting the rocks below my feet, and smelling the salty spray of the waves. Now, that was more like meditation to me.

Donna and Cody were vegetarians and afterward they

served a delicious green salad with every conceivable raw vegetable, accompanied by warm crispy Italian bread. The dinner conversation covered Buddhism, Hinduism's Karma, and reincarnation which took us into bringing up stories about spirits.

"There's a ghost living in my apartment." Loretta's announcement created a silent response in the room. "I can feel a negative force taking over my whole apartment, most predominantly in my bedroom. It's very hard to study in there and it's even affecting my sleep."

Donna offered to come to Loretta's apartment the following Saturday night and exorcise the ghost away. Loretta invited everyone to watch and after Donna got rid of the unwanted spirit, she would serve us her famous homemade spaghetti with tomato sauce and meatballs.

I couldn't wait to see Donna play the part of an exorcist.

Papa always talked about his magical days as a student in Berlin, Germany. I wondered if he had as much fun as I was having.

We were in anatomy lab, and during our ten-minute break, Ralph left to go to the bathroom. I remained seated using my time to go over the notes. Ralph returned as pale as a ghost and noticeably disturbed, "Whatever you do, Mom, do not go into the dissection lab."

"Where is the lab?"

He pointed, "You see the door over there? If you decide to go into that room to investigate, don't open the white buckets standing against the back of the room."

I had no intentions to look inside the dissection lab, but I had to ask, "Why?"

"They keep the cadaver's heads inside the buckets."

Dexter and I got to Loretta's house half-hour early. She waved at us from the kitchen and we stood next to her watching her making spaghetti sauce. She added fresh basil and I asked, "You don't use oregano?"

"Oregano in spaghetti sauce is a gastronomic crime against Italians." She was Italian and so was her mother who still lived in Italy.

The other students started arriving, and finally Donna and Cody. Donna wore black boots, a short black dress with long sleeves over blue jeans and an extra-long purple silk scarf around her neck. But her grand entrance was brought on when she stood in the doorway, while Cody got on his knees and removed her boots. She reached her outstretched hands to the sides of the door frame, like a human gate, and said with a solemn look on her face, "Do not close this door. It must remain open." We all watched silently as she gazed slowly around the room from one side to the other before stepping in. "I can feel the spirit of a young black man who needs just a little help to move on." I gasped along with the other students at her statement. Cody took from his backpack, a three by five inch carved-glass figure of Jesus head with a crown of thorns and handed it to her. She put a finger to her lips to indicate silence from all of us and we followed her as she walked slowly from one room to another, holding the head figure in front of her, like a protective shield. Leila had confided a while back that Donna and Cody were Jewish. Why she didn't use a carved-glass piece of David's star instead, puzzled me. Donna returned to the living room and asked Loretta to turn off the circuit breaker in the apartment. In the semidarkness we followed her once again as she went from one room to another but this time she uttered what sounded like an incantation while holding Jesus' head in one hand and a lit candle in the other. Then she returned to the living room, asked Loretta to turn the breaker back on, blew the candle out, and put both items on the fireplace mantel.

She declared with a broad smile, "Loretta, the young man is gone. From now on, you can relax and enjoy your apartment."

While we ate the spaghetti—which would have been even more delicious with some freshly grated parmesan cheese and a touch of oregano on top of the sauce—I wondered if Donna had done all that as a psychology game to free Loretta of what she believed to be a spirit in her apartment. I didn't share my thoughts with anyone, not even Dexter. Maybe there had been a spirit imprisoned in the apartment after all. I wasn't going to question its validity.

Tamara a friend from school came over to my apartment to study. Like Leila and so many other students, she was stressed out over the curriculum and at home she couldn't concentrate. I told her, "After an hour of studying, I relax for ten minutes with a very slow dance I made up." I showed her my moves but she stopped me. "That's called Tai Chi," she said. "It's older than you and me together."

I didn't care what it was called, or if it had already been invented. I had created it as a poetic dance movement from deep within the soul, and as such it rejuvenated my thinking process while studying. I couldn't help her at all. Everything I showed her to help with studying at home, she didn't even want to try.

I was at the library when Leila walked in with a limp and sat next to me complaining that she could barely walk. She had attended a weekend seminar specializing in instilling self-confidence into people like her who were insecure. They had her and other insecure folks walk on burning hot stones. She was told she lacked self-confidence, the reason she had burned the soles of her feet.

A month earlier at the same seminar they convinced her to climb a telephone pole and stand on top of it and then jump. Even though she was tied to a rope, why would acting like Evel Knievel make anyone self-confident? How naïve could she be, to believe such nonsense?

She not only spent a fortune going from one empowerment seminar to another but she also wasted full weekends, precious time that she could be studying instead. I did my best to rub off some of my self-confidence on her, but I was not a professional psychologist and her boosted self-esteem only lasted a few days before it deflated.

When Ralph and I finished the Spinal Biomechanics exam, we knew we had done poorly. We had paid a tutor a small fortune for nothing. Ralph went home and I stayed on campus. When I felt frustrated, talking about it always calm me down, much like purging out something that made me sick of my stomach. I found Leila sitting on a wooden bench by a flowerbed, and she had a chance to see the worst side of me.

"Leila, I had it with Dr. Shtick and all the other lousy teachers. I want to blow this college to kingdom come." I sat next to her holding my head in my hands. "I need your help; I can't do it by myself."

"Now, take a deep breath; relax and tell me what's happening," Leila had been a psychotherapist before she decided to become a chiropractor.

One thing about being Portuguese, we tended to talk too fast when we were angry, and usually we added bad words to give it more impact. And that's how I described how much dynamite I would need to blow up all the buildings on campus at the same time.

"Veronica, what you're saying makes no sense; you are far from being a terrorist. You can't blow up our college." She put an arm over my shoulder and rocked me side to side as if consoling a child, her voice purred, "Let's work on this together, okay? What would you like to do instead to help with your feelings of exasperation?"

I pointed to the manicured landscape. "How about if I step on all the flowerbeds and smash them hard with my feet?"

"Now, Veronica," her soothing voice rang softly, once again. "Why would you want to hurt the innocent flowers? Can't you think of something less destructive?"

"Instead of spending our tuition to make this place pretty, they should be using the money on qualified teachers, that's all I'm asking for. The flowers need to go."

"Veronica, the flowers bring joy to those walking around the campus. Look at them, they're beautiful."

"Okay since you like the flowers so much and you are my friend, when I blow this place up to smithereens I'll refrain from messing up the flower beds." I tickled her arm pits.

And then she had me laughing too as she told me, she had heard from other students that the manly statue outside the gym—which had an interesting resemblance to Dr. Williams according to many people—had been found one glorious morning missing its penis. The body part had been sent anonymously to his office on campus and as the story went, Dr. Williams was using it as a paperweight on his desk.

Dexter called last night. He had heard from Lisa, a student in one of my classes at school, that I had gone home with a cold. He wanted to come over and do Reiki to help me get better. I had never heard of Reiki. I asked Ralph as he was leaving to meet with another student. "Mom, it's another quackery treatment," he said.

I called Leila and she said, "It has to do with using the energy in our hands, a most amazingly powerful technique to help people with health problems."

Dexter was at my apartment within a half-hour.

Dexter put one of the dining room chairs in the living room, and asked me to sit down, close my eyes, and relax. He stood behind me. I could tell his hands were above my head, from the heat emanating from his hands, and then around my face, and my neck. It felt as if he was working his way down but I was not sure. I opened my right eyelid slightly just enough for a quick peek and it confirmed my suspicion. His hands were facing my chest. A while later I felt my feet being held firmly in his hands. I kept my eyes closed while waiting for what next. He let go of my feet gently. "You can open your eyes now," he said. He was on his knees. "How do you feel? Better?" I didn't feel any different but his expression of self-accomplishment made me respond with several nods and a yes.

I was curious. "So, what were you doing? Can you show me what you did?"

"I can't. You'll need to learn it from a Reiki master like I did. But I can tell you this much, I covered you with gold dustings falling from above."

He left, after telling me to get some rest and get well soon. While heating the chicken soup I had made earlier, I smiled. How nice of Dexter to choose imaginary gold dustings to cover me, instead of silver or even plain dust. I poured the hot chicken broth into a cup and rested it on the old wooden barrel next to my bed. I ran the hot water in the bathroom shower until the bathroom was steaming hot. After a short but very hot shower, I put on my flannel pajamas and sat on my bed to drink the hot chicken broth. Then laid down and covered myself with an extra blanket. I fell asleep with one thought in mind: sweat it out and get well so the next morning I could go back to school. Fever or not, I did not miss a class. Just my luck, the day I did would be the day the teacher would come to class on time and give everyone actual information on what to study.

I awoke in the middle of the night with Dexter's slim naked body against mine. His warm hands held me tight against him. I freaked out! It was too real to be a dream! How dare he take advantage of me while being sick? Obviously, he had sneaked into my apartment during the night and into my bed. What kind of a friend was he? I turned the night lamp on. I was the only one in it and came to the conclusion that what I had just experienced was nothing but voodoo, witchcraft or Reiki as he called it. Dexter had put a spell on me, by projecting himself into my bed, like a hologram. I wasn't complaining, just surprised.

When Dexter called the next evening to see how I was doing, I told him Reiki had definitely worked, and I was feeling a lot better. "When I'm done with my last class, I'll swing by your apartment," he said. "If you don't mind I would like to see how *my* patient is doing." He chuckled.

Ralph was in the dining room eating when Dexter arrived at our apartment. I told Dexter we probably should hang out in my room. We talked, and then he offered to give me a back massage. We took turns massaging each other. Then we started kissing, and one movement led to the next, and soon we were French kissing. I was not thinking about Michael when I gave myself to Dexter. I took the experience as a sign of finally being free to love whoever I wanted.

Feeling the occasion required a demonstration of my womanhood; I stood well aware of my nakedness and walked to my closet to put on my pink silk bathrobe.

"You're in such good shape. You must exercise a lot."

It was a nice compliment since I did not even know the first thing about working out. But when I lay back next to him he moved away from my embrace as if jolted by an electric shock, his whole body stiffened. I asked if he would rather leave, and he said it was a good idea.

The next day at school I didn't see him. When I got home later that afternoon, I was disappointed; he had not called to leave a message. I was going to call him when the doorbell rang. As I opened the door, Dexter walked in swiftly and when I went to hug him, he put one hand up to stop me. Ralph was in the kitchen, waiting for his homemade lasagna to heat up in the microwave.

"Oh hi," Dexter said glancing at Ralph, who waved back at him. Then to me, "Veronica, on second thought, since tomorrow is Saturday, how about if I pick you up to go to the movies and then we can talk afterward? I'll call you in the morning." He left as if in a hurry to catch a bus.

"What in the world was that all about?" I asked Ralph.

"You have very strange friends, Mom," and he sat down to eat.

Dexter picked me up to see "The Virgin Spring" a Swedish film directed by Ingmar Bergman. On the way to the theater and back he made small talk, charming light talk and I responded in the same way. His aloofness vibrating throughout his whole being confused me. I didn't know what to say or do except play along by acting happy. While watching the movie Dexter did not hold my hand. I reached for his, but he drew it away. "I don't like holding hands in public," he said. "And definitely not while watching a movie."

I knew I lacked experience in matters of the heart, but I always thought that after making love, some kind of loving residue would remain between two lovers at least a day or even two. On the way to my apartment the subject of antiques came up. He only liked to collect books. I told him I didn't really care for antiques but I did own a very, very special one, my grandmother's long evening party dress, which was over one-hundred years old. When we walked into my apartment I said, "Would you like to see it? I keep it in my bedroom closet."

He followed me quietly. I went directly to my closet and removed from the top shelve the box where I kept the dress inside in a plastic bag. I sat on my bed and laid the box next to me to take the cover off.

"Stop right there," his voice rang impatiently. "We need to talk about our relationship."

I remained seated, my goodness, he had not even seen the dress, wasn't he the least curious? I stared at him.

"Veronica, I know what you're doing."

"You do?"

"You're using the dress as an excuse to bringing me into your bedroom so you can seduce me."

I was too dumfounded to laugh, instead I shook my head several times while saying, "That was not my intention." And then I broke down with a chuckle. "Are you actually accusing me of wanting to seduce you with my grandmother's dress? Are you for real? That's a terrible accusation." I placed the cover back on the box and stood ready to leave.

But he was not finished, oh no, he went on, "The night we had sex was simply that. Being mutually attracted to each other, our hormones acted upon it, that was all." I looked at him, up and down in total disbelief but he must have interpreted it as the look he had seen on so many of his ex-girlfriends when they told him to pack his bags and leave, because he said, "Please, I don't want to lose you. You mean a lot to me and I need you to understand that I don't deal well with any kind of affection; things such as kissing, hugging, or holding hands, make me feel as if someone is choking me and I can't help going into an uncontrollable panic attack. It doesn't matter if it's in private or in public, I can't handle amorous behavior."

How sad, he was so intelligent and yet mentally defective. Since we met I could tell there was something weird about him, and it had just been confirmed, it was now official. Wow, was I glad the mystery was over, I could relax. I remained in the room standing against a wall and nodded as he continued to speak.

"It's not your fault," he said. "You're the best thing that has happened in my life. Over the years I've been to several psychiatrists and other forms of therapies but nothing helped and the way I am is the reason all my relationships end quickly. But I can't help myself. According to my latest psychologist, all my emotional inadequacies may be the result of what my mother did to me as a child. The doctor mentioned that I was probably sexually abused, even though I can't recall anything out of the normal while growing up. I only know that I don't like my mother."

I had no experience with psychologists, but from other stories I had heard, it sounded like they had the bad habit of putting dumb stuff into the heads of their patients. Instead of teaching them to get over it and go on with life, they would rather link their patients' emotional problems with the past by putting them into a stagnant repetitive mental disorder of victimized lost souls. Dexter was clearly one of those victims.

"Being friends is fine with me," I stood and put the box back in the closet. "Would you like to join me for dinner since it's late?" Poor Dexter didn't realize that being married for thirty years; a serious relationship was the furthest thing from my mind. But I didn't feel I owe him an explanation.

"I can't believe you're not angry with me, or accuse me of using you, or worst." We talked easily through dinner and he left with a smile. I waved at him and said, "See you later." And then I went into my bedroom and cried. It served me right for leaving Al. God was punishing me for wanting too much out of life.

True, I was attracted by a man's intellect, but the human touch, a kiss or even a hug was a serious prerequisite to establishing a loving relationship. For me, sex without romance was far from a balanced relationship. I had learned all about balance from producing the musical "Godspell," years earlier. Unless it was the case of a casual encounter with the stranger in the elevator, a mistake on my part and not worth dwelling on it.

After years and years of professional therapy not helping Dexter I had no hope for him. That night, I prayed before going to sleep, for God to continue to guide my steps so I could make the right decision when it came to future matters of the heart.

When Ralph and I received our mid-term grades in Pathology, we were stunned. He gotten a B and I had beat him with a glorious A. It was usually the other way around.

"I don't want you to think I'm upset about you getting an A on your written exam," Ralph said. "But as you well know, Dr. Frickenson, is an imbecile, and I'm ready to bet my life he switched our grades by accident because of our last name being the same."

Ralph and I paid a visit to Dr. Frickenson's office. He was a tall, obese man with a prominent buffalo hump (fat deposits) in his upper back, a possible sign of Cushing's syndrome. That would also explain his ongoing irritability and red round moon face. He was annoyed when Ralph requested to see his test.

"Why don't you be a good boy, and let your mother have the A? Don't be so greedy."

Ralph argued back, "If I didn't answer right in my test, and the score is a B then that is what I should get. But if I scored an A, I want it."

Dr. Frickenson glanced at me and asked in his typical sarcastic way, "What do you say, Mom. Should I give him the A and you the B instead?"

I hated when people called me mom and we weren't even related. Nasty bastard was all I could think. "No, just give us what is rightly ours." I said.

Dr. Frickenson sat at his desk and went over the tests. Ralph had answered all the answers correctly.

Ralph leaned over the teacher's desk and looked straight into his face. "We expect you to take care of this blunder immediately."

"Big freaking deal," mumbled Dr. Frickenson.

On the way out, Ralph glanced over his shoulder at him, "My mother and I will be checking our grades tomorrow to make sure they were posted correctly." Dr. Frickenson was a bully, but we were not afraid of him.

There were other teachers in school that Ralph and I despised, but the one on top of our list besides Dr. Frickenson was Dr. Shuck. Grrrr that was how I described him, otherwise I would have to use obscene words.

Ralph had been on the dean's list since his first quarter at Life Chiropractic College but that didn't keep him from being frustrated with the academics. "Mom, I don't know how much longer I can stand it. If I have to attend another semester at this college, I'm tempted to quit," he said.

And then a miracle happened that Monday. Ralph had his head on his desk, trying to stay awake while Dr. Shuck rampaged on and then said, "There is a college in Oregon called Western States Chiropractic College promising their chiropractic students a medical degree along with their chiropractic degree. We must do everything we can to shut them down. This is nothing but another medical attempt to corrupt our profession!"

Ralph was now paying a lot of attention and after class; he planned to look further into the college in Oregon. Ralph didn't lose much time. The next day he called the dean at Western States Chiropractic College in Oregon and spoke to him. He made up his mind to transfer to their college as soon as possible.

I would be staying. I couldn't afford to lose my scholarship.

During lunch break at school I was walking to my car when I heard Dexter call, "Hey, Veronica, where you going? I've been looking all over for you."

"I'm going home for lunch."

He walked at a fast pace toward me and visually excited took my hand. "C'mon," he said. "I want you to meet a student at the cafeteria, she's Portuguese like you." It lasted a minute before he let go of my hand and asked me to just follow him. He wanted me to meet Cida, a new chiropractic student from Brazil. Dexter had told her about his issues with intimacy. Cida knew a therapist that offered a unique deep breathing technique so profound that many people had been helped with emotional problems after experiencing their own birth process. She believed the breathing therapy might help Dexter to go back far enough in time to see what happened between him and his mother.

Who the heck would want to go through such trauma again and have their head squeezed out of a vagina and then yanked out by their head? It wasn't that I objected enriching my life with more knowledge, but some stuff being presented at our college and outside seminars, were hard to comprehend as anything but nonsense. No wonder Ralph had given up.

Dexter got the breathing therapist's phone number from Cida, in the hopes of saving our relationship, since he liked everything about it except the affectionate part. Dexter left for a class, and Cida told me she had found the breathing technique very useful, for herself. She had tried it several times and with each time she had gone further and further back in her life to practically the point of her own birth process. No wonder I had no interest in taking recreational drugs; it was trips like those that turned me off.

I found Cida a little on the odd side, but at the same time a very cool person to listen to. And if nothing else, I had a new friend at school to practice my native language with. She loved to talk.

Ralph told me I'd make a great psychiatrist, but what he didn't know was that I actually had no tolerance for people like Dexter. With patients like him, I'd probably slap them across the face and tell them to shut up and get with it.

Our relationship had returned to a crossroad of emotions, at least for me. He would come over to talk and then out of nowhere he would become my bedroom lover. Afterward, I was supposed to stay away from him, as if nothing happened.

Dating was not as great as I thought it would be. I began

to wonder when the breathing technique was going to take effect, and if all men had the same emotional problems.

I was on my way to class when Lucy the girl that had told me she was a witch, called me over to where she sat. "I'm so glad you are also a witch, we have something wonderful in common."

I laughed and said, "Yeah, we do." But then, reconsidering my words—like, what if she started asking me witch questions—I added convincingly, "I'm just not as experienced as you." Then, keeping my fingers crossed that she would not ask me anything else, I waved at her, as I rushed out, "Have to run, bye."

I promised myself to be more careful in the future, and use the other door to exit the classroom. If she knew I was lying, she might get angry and put a spell on me. I wondered if Lucy was her real name. Either way I had no interest in finding out.

Leila invited me to go hiking to Kennesaw Mountain Park. I told her I had never hiked or climbed a mountain before, but she assured me that even though the climb could be a little challenging at times, I would be fine. "The weather this Saturday calls for the high 90's," she said. "Let's each bring a bottle of water to stay hydrated in the scorching heat, and don't forget to dress comfortable."

Excited by the idea of hiking a mountain, before I left the house, I grabbed a pair of scissors and cut my hair as short as I could. I had always wanted to wear my hair, loose and shaggy. It fitted the new me. I put on a thin beat-up t-shirt from my theatre days, and for the fun of it, I wore Dexter's red silk running shorts. Supposedly they were too tight for him. I couldn't even imagine him any skinnier than he already was. They were perfect to wear on a hot day.

Hard to believe the Civil War battlefield had occurred

on such a steep mountain. There were lots of broad-leaf trees, countless rock boulders and grooved, exposed rock all along the way and it was hard for me to comprehend how the soldiers had been able to pull the heavy metal cannons over such tall boulders and then stabilize them on a clearing that seemed too small to be considered a battlefield. When we got to the top of the mountain, I felt as if I had reached the very top of Mount Everest. I opened my arms as wide as possible and let my spirit embrace the Atlanta skyline and Stone Mountain out in the horizon. I sang Alleluia with gusto and then poured half of my water bottle over my head to cool off. Leila and I took several pictures of each other, and she had me pose seated on top of an old cannon. I did the same for her and we laughed and hugged joyfully energized.

"Thank you, Leila, for bringing me to the top of the world." I brought my hands together and bowed to her with gratitude, the way I used to do at the Kobe Japanese Restaurant, to Mr. and Mrs. Ounuma.

"Veronica, you're so easy to please. Now that I see how much you love Nature I'll start taking you with me on other hikes."

All the pictures she took of me, I had them developed and sent them to my parents.

Rosanna called to remind me about our trip to Florida. She expected me to meet her there during my Christmas school break like we had talked about in the Spring. After we hung up I had second thoughts about it. I wanted to put my energy into my relationship with Dexter and the school break was ideal. I called her back and told her that.

"You said that you would meet me in Florida, and now you're backing out? You lied to me!"

She knew the problems I had been experiencing with Dexter's mood swings. "Rosanna, please I need you to understand my predicament. I'm asking you as my friend to be understanding about my situation. He asked me to stay while he's taking a special breathing technique that might help him."

"I totally understand, and you go ahead and have fun with your new boyfriend."

I thanked her for being so understanding, but she hung up.

Ralph left to New Jersey, right after finals.

Dexter called me in the evening. He wanted to know if he could spend the night with me. I was surprised, but I wasn't going to ask questions. As I opened the front door, he whispered, "Let's go to your room."

He closed the bedroom door and proceeded to pull the blankets and the pillows off my bed and laying them carefully on the carpet. I remained quiet and watched while wondering what he had in mind besides messing up my bed. "Please do not do anything in return for the love I want to give you," he said. "I'm not here to satisfy myself but instead to provide you pleasure."

I looked at him wondering what had gotten into him. He must have read my thoughts because he said, "This is my present to you. After all the bullshit you had to go through to finish second quarter, relax and enjoy the night."

Wow, what a guy that was all I could say. I didn't ask if he had already started the breathing therapy, but I took he had and maybe we were on our way to living happily ever after. Either way, I would soon find out; if he stayed until the morning. He did sleep over, but in the morning, he was out the door before I could even say thank you.

Papa called me this afternoon. Mama had come to terms about living in Luisa's house, and he couldn't be happier. I couldn't be more thankful. I was able to stay in Georgia for Christmas without feeling guilty. I used the paint left from the previous quarter to do some more touch ups. I enjoyed having the apartment looking fresh. It made me happy, when at the end of the semester I could clean my desk of all the books and masses of notes gathered from each subject. The idea of clearing my desk was a visual confirmation of my success. My second quarter was visibly done!

Then I got busy making Christmas cards. I used a thicker paper stock for the cards and also bought a paper cutter to cut them to size. For friends I drew a femur bone or a couple of vertebras, and wrote, "I make no bones about it when I say, have a Merry Christmas and a Happy New Year."

To my parents I cut out little heart shapes of colored paper to make the card a little more sentimental. For friends I cut odd shapes pieces of colored paper and glued them together to make the cards look more contemporary.

I received a nasty one-page letter from Rosanna, written with a thick black magic marker across the page, "From now on I will not trust anyone because of what you did to me. I have lost my best friend, YOU!"

I immediately wrote back asking her to forgive me. I didn't mean to hurt her feelings. If she had met someone special and had been the one to cancel her trip, I would be disappointed but as a friend I would been happy for her. I added that I looked forward to seeing her again and would get in touch with her the next time I went to New Jersey.

I also got a card from Dr. Peruzzi. "You promised to be my slave, so what are you doing so far away? Love, Francesco."

At first, I wondered who Francesco was, until I read the return address from his chiropractic office and realized Francesco was Dr. Peruzzi's first name. I did say I would be his slave, but that was due to the elation of being pain free after he adjusted my spine. I had not meant it literally. I sent back a simple hand-made card with a small origami bird glued to it and wrote, "Dear Dr. Peruzzi, I'm not that far away. Love from your friend, Ronnie."

When I lived in New Jersey, I had introduced Rosanna to Dr. Peruzzi, since they were single and the same age, they might make a good match. They hated each other at first sight.

The relationship between Dexter and me during the school break didn't improve as I had hoped. Yes, we watched movies, went for walks, ate at home, and as always, we shared precious moments of laughter and meaningful long conversations. Even sex did not lose its sparkling blissful quality; but, very much like before, it was all and then nothing. If Dexter had been born a caterpillar I doubt anyone could beat him at building his cocoon right after we had sex, except that he didn't emerge as a butterfly or even a moth.

One evening, we had dinner and then without a word he went into my room, climbed into bed and covered himself with a bunch of blankets. He remained distant and quiet, reminding me of a terrified child afraid of the boogey man. I laid next to him, talking, but I was very careful not to touch him. When he fell asleep I cried from within, feeling sorry for the broken-down human being next to me. That night I began distancing myself emotionally so I wouldn't get hurt when we finally broke up.

Winter of 1994

Third quarter classes promised to keep me busy with exciting new subjects like Visceral Gross Anatomy, Bacteriology & Virology, Visceral Physiology, Basic Nutrition, and Anatomy/Anomalies I, including more advanced classes in Motion & Static Palpation, Clinical Observation, Chiropractic Principles, and Business Principles, and the customary Chiropractic Assembly, with inspiring guest speakers. Schoolwork no longer overwhelmed me like it used to, I had gotten so used to studying on my own that I could skip classes and still feel confident enough to take the exams. Ralph would not be taking third quarter with me. He was busy transferring his credits and other necessary paperwork for admission to the college in Oregon. He was leaving as soon as he received confirmation of being accepted at Western States Chiropractic College. He planned on driving to New Jersey, visit the family and his friends, and then drive on to Oregon.

The academics at Western States College were no joking matter. Ralph called several students attending the college, and they all had one thing in common to say, the teachers were outstanding and the curriculum extremely challenging. Ralph become alive with excitement and looked forward to his future again as a chiropractor.

My comfort zone was in Georgia. Even though the teachers' qualifications left much to be desired, I still had half a year more of free tuition, I would be a fool to leave. It wasn't even about losing half a year more of tuition anymore; I was doing well studying on my own.

Ralph finally had a chance to see for himself I had not exaggerated the size of the cockroach that had fallen out of the toilet paper a few months prior; I couldn't tell if it was the same one, but this one was just as big if not bigger. She was hanging from the ceiling close to the corner wall in the living room. Her ability to grab on to the ceiling with the weight of her humongous body, plus gravity, was impressive. Ralph picked her up with a broom and put her outside.

Friday night Ralph came home in awe after visiting a Jewish Temple in Atlanta.

The Rabbi asked Ralph to carry the Torah scrolls during the religious ceremony at the Temple, and Ralph told him,

"I don't feel I have the right to hold in my hands something as sacred as God's written words. I barely know anything about Judaism."

"Of all the people here, I chose you to carry the Torah. You're honest about your feelings and God wants his people to be Jewish by choice, from the heart, and not because they have to do it."

Ralph felt very moved and honored that he was allowed to carry the Torah scrolls and decided to investigate further into our religion. Then he would decide if he wanted to be a practicing Jew or not. I was very proud of Ralph for taking on such an endeavor.

This afternoon, I received an odd phone call from Donna. "Would you mind if I stop over in about an hour? It won't take more than ten or fifteen minutes of your time."

"Anything special?" I asked curious since we didn't really talk much to each other in school, and never on the phone.

"I had a dream about you and I need to be in your presence."

"Oh, okay," I said. "Sure, I'll see you later then." My presence? What was I the queen of England?

Donna requested we sit on two chairs facing each other. She leaned forward and grasping my hands she held them firmly as she closed her eyes and raised her chin up as if beholding to something above. I wondered what was going through her mind and waited what felt like five minutes or more.

"Veronica," she whispered my name followed by a soft tiny moan, then added in the same soft tone, "How are you doing?"

"Fine." I waited for another question.

"Veronica," She opened her eyes and let go of my hands. "You probably don't know this but you're a true inspiration to me."

"Thank you." I was too nervous to ask her why and also a bit overwhelmed—even uncomfortable—by her strange behavior. I instinctively didn't want to know what her visit was about. She was into spirits and the world beyond, and the thought crossed my mind that maybe she was saying goodbye as she had seen me die or something worse. "I'm so happy to have seen you," she said. "You truly are a blessing." Then she stood, hugged me and I hugged her back and then she left.

Like Ralph said, my friends were weird; I guess I attracted the type because I was also odd in my own way.

With each passing day, Dexter became more and more of a disappointment. I knew nobody was perfect, but at his age I figured he would have outgrown the drug scene. Dexter latest fantasy was to use a new psychedelic drug—which he would do anything to get his hands on, because it provided the exhilarating experience of seeing paintings melt. What the heck was the big deal about seeing anything melt at the possible cost of melting your own brain?

Dexter was visiting on Sunday and brought up once again his peculiar desire. I got so upset that I called Ralph, who was in his bedroom, to come out, and then I asked him if he would mind taking Dexter for a drive around the block.

Ralph was puzzled with my request. So, I told him, "I'm not being a smartass okay? Dexter is looking for a thrilling, mind bogging, melting experience, and I figured that after he takes a ride with you, he'll be satisfied."

Dexter was laughing and so was Ralph, but I was very serious. Whenever we went out and Ralph insisted on driving, I did a mental prayer that we would survive the crash in one piece. I always offered to drive, but he believed I drove worse than him.

I would never forget the time when Ralph drove his car from New Jersey to Long Island and I was the front seat passenger. Seeing melting paintings was nothing to compare with seeing my whole life flashing in front of me. Matter of a fact, just a month ago Ralph totaled his car while driving home from a club not far from where we lived. When he drove around a corner he lost control of the wheel and the car fell into an abyss. Now that had to be better than watching a stupid painting melting on the wall. At least it was a real experience!

Ralph made arrangements to have a trailer hitch attachment to the back of his new car. The dealership promised him that the new Plymouth Duster would do fine pulling a small storage trailer. He was thrilled to know that when he drove to Oregon he could take all his belongings with him and not depend on a moving company.

Lucy came by my desk during Visceral Gross Anatomy class and handed me a medium sized pink paper bag. "This is a little gift for you." She winked at me. "Don't look inside until you get home. Enjoy."
 As soon as I sat in my car I looked into the bag. I was horrified to find a book on witchcraft and four white candles. The card read, "To Veronica, from one witch to another, my very best, Lucy."
 I showed the bag and the contents to Ralph. "Great," he said. "All you needed now, a witch's incantation book. Mom, just throw that garbage away!"
 I was going to but I was an adult, a curious adult. I sat at my desk and after a couple of pages here and there I agreed with Ralph. It was nothing but mumbo jumbo, and it did belong in the garbage. I placed it into the small, plastic grocery bag at the front door where I kept my daily garbage to be disposed in the morning on the way to school.
 I didn't throw away the candles. I placed them in the kitchen drawer in case we lost electricity during the night.
 On the way out of the house the next morning I

reconsidered throwing away the book. I had no intention of ever inviting Lucy over, but with my luck she could show up at our apartment unexpectedly and ask to borrow the book. It was called Murphy's Law, and I couldn't take a chance. I inserted the book at the bottom of the homemade bookcase by my desk, and asked God to forgive me.

No one had called to rent the extra bedroom in the apartment and Ralph would be leaving the following month. I was getting concerned when one evening I got a call from New York. I had forgotten how far in the country the school ads reached. His name was Sam and would be starting his first quarter the following month. I told him how spacious the apartment was and for $200 a month he would have a nice-size bedroom and a bathroom across the hallway. I had made plans to move into Ralph's bedroom which was bigger and boasted its own bathroom. Sam was more interested in knowing how old I was.
"How old are you?" I asked back.
"I'm twenty-four and single."
I remarked sassily, "I'm old enough to be your mother and let's leave it at that."
Mama would not have been proud of me for basically telling him my age, but it felt good to show my boundaries.

When I complained to Ralph concerning the excruciating pain in my legs for the last two days he said, "Stop complaining around me. I don't feel sorry for you. You know better than to eat chocolate. You know how it affects you, but you keep eating it anyway."
"I swear it's the last time." I hoped he would feel at least a little sorry for me. "I will never eat chocolate again. I promise!"
"Yeah, sure; like the last time you promised. Mom, you're addicted to chocolate, just like an alcoholic to alcohol." He went into his bedroom and slammed the door.

He was right to be angry at me. I was a chocoholic. Oh my God, the pain was so debilitating, I couldn't even sleep at night. I considered taking a pain killer but I couldn't allow that to happen, it would be something a coward would do. I swore to myself that I'd never ever eat another piece of chocolate for the rest of my life.

Three students I knew from the fourth quarter asked me if they could come to our apartment so they could show me how the Toughness Adjusting Technique worked They were trying to recruit students to join their adjusting club. They brought a portable adjusting table. It reminded me that I needed to buy an adjusting table too, so I could practice adjusting on my buddy Joe. He had a regular size head and the perfect plastic consistency of a neck, ideal for practicing.

When Ralph heard about the three students coming over, he announced flatly, "I'm staying in my bedroom. I can't stand any more of the stupid nonsense being taught at this school as techniques for adjusting the spine. I can't wait to attend a real chiropractic college, Western States Chiropractic College."

I understood how he felt, but I liked staying open minded. I watched the Toughness Technique being used on one of the other students, and then agreed to lay face down on their adjusting table. One of them rubbed his fingers on what looked like a small tambourine about five inches from my back until the tambourine made a high pitched squeaky sound. The sound indicated where to adjust the spine. Incredibly enough it squeaked right over my L4-L5 where my back was the weakest. With the Toughness Adjusting Technique, kind of an ironic name for something so gentle, the doctor of chiropractic didn't have to do spinal motion or palpation to find the subluxation; the little tambourine did all the work by squeaking at the spinal level that needed the adjustment.

I was sold on the power of the tambourine until I was adjusted by one of the students. He barely touched my back, and as far as I could detect, nothing had been achieved. I let the subject drop because I didn't want him to feel bad, but from extending my back lying face down for so long, my lower back hurt more when I stood.

In the old days I used to sleep face down but once I started waking up with back pain from extending my spine, I realized that I had to acclimatize my brain not to allow me to sleep on my stomach. It took me years to achieve that but I did it. My clinician at school took x-rays of my neck and back and she diagnosed me with lower back facet syndrome, which explained why I should never sleep face down. Such position forced the facets of the spine to compress into each other and put pressure on the nerves. It was my intention, when I became a chiropractor to pass that important bit of knowledge to my patients who had the same condition as me.

Anyway, I was not impressed with the Toughness Technique, and had no intentions of joining their club.

The weekend before Ralph was leaving for Oregon; I made a dinner fit for a Portuguese king and invited Dexter, Ralph's best friend Russell and his wife, Leila and also Sarah, our mutual friend from school.

In Ralph's honor, and to wish him good luck, Russell brought a very special gift, a rare and extremely expensive bottle of wine. Ralph was quite touched by Russell's show of friendship. It was like opening a one-of-a-kind national treasure and they all took their time savoring it. I took a sip from Dexter's glass. Then I put my hand on his shoulder and said, "I'm so happy that you're here to share this meal with us." I should have known better than to touch him. He stood from the table and sat on the floor in the corner of the living room away from everyone. We all exchanged glances.

After half an hour, he left without a word. We felt relieved and resumed our joyful evening.

On the morning of February 2nd Ralph left for Oregon. Before he left he reminded me that if I changed my mind after my scholarship was over, I could always transfer to *his* college in Oregon. I thanked God, for putting Ralph into my life as my son and my best friend.

Aware of having a new roommate soon, I began unpacking my boxes and taking all my personal things into my new bedroom over the weekend.

My bedroom was slowly turning into a dream room. Inside one of the boxes I was thrilled to find my favorite cream-color lace curtains and matching bedspread used as stage props for "Veronica's Room," a murder mystery I had produced at Kobe.

On the left corner of my room, between the two shaded large windows, I placed a beat-up round table I found for two dollars at Goodwill and covered it with the Japanese silk cloth Katherine, my costume designer and friend at The Simy Dinner Theatre, had given me. On top of the table I placed Mrs. Ounuma's maroon flowers, appropriately arranged inside a tall crystal glass jar I bought at the local flea market and used Grandmother Mutter's crystals, to decorate around it.

On the nightstand, I positioned my old fashioned black telephone, an old prop from my theatre days but still working; and a dainty lamp I found at a garage sale. The lamp caught my eye because the shade matched the bedspread and curtains.

The bathroom was a lot larger than my old one and I was able to decorate it with all my duck paraphernalia of luxuriously thick, soft duck towels, duck dish soap, tissue duck box, green carpet with matching toilet green seat cover and a see-through plastic shower curtain with perfect examples of every conceivable duck breed to be enjoyed and familiarized with—while sitting on the toilet. Thanks to Katherine's more than kind handouts when I helped her move, I now had a very warm and inviting bathroom. When Leila came over I showed it to her. Leila was beyond impressed, "Do you mind if I take a shower right now, it's so luxurious. I just love it."

I told her my bathroom was her bathroom, just like, mi casa es su casa, in Spanish or a minha casa a sua casa, in Portuguese.

I admired Leila, how she kept repeating class after class and would not give up. The previous quarter Leila was studying in the library for chiropractic philosophy finals and forgot that was the exact time she was supposed to be taking the test. She ran out of the library and into the testing center, but it was already too late and the teacher would not allow her in. It was absolutely ridiculous, if anybody should win an A for chiropractic philosophy it should be Leila. She was the epitome of commitment and knowledge when it came to being eloquent about chiropractic.

In her younger days she smoked pot, but she had also experimented with hard drugs. That might explain why she was such a space cadet, unless she was already that way before she did the mushrooms and LSD. Dexter also did a lot of drugs in his younger days. I wonder if the drugs they had used were the cause of their emotional inadequacy. When it came to being out of touch with reality, both had a lot in common.

Besides being a lousy teacher Dr. Frickenson was a despicable human being. On Thursday, he came into the classroom, and instead of teaching, which was the job he was being paid to do, he began attacking us with his usual verbal abuse.

"You, young men in this classroom, you better enjoy it while you're still young, because in a few more years from now, you're all going to wind up with prostate cancer, and croak." He laughed disdainfully before going on, "Read chapters five through nine for the test in two weeks. Just so you know it, I won't be here tomorrow; I have better things to do." Then, he left the classroom.

We were dumbfounded. No one stood; we just looked at each other. The student behind me said, "Let's lynch the son of a b****."

Another angry voice was heard, "I'm with you man."

"If you need me as a lookout, let me know," I offered. It felt good to imagine Dr. Frickenson on his knees begging for mercy. I began to wonder if I had made a mistake not going with Ralph to the chiropractic college in Oregon.

The following Thursday he walked into class, threw us some more insults and then proceeded to describe his latest criminal case. Supposedly he was also a lawyer.

He stopped in the middle of his story concerning his case in court when he noticed Susan one of the students, walking quietly through the back door of the room. He pointed a finger at her and shouted, "You, loser, get the hell out of my class."

"I'm sorry Dr. Frickenson, but it took me a while to find a parking space." She put her books down on her desk and was about to sit.

"Are you deaf? Didn't you hear me? I said get the hell out of this class if you know what's good for you!"

Susan left crying, and he went on bragging about his court case story.

There was another serious problem with him. He would open the lab room and say, "You guys have fun. I'll be back in an hour."

We had no idea what he wanted us to do for an hour, since he gave us no instructions.

When he returned and say, "Don't ask me any questions, I have no time for that. Just go home and read your books."

That night I experienced a horrible nightmare. It was the

kind of thing you could only confide to a good friend. I called Leila.

"That is gross!" she said audibly disgusted.

"You bet. Having sex with Dr. Frickenson is not a pretty picture."

"You must be attracted to him to even come up with such disgusting dream." She laughed.

"Leila, it wasn't a dream, believe me. I awoke sick to my stomach. It was a repulsive experience, a real nightmare!"

"Veronica, my dear, you always make me laugh with your stories. Thank you."

"Please, don't mention it. It's my pleasure to make you laugh."

I did like telling her outrageous stories just to hear the sound of her laughter. I never told Leila, but she laughed exactly like the famous cartoon Muttley the dog.

I had a frightening experience this afternoon. After parking my car and locking the door I turned to walk to the supermarket when I noticed a skinny white man, probably in his late thirties, with a stubbly looking face that matched his stained jeans and oversized buttoned up gray jacket, and he walked at a rapid pace toward me. "Your plate says New Jersey. Is that where you're from, honey?" he grinned. His front teeth were missing.

Even though it was only three in the afternoon, my instinct warned me of danger. My hand was shaking as I reached into my backpack to search for the pepper spray Al had given me the first time I left New Jersey to come to Georgia.

I shook so bad that I was forced to use both hands to hold the pepper sprayer in front of me; the nozzle faced him. *Oh, God what if I'm jumping to conclusions and he's just being friendly.* My thoughts got cut off when about ten feet from me he stopped, stared at me momentarily with his eyes wide open, and with an abrupt turnaround, he ran away. I assumed I had frightened him when he saw the pepper sprayer in my hand, when a heavy man's hand flopped down on my right shoulder, from behind me. "Miss, don't worry about him. He won't bother you anymore," he said.

I ran into the store where I asked to speak to the manager. I told him what had happened in the parking lot and he said, "Oh, good he's doing his job. We pay him to stay outside protecting our customers."

Al was still calling me every week to know how I was doing. He was a good person and I knew I should be thankful for his kindness but I felt uncomfortable that he kept sending me money each month even though we were no longer married. He accepted the way I was, and all he wanted was for me to be safe and happy. I kept hoping he would find someone else to focus his love on besides me, but it wasn't happening. Steve told me he had tried twice to connect Al with a woman, but he had given up. The teacher Steve invited for dinner at his house to meet Al didn't work out; Al ignored her and had been very rude toward her.

Our teacher, Dr. Boyle, who had worked at a water sewage plan before he became a teacher brought to our attention some very interesting facts concerning the water we drank. I was so grossed out by his data that the next day I bought a water purifier machine at Sears. It guaranteed to boil a gallon of water overnight and put out a sparkling clean gallon of water by the next morning.

The first time he lectured us Dr. Boyle obviously proud of his family shared with us a homemade videotape of his children which seriously offended Doug, one of my classmates. "I don't appreciate being forced to see two kids naked. This is nothing but child pornography and we shouldn't have to be put through such an emotional ordeal!" he said as we left the classroom. I remained quiet. How could a three-year-old boy and his two-year-old baby brother, running around naked on the front lawn of Dr. Boyle's garden while being sprayed with the garden hose be considered an obscenity?

Before Ralph left for Oregon we used to refer to him as, Doug the Degenerate because everything coming out of his mouth was sexual and lewd. But since Ralph left, Doug had been watching his language near me and even took upon himself to act as my protector. Still, he had a distorted way of analyzing situations I considered perfectly normal. He was the epitome of weird!

I got myself a 3x3 trampoline and set it close to my desk at home, along with my radio tape recorder. It was my modus operandi for taking a mental and physical break. Every hour the kitchen timer went off, I stood from my seat and danced around the room to one tune on the radio. Then I got on the trampoline and jumped up and down for two or three minutes until I felt re-energized enough to go back to sitting at my desk. When in the mood, I did what my friend called, Tai Chi.

Dexter came over Saturday to hang out and talk, but soon afterward we were doing what came naturally. When I came out of my room I found him in the kitchen making tea. I tiptoe to him and put my arms around his waist.

He gently wiggled away from my embrace. "Why do you have to be so affectionate? We just had sex, so why do you still need to hug me?"

I started to cry softly, and then I shouted angrily, "Our relationship is a joke. It's… it's…" I finally found the proper image in my head. "It's like a nicely wrapped gift box with all the trimmings, but when I open it, its empty inside."

"Is that an analogy of some kind?" His calm voice

exasperated me to no end.

"Don't you get it?" I cried as loud as I could. "You're empty of human feelings. You don't have a heart. I curse you for not allowing us to be happy and putting me through these spouts of anger."

I ran to my bedroom and locked the door. After a short while I heard the front door closing. I waited a few minutes then opened my door cautiously. On the carpet he had left a cup of tea on one of my duck trays.

I laid in bed and thought about Michael. He lived way in back of my mind, a nearly vanished shapeless shadow, but thanks to my mind's eye I could recover him any time I needed him to lay next to me and hold me the way we used to. Those few intimate hours I had with Michael had been kept dormant, burrowed deep into every part of my being but when I summoned his presence he came, like a glistening mist covering my body and breathing life back into me. It was pure nonsense but that's what fantasies were made for, to help keep the harsh reality of life bearable. I couldn't deal with Dexter anymore but lacked the courage to break up with him. My life would be a lot simpler if he moved away Donna and Cody and a few other students were leaving at the end of the quarter to attend the chiropractic college in California. They had asked him several times to join them, but he wasn't sure. I prayed that Dexter would leave with them.

The next day Dexter called to say he had something important to tell me and needed to come over at the end of the day. I stood emotionless when I opened my apartment door. I knew he would be pleased with that.

"Veronica, I know you're not going to believe this, but last night I woke up after hearing a voice telling me, 'Dexter, go to California.' I'm taking it as a sign that I must leave Georgia and transfer to the other college. Veronica, I want you to come with me."

I almost freaked out when I heard the good news. "You know I can't go with you. I'm on a scholarship," I said. "But tell me more."

"I've heard nothing but good things about the teachers there, and my mind is made up, to go. Are you sure you can't go with me? Veronica, if you come along, I promise to see a psychiatrist in California. I know if I get the right help, we can work it out."

"I can't go and please don't ask me again." I summoned a slight frown and then smiled, "But you should still see the psychiatrist anyway; it would be good for you."

"Yes, you're right," he took a deep breath. "I'll need to get rid of all my belongings too, I don't want to travel across country with all of that I'm planning on renting a truck this weekend and dumping everything at Goodwill."

"Oh, my goodness, I know you're not rich, how about selling your stuff this Saturday morning at the Farmers Market?"

"I'm not good at talking to people and I can't do it on my own."

I told him I'd help. All he had to do was pick me up early Saturday morning.

Thursday night, I was talking on the phone to Leila, trying to lift her spirits and telling her not to give up, because when you least expect it that's when our wishes come true and she said in her slow understanding psychotherapist tone, "And what is it that you wish for right now, Veronica?" She always tended to see more meaning in what I said than what I really meant.

"A couch, I need a couch, badly. Every time I have company they have to sit at the dining room table or on the floor. A nice comfortable couch would be great!"

Just then I saw through the open sliding glass doors of the living room a couch on the lawn very close to my patio. No, I was not surprised.

"Leila, I hate to hang up, but guess what? My couch just arrived."

"You didn't tell me you bought a couch."

"I didn't buy it. I wished for one, and it's here! Talk to you later."

She was doing her Muttley laugh, when I hung up.

I ran outside. A super long stained brown corduroy couch sat on the front lawn. I was disappointed with the style and color but it was a couch. Then I heard my two new neighbors coming down the steps from the second floor. One of them said with a sound of relief, "Let's get our couch, and we're done moving in."

I had just learned a big lesson when wishing for a couch. I needed to visualize the size, and it had to be light enough so I could move it by myself around the living room without hurting my back. I'd also like my couch to have an exotic Asian flare and not be dirty and beat up like the other one.

Dexter picked me up on Saturday morning. His rented pickup truck was full to capacity. I was shocked to see how many beautiful things he was ready to get rid of. He encouraged me to take anything I wanted for myself before we left for the Farmers Market.

I told him our mission was to sell his stuff, not give it to me. "I'd rather you have it than sell it at the market for nothing or donating it at the end of the day," he insisted.

I took three super large cream color pillows, perfect to use on the floor to sit on, a set of four 25" by 20" black ink hand painted Chinese drawings already framed. I loved Asian stuff. I was also attracted to a 3" by 6" framed Batik cloth painted deer with a variety of maroon and gold shades. It reminded me of Dexter, innocently standing at a crossroad staring at the headlights coming toward him. I intended to hang all the framed artwork on my bare bedroom walls.

Dexter made a small fortune at the market. He had enough to cover his traveling expenses to California, and still would have plenty left over. "This only proves we make a good team," he said.

It didn't matter how wonderful we worked together, no way was I going to California. My mother already had warned me not to go west; she had a bad premonition about the deadly earthquakes all along the west coast.

We packed what little we had not sold at the Farmers Market and put it into the back of the pickup truck. He drove directly to Goodwill. There it had been patiently waiting, my like-new, silky cotton, red with white crane birds and golden flowers, medium sized Asian couch, with matching pillows. Special of the day: $15!

Dexter wanted to pay for the couch, but in order to be truly mine I told him I had to pay for it. But I did take advantage of his offer to use the rented pickup truck to deliver the couch to my apartment. That in itself was a transportation miracle.

I told Leila about the couch, "It's called Karma. You did something good for him and it bounced back."

I prayed with all my heart, "Dear God, please give Alice the woman that killed my brother and destroyed my parents' life, the Karma back she deserves."

Steve and I were talking on the phone when he said hurriedly, "Mom, I'll call you right back. Jacob needs to have his diapers changed."

Wow, my son was changing his son's diapers. My son was a caring father!

The phone rang again.

It was Steve, and he was a lot more relaxed.

"Mom, I'm so lucky to have Jacob. I was changing his diapers and he smiled back at me when I cleaned his poop. He can't talk yet, so he smiled at me as if he was saying, thank you dad for cleaning me up."

"I bet his poop smelled pretty bad…"

He interrupted me, "Are you kidding? Mom, Jacob's poop is never stinky. Everything about him is perfect."

Now that, was a truly inconceivable statement, only a loving parent could say wholeheartedly.

"Mom, I hope to be as good father to my children, as you were a mother to Ralph and me. I could not have wished for a better mom than you. We sure had some great times together, didn't we?"

I was not an expert mom as he made me sound. I was just doing my best. "Thank you, Steve. Guess what? After my finals next week, I'll be coming to New Jersey."

Leila believed the reason Al sent me money each month was because I had told him not to do it. "I'm going to use the same psychology on my ex-husband," she said.

I felt the real reason Al sent me money was because to him we were still married. The only way to stop him would be to face him and make him understand that he did not owe me anything. I did not deserve alimony, I had no children to take care of; and I had been the one who requested the divorce, so why should he compensate me for the rest of his life? Between the government loan and my tuition being paid for the year, I was doing great financially and was even putting money away.

Except for two more exams, I was about done with all my finals. I couldn't help feeling a little nervous about meeting with Al. We had not seen each other, since I had moved to Georgia and had asked for our separation to be permanent.

While in New Jersey, I planned on staying with Steve and Diane. My grandson, Jacob, had just turned six months old. My main reason for going to New Jersey was to meet him. I couldn't wait. Instead of driving I planned on taking the train but remembering how difficult it was for me sleeping seated on a train to Florida a few years back, I booked a private cabin with a bed.

While waiting to go back into the testing center to take my final test on Visceral Physiology, I met Robert, a black student, taking his finals for first quarter. What got my attention while we talked was not his athletic body but his light green eyes, and his mellow deep voice like that of a blues singer. I couldn't help myself, I loved the blues. He asked me all kinds of questions about second quarter and what he should expect since I already had gone through it. He wanted to know what my secret was for memorizing so much material I told him doodling and taking notes while studying helped me a lot, and I also made cards with questions on one side and answers on the other side. He asked me if he could borrow the cards. We exchanged phone numbers.

Robert called me later that night. He was thirty-nine, divorced and had two small children. He was going to stop by my apartment the next morning to pick up the study cards.

Dexter had left the day before for California with the other students. We said goodbye over the phone. It was better that way. I wished him and the others my very best. They were doing what felt was best for them, just like Ralph. And I was doing the same, by remaining in the school in Georgia.

I was about done packing for my trip, when the doorbell rang. It was Robert. As it was customary between all students, we hugged but I kept it short, "Let me get the cards before I forget." I could feel my face flushed as I walked to my desk to get them. I handed them to him but he held my hand in his. "I'm staying in town during this break and I'd love to spend time with you."

"I'm about to leave to New Jersey to visit my family," I evaded his glance and opened the front door to encourage him to leave. "Now if you'll excuse me, Robert, I have to get ready, a friend is picking me up soon to take me to the train station."

When he left I couldn't help feeling confused because I didn't really want to let go when we hugged. His arms were muscular, strong and the feeling I got from his hug had nothing to do with love. Plain and simple, I was sexually attracted to him even though I rationalized that such a feeling was most likely due to feeling lonely, and as a human being I needed human contact. After hugging Robert, I couldn't help wonder if perhaps I never loved Dexter, and I was just having a good time. Could it be that sex was just as fulfilling without love? That would mean I was just as cold as Dexter. What a horrible thought!

Cida took me to the train station, and I was relieved when we said goodbye. The ride to the station was beyond my endurance, not only because she drove with the heat on full blast but she was the perfect example of a one-way conversation. We were friends, but there was only so much I could take listening to a person speaking Portuguese, without ever taking a breather.

Seated in my private train cabin I found it smaller than I expected. In the James Bond movies, the train cabins seemed to be so much bigger. When I brought to the conductor's attention that it was very hot inside the cabin, he said, "No problem. Once the train starts to move, the air conditioner will kick in."

The train left the station making a steadily chugging sound and the continuing motion gave me a tranquil overall feeling. I closed my eyes and allowed my body to sway along as I listened to the sound of the wheels hitting the tracks like a professional tap dancer, clickity-clack, clickety-clack over and over again. The howling sound of the whistle and the brakes hissing and screeching as we went around a curve made me sit up and open my eyes.

From my window I caught the glimpses of small town communities and whole forests moving away from me.

   I didn't bring any books to read, but I did take my journal, which begged me to fill its blank white pages with my next diary. I wrote, "I look forward to the journey ahead and I'm ready to face what life will bring my way." And then I stood and went to look for the dining car.

ABOUT THE AUTHOR

Dr. Veronica Esagui is a chiropractic physician and the internationally and critically acclaimed author of *The Scoliosis Self-Help Resource Book*. In addition to maintaining a successful practice in West Linn, Oregon, she hosts *The Author's Forum*, a television talk show featuring authors, publishers, editors, and others involved in the production of books. She is a member of The Northwest Association of Book Publishers, Pacific Northwest Literacy Alliance and the recipient of the NABP Member of the Year Award. She is the Chief Executive Officer of the Northwest Annual Book Festival, The Northwest Writers and Publishers Association, (NWPA) and Papyrus Press LLC, Publishing Company. She is an active member of the Northwest Independent Writers Association (NIWA).

Additional Works by Veronica Esagui

Veronica's Adventures Series:

Book I: *The Journey of Innocence* (1944-1962)
Describes in the most candid manner the first eighteen years of Veronica's life growing up in Portugal, until a pre-arranged marriage with her cousin brings her to the USA in 1962.

Book II: *Braving a New World* (1962-1988)
Follow Veronica's trail blazing accomplishments as a music teacher, performer, news reporter, playwright, owner of three music centers, theatre producer, director, and owner of the only American dinner theatre in the world in a Japanese Restaurant

Book IV: *Angels Among Us* (1994-1996)
Experiencing the darkest days of her life, Veronica is thankful for the angels along her path, some of who were still exorcising their ghostly past as they strived to earn their wings.

Book V: *The Gift* (1996-2003)
A stranger follows Veronica into a supermarket and hands her a small pottery, insisting that the gift is meant only for her. Veronica's rich life experiences as a time traveler have finally taught her to recognize that her quest for happiness has finally been granted.

Mary Celeste – The Solved Mystery of a Ghost Ship
Historical fiction. Mary Celeste was an American Brigantine ship found adrift and deserted off the coast of Azores, on December 4, 1872. The vanishing of Captain Briggs, his wife, child and crew remained a ghostly

mystery for over a century and a half until now. (Massachusetts mid 1800's)

The Scoliosis Self-Help Resource Book
(is available in English and Japanese.)
It includes the illustrated step-by-step approach to TESP (The Esagui Scoliosis Protocol) a very specific group of exercises for the spine. With this book, a person with scoliosis will discover that they may have options other than drugs or surgery.

To learn more about the author and her books, visit her website: www.veronicaesagui.com

www.ingramcontent.com/pod-product-compliance
Lightning Source LLC
LaVergne TN
LVHW010147070526
838199LV00062B/4279